A COOK'S TOUR OF
SEAPORT
H I S T O R I C
SAVORIES
ALEXANDRIA, VIRGINIA

PRESENTED BY THE TWIG
FOR THE BENEFIT OF
ALEXANDRIA HOSPITAL

ISBN 0-9639652-0-4

Library of Congress Number 93-061604

Cover illustration by Margitta Hanff

Art direction and design by William Shuyler

Seaport Savories, P.O. Box 3614, Alexandria, Virginia 22302

Printed in the United States of America

First printing May 1994

The Twig

THE TWIG is the Junior Auxiliary of Alexandria Hospital — an organization of women dedicated to providing financial aid, volunteer service and support to Alexandria Hospital — itself originally established by volunteers.

From its very first days, Alexandria has been home to distinguished physicians — from Dr. William Brown who prepared and published the first American *Pharmacopeia* while he served as the Physician-General and Director of Hospitals for the Continental Army — to Dr. James Craik, who served with a young Major George Washington in the French and Indian Wars, and later became Chief Physician and Surgeon of the Continental Army (and on whose country estate, Vaucleuse, the Alexandria Hospital was later built).

For the city's first hundred years, though, physicians cared for their patients at home or in their offices, and there was no central facility to care for those who suffered from contagious diseases such as smallpox. After the Civil War, however, when an outbreak of typhoid fever occurred on board a ship in the harbor, several sailors were brought to the home of a local doctor. Answering a plea for assistance, Miss Julia Johns, daughter of the Episcopal Bishop of Alexandria, called together a group of concerned women to "form a society to establish and control a hospital for the sick."

After this small group of "charitably disposed friends" met in 1872, the Alexandria Infirmary opened its doors in a converted house on the southwest corner of Duke and Fairfax Streets. The staff consisted of three doctors, one matron, one nurse, and a cook. Miss Johns and the Board of Lady Managers continued to oversee the operation of the hospital, establishing a Nurses Training School, a dispensary, a surgery, and a horse-drawn ambulance service. These first "volunteers" established more than the fledgling infirmary. They set the precedent for Alexandrians to rise to the responsibility of supporting and operating a community hospital.

In 1933, a group of 24 young women gathered at the home of Mrs. Julian T. Burke to form the Junior Auxiliary of the Alexandria Hospital. They took the name "Twig" from a contest entry by Mrs. Nellie Sommers Blackwell, which described the new organization's relationship to the "tree" which represented the Hospital.

The Twig and Alexandria Hospital both have grown along with the city of Alexandria. For over 60 years, the Twig has remained true to the goals of its charter members by helping Alexandria Hospital provide the highest quality medical service. Today's members carry on that tradition of community support and individual dedication.

Acknowledgements

Three extremely talented members of The Twig are responsible for the beautiful artwork in *Seaport Savories*. The Twig thanks them for donating their artistic talents to our new cookbook.

MARGITTA HANFF contributed the cover illustration and additional sketches. A Sustaining Member of The Twig, Margitta has been the illustrator for two of Twig's *Cook's Tours*. Raised in Switzerland, Margitta earned a degree in biology but is currently a student at Northern Virginia Community College pursuing a new career in illustration/graphic design. Her work has won prizes in juried student shows and has been published in *Warehouse Journal*, the college arts magazine. An avid gardener, Margitta enjoys creating botanical watercolors of specimens from her yard. She is married to an Alexandria orthopaedic surgeon and has two grown children.

ASHLEY SPENCER contributed illustrations for chapter headings and additional illustrations. Ashley is a free-lance illustrator specializing in portraits for birth announcements as well as house renderings, invitation designs and special illustration projects. She is also the staff artist for *Consumers' Research* magazine. She was graduated from the University of the South (Sewanee) with a degree in art history and also studied at Parsons School of Design in Paris. She has worked at Arena Stage, the National Museum for Women in the Arts and the National Gallery of Art. Ashley lives in Old Town Alexandria with her husband and two young boys.

PATRICIA MILLER UCHELLO also contributed illustrations for chapter headings. Patsie is a professional artist who specializes in portraits in oil. She holds a Master's of Fine Arts degree in painting from Pratt Institute in New York and a Bachelor's of Fine Arts in painting from Newcomb College of Tulane University, *cum laude*. Patsie's work has been collected by firms such as IBM, Tulane University and the International Monetary Fund as well as by private collectors. She is represented by art galleries in the United States and Italy. Currently, she is an instructor of portrait painting for Northern Virginia Community College. Patsie served for three years as a Visual Arts Panelist with the Alexandria Commission for the Arts.

The Twig extends its sincere appreciation to William Shuyler for his professional guidance and generous help in the conception, design and production of *Seaport Savories*. We would also like to thank the Cardiovascular Service Program at Alexandria Hospital for its contributions from "Favorite Heart-Healthy Recipes."

Contents

Heart-healthy recipes are marked with a ❤

Starters

Menu

**Hors d'Oeuvres Before the Symphony at the
George Washington National Masonic Memorial**

This towering monument, with its sweeping green lawns, was
dedicated in 1932 by the Masonic Fraternity of the United States in
honor of the nation's first president — and the Alexandria Lodge's
first Master — George Washington. Today it is the site of many
cultural events in Alexandria, including performances by Opera
Americana and the Alexandria Symphony Orchestra.

Red Pepper Pesto

6 medium red bell peppers (2 lbs)
½ teaspoon peanut oil
¼ cup pine nuts
4-6 peeled medium garlic cloves

¼ cup grated Parmesan cheese
¼ cup olive oil
¼ teaspoon salt
French bread* or crackers

Heat oven to 500 degrees. Place peppers on oven rack and roast, turning, until skins are charred all over. Place in a paper bag. Close bag and let steam for 10 minutes. Use a paring knife and fingers to remove skins, seeds, and cores. Heat peanut oil in small frying pan until it begins to smoke. Add pine nuts and stir quickly to brown, about 2 minutes. Remove from pan to cool. Combine chopped peppers, pine nuts, garlic, cheese, olive oil, and salt in food processor. Process until smooth, then chill in serving bowl. Serve with toasted bread slices* or crackers. **SERVES 16.**

  *_Toasted French Bread Slices_ — Slice French bread into ¼ inch slices. Brush with olive oil on both sides and bake 6 minutes on each side.

Marinated Goat Cheese with Sun-Dried Tomatoes

½ cup sun-dried tomatoes,
  packed in oil
3 garlic cloves, minced
1 small goat cheese, about 4 oz.
  (preferably mild such as
  Chevre de Bellay or Boucheron)

1 teaspoon Italian herbs
  (or combination of rosemary, thyme,
  sage or oregano, as you desire)
Fresh ground pepper, to taste

Slice sun-dried tomatoes, reserving oil. Place cheese in bottom of serving dish or bowl. Cover with reserved oil. (If you use tomatoes not packed in oil, use ¼ cup olive oil to cover cheese). Sprinkle tomatoes, garlic, herbs and pepper on top. Cover. Marinate for several hours in a cool place or overnight in the refrigerator. Serve at room temperature with Italian or peasant bread slices. **SERVES 4 - 6.**

Mushrooms Escargot

¼ cup white vinegar
1 minced garlic clove
¾ cup olive oil
1 teaspoon minced fresh parsley

2 tablespoons coarsely chopped chives
1 7-oz. can (24) snails, drained
24 medium mushroom caps,
   lightly sautéed in butter or margarine

Combine vinegar, garlic, oil, parsley and 1 tablespoon of the chives and whisk to make a vinaigrette. Place snails in bowl and cover with vinaigrette. Chill for at least 1 hour. Drain, reserving vinaigrette for other uses, and insert snails into mushroom caps. Sprinkle with remaining chives. Serve cold. **SERVES 6.**

Asparagus Canapés

1 loaf good thin-sliced bread
1 15-oz. can asparagus
8 oz. Roquefort cheese
   at room temperature
8 oz. cream cheese
   at room temperature

1 tablespoon mayonnaise
1 egg, beaten
Melted butter

Cut crust from bread. Roll bread flat and spread with mixture made of both cheeses, mayonnaise and egg combined. Roll one stalk of asparagus in each bread slice. Secure with toothpick. Dip each bread roll in melted butter. Place in freezer for 1 hour. Cut each roll into thirds. Bake at 350 degrees for 15 minutes. These can be made ahead and frozen until ready to use. For a variation, flatten bread. Place asparagus diagonally on bread spread with mixture. Fold two opposite corners into center. Brush with melted butter and freeze and bake as directed. Do not cut. These make a larger serving for luncheons, etc. If stored in freezer before baking, cover airtight. **MAKES 36 SMALL OR 12 LARGE SERVINGS.**

Hearts of Palm with Prosciutto

2 13½-oz. cans hearts of palm
½ pound prosciutto, thinly sliced
¼ cup white wine vinegar
½ cup olive oil

4 sprigs fresh thyme or
  ½ teaspoon dried thyme
¼ teaspoon pepper

Cut the hearts of palm lengthwise into quarters or thirds depending on the thickness of the hearts. Drain. Wrap each with a small piece of prosciutto and secure with a toothpick. Place in a shallow casserole dish. Whisk together the remaining ingredients and pour over prosciutto-wrapped hearts of palm. Cover and refrigerate overnight. Serve at room temperature. Makes an excellent first course when served over a bed of lettuce, drizzled with reserved dressing. SERVES 4-6.

Broccoli-Cheddar Cheese Triangles

1½ pounds broccoli
2 oz. Parmesan cheese, grated
8 oz. sharp Cheddar, shredded
3 medium scallions, thinly sliced
2 large eggs, lightly beaten
½ teaspoon dry mustard
½ teaspoon cayenne pepper

1 large white onion, peeled and chopped
½ pound plus 1 tablespoon
  unsalted butter
1 teaspoon vegetable oil
Salt to taste
Pepper, freshly ground, to taste
1 16-oz. package of phyllo dough

To prepare filling: Trim broccoli flowerets from stalks. Cut about one inch from stalk ends and discard. Peel remaining stalks and cut into 1-inch pieces. Steam all broccoli until tender, about 10 minutes. Using a food processor or blender, puree all broccoli until smooth. Cool in a large bowl and add cheeses, scallions, eggs, mustard and pepper. Sauté onion in one tablespoon of butter and one tablespoon of oil until soft and golden. Add to filling mixture.

　　To prepare triangles: Melt remaining butter. Place one sheet of phyllo onto a flat surface with long side facing you. Brush with melted butter. Add another sheet. While working, keep remaining phyllo covered with a damp towel to prevent drying. Cut 2 layers of phyllo with a sharp knife into two strips, each about 2¾ inches wide. Place 2 teaspoons of filling on one corner of each strip. Fold the filled corner over to enclose the filling and form a triangle. Continue to fold each strip as if you were folding a flag.

As you need strips, remove from dough covered with damp cloth and continue as directed until all filling is used.

Place triangles, seam side down, on buttered cookie sheet and brush tops with melted butter. Place cookie sheet in a 375 degree preheated oven until golden brown, about 12 minutes and serve warm. **MAKES ABOUT 72 TRIANGLES.**

Fromage Chaud Canapés

2 small loaves French bread
(or loaf of party rye,
pumpernickel, etc.)
2 cups grated cheese (Cheddar,
Swiss, Monterey Jack, etc.)

½ cup crumbled bacon
½ cup mayonnaise
½ cup chopped olives (ripe or green)
2 teaspoons minced chives

Cut bread into ¼ -inch slices. Mix remaining ingredients and spread thickly on one side of bread slices. Place on baking sheet and broil until cheese begins to sizzle. Serve hot. **APPROXIMATELY 40 CANAPES.**

Rarebit Canapes

¼ cup dark ale
2 egg yolks
1 pound sharp Cheddar, shredded
2 tablespoons butter

1 teaspoon paprika
1 teaspoon dry mustard
or more, to taste
6-10 slices toasted white bread

Whisk 2 tablespoons of the ale with the egg yolks. Place cheese and butter in heavy saucepan or double boiler. Heat, stirring constantly, until the cheese starts to melt. Gradually stir in the remaining ale to form a smooth mixture. Do not overcook! Stir in paprika, mustard and egg yolks to the ale mixture. Continue cooking 3-5 minutes or until mixture is creamy. Can be prepared up to two days ahead to this point and refrigerated. When ready to use, heat broiler. Spread rarebit on toasted bread slices. Broil until brown. Remove crusts and discard. Slice in quarters and serve immediately.

NOTE: A favorite of Edward VII, this makes a wonderful late night snack as well as an hors d'oeuvre.

The Brie Torte

The following recipes give a variety of uses for Brie. Although a small jar of pesto sauce over a 6-oz. wheel of Brie will provide a wonderful and easy solution to a last minute appetizer, try one of the following for an exciting variation of your "old standby"! If you wish to place any filling in the center of a wheel of Brie, freeze the wheel first for at least 30 minutes. It will slice nicely!

I — Brie Torte With Olives

1 14-oz. wheel of mature Brie
½ cup butter, softened
1 large garlic clove, pressed
⅓ cup finely chopped walnuts

⅓ cup finely chopped ripe olives
2 tablespoons chopped fresh basil
　or 2 teaspoons dried

Place cheese in freezer about 30 minutes or until very firm. Carefully cut into halves, horizontally. Set aside. In a small bowl, cream butter and garlic (a food processor is great!). Mix walnuts, olives and basil to blend thoroughly. Spread evenly on cut side of one of the Brie halves. Top with the other half, cut side down. Press together lightly; wrap and chill. Bring to room temperature. NOTE: If wheel of Brie is thick enough, it may be sliced, horizontally, into thirds. **MAKES 12 GENEROUS SERVINGS.**

II — Brie Torte with Apricot Filling

1 14-oz. wheel of mature Brie
4 oz. dried apricots
⅔ cup water

Strip of lemon rind, about ½" by 1"
Juice of ½ lemon
2 oz. sliced almonds, toasted

Freeze Brie for at least 30 minutes. Toast almonds in slow oven, 200 degrees, until light brown. Set aside. Simmer apricots in water with lemon rind and juice for 20 minutes. Puree in food processor and set aside to cool. Remove Brie from freezer and slice horizontally. Heat in microwave oven on high for 1¼ minutes. Spread ¼ of apricot mixture on cut side of Brie. Top with other side of Brie, cut side down. Spread rest of apricot mixture on top of Brie and sprinkle with toasted, sliced almonds. Serve with crackers. **MAKES 12 GENEROUS SERVINGS.**

III — Truffled Brie

1 8-inch wheel Brie
  or Brillat-Savarin
1-2 fresh truffles, shaved

Sliced pears
Toasted brioche slices

Chill Brie or Brillat-Savarin wheel in freezer for 30 minutes and slice in half, or use a cheese wire or heavy thread to slice. Sprinkle each layer with truffles. Stack, cut sides together, and wrap airtight. Store in refrigerator about 3 days to flavor cheese. When ready to serve, slice into 16 wedges and serve on platter with sliced pears and toasted brioche slices.

NOTE: Fried sage or spinach leaves can be substituted for the truffles.

IV — Brie with Kahlúa

1 14-oz. wheel of mature Brie
¾ cup finely chopped pecans
¼ cup Kahlúa or other
  coffee-flavored liqueur

3 tablespoons brown sugar
Tart apples, washed and
  cut into thin slices

Spread pecans in a pie plate and microwave at high 4-6 minutes, stirring every 2 minutes until toasted. Add Kahlúa and sugar. Stir well. Remove rind from top of Brie. Discard rind. Place Brie on a microwave-safe plate. Spoon pecan mixture over top of Brie. Microwave, uncovered, at high 1¼-2 minutes or until Brie softens to desired consistency. This is an exceptional dessert or sweet treat! The apples make an excellent variation to crackers. **MAKES 12 GENEROUS SERVINGS.**

Le Fromage Aux Herbes I

2 8-oz. packages cream cheese,
  softened
¼ cup mayonnaise
2 teaspoons Dijon mustard

1 clove garlic, finely minced
2 tablespoons chopped,
  dried chives
1 teaspoon dried dill

Beat cream cheese, mayonnaise, mustard, dill, chives and garlic until well blended or use food processor. Cover and place in refrigerator up to one week or freeze. Serve at room temperature with crackers or rounds of French bread.

Le Fromage Aux Herbes II

8 oz. whipped butter
2 8-oz. packages cream cheese,
  softened
2 cloves garlic, mashed

½ teaspoon dried oregano
¼ teaspoon each dried marjoram,
  thyme, basil, dill, and pepper

Mix all ingredients until smooth in food processor or with electric beater. Store in refrigerator for several days or freeze. Serve with crackers or rounds of French bread.

Le Fromage Aux Fines Herbes

1 8-oz. package cream cheese
⅓ cup sour cream
⅓ cup chopped fresh parsley
2½ tablespoons chopped shallots
¾ teaspoon chopped garlic
1½ tablespoons chopped chives
1 teaspoon tarragon
  from tarragon vinegar

Salt and pepper to taste
⅓ cup whipping cream
Parsley sprigs, drained capers
  and slivered almonds if desired
  for garnish
Cucumber slices

Soften cheese and add all ingredients, except the whipping cream, cucumber slices and garnishes. Beat the whipping cream into soft peaks and fold into the cheese mixture.

Mixture should be refrigerated for 1 week to thicken. Using a pastry bag, squeeze a small amount on cucumber slices and top with a sprig of parsley, a caper and an almond slice. Use also as a spread with crackers.

NOTE: These faux Boursin recipes are excellent to make ahead and have on hand for last minute entertaining!

Hot Jezebel

1 18-oz. jar pineapple preserves
1 18-oz. jar apple jelly
1 5-oz. jar prepared horseradish

1 oz. dry mustard
1 tablespoon crushed peppercorns

Mix all ingredients well in a quart jar and store in refrigerator. This will keep indefinitely. Serve 2-3 tablespoons over a large block of cream cheese with water biscuits. NOTE: This is an old recipe passed along for years in the hunt country of Virginia.

Shenandoah Cheese Spread

2½ cups shredded sharp
  white Cheddar cheese
¼ cup grated onion

2 tablespoons mayonnaise
½ cup raspberry preserves

Using a food processor with a metal blade, combine cheese, onion and mayonnaise. Blend. Form into an upside-down saucer shape on serving platter. Top with preserves. Serve with shredded wheat crackers. NOTE: A great recipe for Christmas or Valentine's Day!

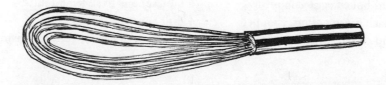

Chutney Cheese Pâté

¼ pound sharp Cheddar cheese,
    grated
6 oz. cream cheese
3 tablespoons sherry

½ teaspoon curry powder
¼ - ½ jar mango chutney
2-3 scallions
Crackers

Cream Cheddar and cream cheese in food processor. Gradually add sherry. Sprinkle in curry powder, scraping down the sides of container and continue to process until pâté is of uniform consistency. Spread on round tray and cover with foil; refrigerate at least 24 hours to develop flavors. An hour before serving, remove from refrigerator. Spread chutney on top. Cut green tops of scallions in ¼ inch lengths and sprinkle on top. Serve surrounded by crackers. Can be frozen without chutney and scallions for later use.

White Oak Pâté

3 Mackintosh apples
3 medium white onions
1 pound fresh mushrooms, sliced

¼ pound butter
2 pounds chicken livers
Salt and pepper, to taste

Peel and slice onions and apples. Sauté apples and onions with mushrooms in butter until onions are translucent. Add chicken livers and simmer until well done. Drain off excess liquid, place mixture into processor and puree. Shape pâté on one or two large serving plates and chill. Serve with crackers, toast points or thinly sliced baguettes.

Caviar Cocktail Torte

Vegetable oil
2 envelopes Knox gelatin
½ cup cold water
8 hard-boiled eggs, chopped
1 bunch green onions, chopped
½ cup chopped fresh parsley

Salt and pepper, to taste
4 ripe avocados, coarsely mashed
¾ cup minced onion, divided
4 tablespoons fresh lemon juice
1 pint sour cream
4 oz. black caviar (or red at Christmas)

1 cup mayonnaise, divided   Pumpernickel cocktail bread
Hot sauce

Lightly oil the bottom and sides of a 9-inch springform pan. Soften gelatin in the water and heat in microwave to liquefy. Combine eggs, ¾ cup of the mayonnaise, green onions, parsley, several dashes of hot sauce, salt and pepper to taste. Add 2 tablespoons of the gelatin and fold together gently. Spread into the prepared pan and smooth top.

Combine mashed avocados, ¼ cup of the minced onion, remaining ¼ cup of the mayonnaise, several dashes of hot sauce, salt, pepper and 2 tablespoons of the gelatin. Carefully spread over the egg mixture and smooth top. Mix the sour cream with the remaining minced onion and gelatin. Spread over the avocado layer.

Cover the pan with plastic wrap and refrigerate overnight. Remove pie from springform pan just before serving. Top with drained caviar and serve with pumpernickel bread slices. **MAKES 25 SERVINGS.**

Eggplant Caviar in Radicchio Leaves

1 1¼-pound eggplant, halved   8 oz. goat cheese or fresh
2 tablespoons olive oil   mozzarella, diced or chopped
2 cloves garlic, minced   16 radicchio leaves
Salt and pepper to taste

Pierce eggplant in several places and cook in microwave on high for about 6-8 minutes or until tender. Cool, then scoop out flesh, discarding seedy portion. Mash flesh with fork or puree in food processor. Whisk olive oil into eggplant. Add garlic. Season to taste with salt and pepper. Mix in goat cheese. Spread 1 tablespoon eggplant mixture over each radicchio leaf and roll, jelly-roll fashion. Continue until all filling and leaves are used. Wrap in plastic wrap and chill for several hours. Serve whole rolls or cut rolls into ¼-inch slices and serve as appetizers. **SERVES 16.**

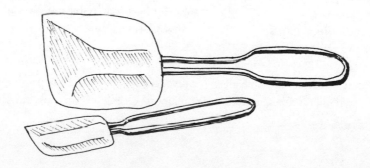

Joanne's Caponata (Eggplant Appetizer)

1 pound eggplant, peeled and
  cut into ½-inch cubes
1 cup minced celery
5 tablespoons olive oil
1 cup minced onion
1½ cups drained, coarsely chopped
  Italian plum tomatoes

2½ tablespoons red wine vinegar
2 teaspoons sugar
2 tablespoons sliced green olives
1 tablespoon capers
2 anchovy filets, minced (optional)
¼ cup pine nuts
Salt and pepper

Sprinkle eggplant with salt and allow to drain in colander for 30 minutes. Pat dry with paper towels. In large skillet cook celery in 2 tablespoons of the olive oil, stirring, for 10 minutes. Add onions and cook until tender. Transfer celery and onions to another bowl. Sauté eggplant in remaining oil until lightly browned. Return onions and celery to skillet. Add tomatoes. Mix vinegar and sugar and pour into skillet. Add olives, capers and anchovies. Bring entire mixture to a boil and simmer for 15 minutes stirring occasionally. Add pine nuts and salt and pepper to taste. Chill. Serve with crackers or toasted Italian bread rounds. MAKES 4 CUPS.

Hot Black-Eyed Pea Dip

½ green bell pepper, finely chopped
2 stalks celery, finely chopped
1 onion, finely chopped
1 teaspoon black pepper
2 tablespoons hot sauce
  (use less for a milder flavor)
½ cup catsup
1 tablespoon salt
3 chicken bouillon cubes
¼ teaspoon nutmeg

½ teaspoon cinnamon
2 15-oz. cans black-eyed peas
  (one can should include jalapenos)
1 15-oz. can tomatoes with
  green chiles
1 clove garlic, pressed
1 teaspoon sugar
½ cup bacon drippings or olive oil
3 tablespoons flour

In a medium saucepan combine green pepper, celery, onion, black pepper, hot sauce, catsup, salt, bouillon cubes, nutmeg and cinnamon. Over low heat, cook and stir until it reaches a boil and the cubes have completely dissolved. Add peas, tomatoes, garlic and sugar. Simmer for 30 minutes. Combine bacon drippings or oil with flour and stir into pea mixture. Cook for 10 minutes more. Stir well and serve hot with plenty of corn chips for dipping.

NOTE: This is a special holiday recipe to bring good luck to those who taste on New Year's Eve or New Year's Day.

Hummus

1 16-oz. can chick peas	4 tablespoons tahini (ground sesame)
Water	Pinch salt
1 clove garlic, peeled	Chopped parsley and olive oil
1½ lemons	for decoration

Drain chick peas. Place the peas in a pan of water and bring it to a boil. Remove from the heat and drain except for 2 tablespoons of the water. Place peas and 2 tablespoons of water in food processor or blender (preferable). Blend briefly and add clove of garlic, juice of the lemons, tahini and salt. Blend until smooth. Spread on a serving plate and garnish with parsley and olive oil. Serve with slices of pita bread. A traditional Lebanese dish. SERVES 4.

Diana's Sun-Dried Tomato Spread

1 8½-oz. jar sun-dried tomatoes in oil	Dash of cayenne pepper
1 8-oz. cream cheese	2-3 tablespoons table cream as needed

Combine first three ingredients in processor until completely blended. Thin with table cream to desired consistency. Spread on crackers or use as a filling for Chicken Medallions. MAKES 1 CUP.

Vegetable Quesadillas

Non-stick cooking spray
1 green pepper, chopped
1 red pepper, chopped
1 small onion, chopped
12-15 mushrooms, sliced
8 flour tortillas

1 cup shredded Mozzarella
  or Cheddar cheese (low fat)
6 scallions, chopped for garnish
Fresh Salsa
Sour cream

Spray skillet with cooking spray. Sauté vegetables until tender. Remove from pan and set aside. Respray pan and put one flour tortilla in pan. Put ⅛ of vegetable mixture and ⅛ of cheese on one half of the tortilla. Fold over as for an omelette. Brown over low heat on both sides until cheese melts and shell is crispy. Keep warm while continuing process with other 7 tortillas. Arrange 2 tortillas on a plate and cut as you would a pizza. Garnish with Fresh Salsa, sour cream and chopped scallions. SERVES 4 AS A MAIN COURSE AND 8-10 AS AN APPETIZER.

Salmon Quesadillas

1 16-oz. can red salmon
  or 2 cups fresh cooked salmon
½ teaspoon dried dill weed
  or 2 tablespoons fresh

¼ cup mayonnaise
2 tablespoons capers
2 cans crescent rolls

Drain canned salmon and remove bones, etc. Blend with mayonnaise, dill and capers. Roll out crescent rolls to flatten and enlarge them. Cut each triangle into two smaller ones, making 16 triangles per can. Put a teaspoonful of salmon mixture on each triangle, fold in 2 ends and roll towards point to seal the filling inside. Place on cookie sheet and bake at 375 degrees for 12 minutes or until brown. Can be served hot or cold. For a variation, add ¼ small onion, finely chopped, to filling and serve with horseradish. MAKES 32 PIECES.

Goat Cheese Quesadilla

½ cup shredded Monterey Jack
¼ cup crumbled goat cheese
2 tablespoons chopped red onion

½ cup finely chopped fresh basil
Salt and pepper, to taste
6 10-inch flour tortillas

Mix cheeses, onion, basil, salt and pepper in a small bowl. Place one tortilla on an oven-safe platter. Spread ¼ of mixture on the tortilla. Place another tortilla on top and spread with ¼ of mixture. Top with third tortilla. Repeat with other 3 tortillas. Bake at 450 degrees for 8 minutes or until cheese melts and tortillas are hot. Cool slightly and slice in 8 pie sections to serve. Garnish with Fresh Salsa. **SERVES 4.**

Baja Quesadilla

1 medium potato, peeled and
   diced or mashed
1 Maui or Spanish onion, chopped
1 small leek, thinly sliced
3 tablespoons butter
1 Anaheim chile, roasted,
   peeled and chopped
3 asparagus spears, diced

Salt and pepper to taste
4 10-inch flour tortillas
½ avocado sliced
Cilantro, chopped
4 oz. Canadian white Cheddar
   cheese, grated or finely diced
Fresh Salsa

Sauté potato, onion and leek in 2 tablespoons of the butter until potato is tender, about 7 minutes. Add asparagus and chile; sauté 3 minutes. Season to taste with salt and pepper. Spoon ¼ potato mixture over 2 of the tortillas. Top with avocado slices and sprinkle with cilantro and cheese. Top with remaining tortillas, pressing down slightly. Brush with remaining 2 tablespoons butter, melted. Bake at 400 degrees until cheese begins to melt and tortillas are crisp. Broil briefly until lightly browned. Cut into wedges and arrange around edge of platter. Place bowl of Fresh Salsa in center. Garnish with cilantro.

Tortilla Spirals with Sun-Dried Tomatoes

4 oz. mild goat cheese,
  such as Montrachet or Chevre
6 oz. cream cheese
3 scallions, minced
1 clove garlic, mashed
1 4-oz. can chopped green chiles
6 sun-dried tomatoes in oil,
  drained and sliced (reserve oil)
⅓ cup minced black olives

4 oz. Monterey Jack shredded
1 cup finely diced, cooked
  chicken meat
3 tablespoons minced fresh
  cilantro
2 teaspoons chili powder
Cayenne pepper to taste
Salt to taste
14 large (10-inch) flour tortillas

Beat cream cheese and goat cheese together until smooth. Add rest of ingredients except tortillas and reserved oil. Beat until smooth. Spread 1 tortilla with 2 heaping tablespoons of the mixture, top with another tortilla and spread filling on top, as directed. Roll up as tightly as possible into a jelly roll. Wrap in plastic wrap. Repeat with other tortillas. Refrigerate for at least two hours.

Preheat oven to 400 degrees when nearly ready to serve. Remove plastic wrap and cut each tortilla roll into ¼-inch slices. Place, cut-side up, on a non-stick baking sheet. Brush tops with reserved oil from the sun-dried tomatoes. Bake in oven until puffy and lightly browned, about 12-15 minutes. Let cool for one minute and serve. MAKES 9 DOZEN.

Fresh Salsa

2 cups chopped fresh tomatoes
1 cup chopped red onion
¼ cup finely chopped cilantro
Dash of salt and pepper
2 tablespoons fresh lime juice

¾ jalapeno pepper, seeded and
  finely chopped (more for a
  spicier taste)
1 tablespoon or more red wine vinegar
½ tablespoon or more light olive oil

Mix together all ingredients. Cover and chill until ready to use.

Pâte à Choux (Cream Puff Pastry)

1 cup water	Pinch of nutmeg
3 oz. butter, cut in pieces	1 cup sifted all-purpose flour
1 teaspoon salt	4 large eggs
1/8 teaspoon white pepper	

In a heavy-bottomed saucepan, bring water to boil with butter, salt, pepper and nutmeg. Boil until all butter has melted. Remove from heat and immediately pour all the flour into the water mixture. With a wooden spoon, beat the mixture until blended thoroughly. Return to stove, over medium-high heat and beat for 1-2 minutes, until mixture leaves the sides of the pan, forms a ball and begins to make a film at the bottom of the pan. Remove from heat again and make a well in the center of the ball with the back of the spoon. Immediately add one egg to the mixture and beat until completely absorbed. Continue with each egg. Finally, beat a few minutes more to make sure the mixture is smooth and blended well. **MAKES ABOUT 2 CUPS.**

NOTE: Pâte à Choux is simple to prepare and it can be used with a variety of fillings. For a dessert puff, add 1 teaspoon of sugar to the water and butter and add only a pinch of salt instead of 1 teaspoon. Puffs also freeze well. Just before using, set puffs in a 425 degree oven for 3-4 minutes to thaw and crisp.

Pâte à Choux with Curried Walnut and Chicken Filling

1 recipe warm Pâte à Choux	1 egg beaten with 1/2 teaspoon water

Preheat oven to 425 degrees. Butter two baking sheets. Using a pastry bag or a spoon, make circular mound of Pâte à Choux, about 1/4-inch high and 1-inch in diameter. Place about 2 inches apart. With a pastry brush, brush tops of mounds with egg and water mixture. Do not allow the egg to run down the sides as it will keep the puff from rising properly. Bake for 20 minutes in the oven or until puffs are golden brown, firm, crusty to the touch and have doubled in size. Remove from oven and pierce with a knife. Turn off oven and place back in oven for 10 minutes with the door ajar. Remove again from oven and cool on a rack. Make one recipe of Curried Walnut and Chicken Filling (on following page). Cut each puff in half and place 1 teaspoon of filling on each puff and cover with top of puff. **MAKES 36-40 PUFFS.**

CURRIED WALNUT AND CHICKEN FILLING

2 chicken breast halves
2 tablespoons butter
2½ tablespoons flour
1 teaspoon curry powder

1 cup milk
½ teaspoon salt
½ cup finely chopped walnuts

Wrap chicken breast in foil. Bake at 375 degrees for 45 minutes. Unwrap breasts and cool. Remove skin and bones and cut into very small pieces. Melt butter in a medium pan. Add flour and curry powder and heat over low heat, stirring constantly, for 2 minutes. Add milk and whisk over the heat until thick. Season with salt. Add walnuts and fold in chicken. Can be made ahead, covered, and placed in refrigerator.

Chicken and Satay Sauce

CHICKEN

1½ pounds boneless, skinless
   chicken breasts
2 tablespoons sesame oil
2 tablespoons vegetable oil
¼ cup dry sherry
¼ cup soy sauce

2 tablespoons lemon juice
1½ teaspoons minced ginger root
1½ teaspoon minced garlic
¼ teaspoon salt
¼ teaspoon pepper
Dash hot sauce

Cut up chicken breasts into ¼-inch wide, 3-inch long strips. Combine with remaining ingredients and marinate in refrigerator at least 4 hours.

SATAY SAUCE

4 teaspoons vegetable oil
2 teaspoons sesame oil
½ cup minced red onion
2 tablespoons minced garlic
1 teaspoon minced ginger root
1 tablespoon brown sugar
1 tablespoon red wine vinegar
⅓ cup smooth peanut butter

½ teaspoon ground coriander
3 tablespoons ketchup
3 tablespoons soy sauce
1 tablespoon lemon or lime juice
½ teaspoon pepper
½ cup hot water
½ teaspoon tumeric
Dash hot sauce

Heat oils in a small saucepan. Add the onion, garlic and ginger and sauté over medium heat until soft. Add the sugar and vinegar. Continue to cook, stirring until sugar dissolves. Remove from heat and stir in the remaining ingredients (or use food processor).

To Serve: Preheat the oven to 375 degrees. Thread each chicken piece onto a small skewer or toothpick. Place on a baking sheet. Bake for 5-10 minutes. Serve hot with room-temperature sauce for dipping. **Serves 10.**

Note: Although time consuming, the above recipe can be made ahead and baked at the last minute. Not only wonderful for cocktail parties, the chicken can be served over a bed of rice flavored with orange zest for a superb main course. The dipping sauce can also be spread on French bread rounds. Do not use a microwave for this recipe.

Swiss Crab Hors d'Oeuvres

1 6½-oz. can crab meat
4 oz. Swiss cheese, grated
1 teaspoon onion, minced
¼ teaspoon curry powder

½ teaspoon lemon juice
½ cup mayonnaise
Croustades (miniature crispy shells)
  or Pâte à Choux shells

Mix together all ingredients except shells. Place in ovenproof dish. Bake at 400 degrees until warm and bubbly. Place on croustades or stuff Pâte à Choux puffs. If puffs have been frozen, see thawing instructions and warm slightly before stuffing.

Sherried Crab

1 cup crabmeat
1 8-oz. package cream cheese,
  softened
¼ cup dry sherry

1 teaspoon brown (Creole-style)
  mustard
Crackers

Soak crab meat in sherry for several hours. Add cream cheese, and mustard to crabmeat and sherry and mix until combined. Heat over low heat until thoroughly warmed. Serve with an assortment of crackers. Can be doubled easily.

Crab Mousse

Mayonnaise for mold
1 envelope unflavored gelatin
   dissolved in 3 tablespoons
   cold water
1 can cream of mushroom soup
8 oz. cream cheese

¾ cup finely chopped green onions
½ cup finely chopped celery
   (optional)
1 cup mayonnaise
1 pound fresh crabmeat, well picked

Prepare a mold by wiping it with mayonnaise, making sure all crevices and dips are completely covered. Dissolve gelatin in the cold water. Melt the cream cheese in soup over low heat. Add the gelatin and cool slightly. Stir in the onions, celery and mayonnaise and mix well. Add the crab and mix well, but gently. Pour into prepared mold and refrigerate for several hours. It is best if refrigerated overnight. Unmold and serve with a variety of crackers.

Marinated Shrimp

2½ pounds raw, peeled,
   headless shrimp
3 teaspoons salt
1 box crab boil, tied in a cheese
   clothbag or purchased in a bag
2 cups thinly sliced onions
7 bay leaves
1¼ cups vegetable oil

¾ cup white vinegar
2½ tablespoons capers and juice
3 lemons thinly sliced and seeded
¼ cup Worchestershire sauce
Dash hot sauce
2½ teaspoons celery seeds
1 tablespoon prepared mustard
1½ teaspoons salt

Boil water in large pot and add shrimp. Add salt and crab boil bag. Cook 10-12 minutes. Drain in colander. Combine remaining ingredients in large bowl. Add shrimp. Mix and cover tightly. Marinate overnight. Serve with toothpicks or serve on a bed of lettuce on salad plates as a first course. Do not freeze. NOTE: Great do-ahead recipe for parties. **SERVES 10-18.**

Salmon Mousse

1 16 oz.-can salmon
2 envelopes unflavored gelatin
2 tablespoons lemon juice
1 cup mayonnaise
2 tablespoons prepared horseradish

½ teaspoon paprika
½ cup diced celery
1 tablespoon diced onion
¼ cup chopped olives
½ cup whipping cream

Drain salmon, reserving liquid. Remove skin and bones. Flake salmon. Add enough cold water to reserved liquid to equal 1¾ cups. Soften gelatin in liquid over low heat until gelatin dissolves. Cool slightly. Blend together lemon juice, mayonnaise, horseradish and paprika. Gradually stir in cooled gelatin mixture. Chill until partially set. Fold in salmon, celery, olives and onion. Whip cream until soft peaks form. Fold into salmon mixture. Chill in oiled 6-cup mold until firm.

NOTE: Also makes a great summer salad served on a bed of lettuce with marinated vegetables and croissants. As a starter, serve with crackers. If you use a fish mold, unmold the fish shape on a platter covered with a bed of leafy lettuce. Decorate the fish with thinly sliced radishes as scales and a slice of stuffed green olive for the eye.

Cajun Fried Catfish Bits

4 catfish filets
Salt and cayenne pepper to taste
2 tablespoon lemon juice

1 cup corn meal
1 egg, beaten with 1 tablespoon milk
Oil for frying

Wash fish filets and cut into bite-sized pieces. Season fish with salt and cayenne pepper and sprinkle with lemon juice. Dip fish in egg and milk that has been mixed together. Roll fish in corn meal to coat. Heat oil in skillet and fry pieces, a few at a time. Drain thoroughly on paper towels and serve with toothpicks and dipping sauce. SERVES 14.

DIPPING SAUCE FOR CAJUN CATFISH

½ - ¾ teaspoon salt
2 tablespoons prepared horseradish
1 tablespoon mayonnaise

1 large clove garlic, minced or pressed
2 dashes Tabasco

Combine ingredients. Stir well. Chill overnight.

Brasalathini (Skewered Beef)

1 cup fine bread crumbs
½ cup Parmesan cheese
½ teaspoon garlic powder
1-2 teaspoons finely chopped parsley

Salt and pepper, to taste
Oil for coating
2 pounds London broil

Combine bread crumbs, cheese, garlic powder and parsley. Season with salt and pepper. Pound meat until flat. Cut meat in strips about 1-inch wide. Dip in oil and then in bread crumb coating. Roll up jelly roll fashion and secure with toothpick (can be made ahead to this point). When ready to use, broil until done. **SERVES 8.**

Curried Pecans

1 pound pecan halves
½ cup butter
¼ cup peanut oil
2 tablespoons brown sugar

2 tablespoons curry powder
1 tablespoon ground ginger
1 tablespoon mango chutney
Salt to taste

Preheat oven to 350 degrees. Place pecans on cookie sheet and toast in oven for 10 minutes. Do not let pecans brown. Leave the oven on. Melt butter and oil in a large skillet. Add the brown sugar, curry powder and ginger; blend well. Add pecans to the skillet and stir with a wooden spoon until well coated. Add chutney sauce and mix well. Turn off heat in oven. Place pecans on paper towels on cookie sheet and place in oven. Let pecans dry in oven for about ten minutes. Remove from oven; salt very lightly and store in airtight container when cool. NOTE: These make an excellent holiday gift!

Toasted Pecans

¼ cup butter
4 teaspoons Worcestershire sauce
1 tablespoon garlic salt

½ teaspoon hot pepper sauce
4 cups pecan halves

Melt butter in heavy skillet. Add remaining ingredients. Stir and mix well. Spread out on a large flat pan and toast in 375 degree oven for 30 minutes. Stir while toasting.

Bermuda Bloody Mary

1 46-oz. can V-8 juice
9½ oz. vodka
2 teaspoons sugar
½ teaspoon pepper
½ teaspoon celery salt

½ teaspoon MSG (optional)
8 full shakes Worcestershire sauce
4 shakes Tabasco
4 oz. freshly squeezed lemon
  juice (about 3 lemons)

Combine all ingredients. The secret is not too much vodka. SERVES 6-8.

Summer Sangria

1 orange
1 lemon
1 lime
1 bottle (750ml) white wine

½ cup Curaçoa
¼ cup sugar
5 strawberries
1 10-oz. bottle club soda

Chop orange, lemon and lime into small pieces (or slices if you wish, but pieces are easier to fit into cups when serving). Combine wine, Curaçoa and sugar in pitcher. Stir until sugar is dissolved. Add fruit to pitcher. Cover and chill in refrigerator at least one hour to let flavors blend. Just before serving add club soda and stir gently to mix. SERVES APPROXIMATELY 8-10.

Virginia Cider

2 quarts apple cider
½ cup brown sugar
1 stick whole cinnamon
6 whole cloves

1 teaspoon ground allspice
1 orange, sliced
Nutmeg, freshly grated

Place cider in saucepan; add sugar, spices and orange slices. Simmer for 15 minutes. Strain. Serve hot with a dash of nutmeg. NOTE: This can also be made in a crockpot. Add all ingredients except nutmeg and simmer at least 3 hours on low. Serve hot with a dash of nutmeg. SERVES 8.

Halloween Pumpkin Punch

1 large pumpkin, cleaned inside
   to serve as the punch bowl
Apple cider, chilled

Cranberry juice, chilled
Ginger ale, chilled
Rum (optional)

Mix equal parts of cider, cranberry juice and ginger ale to fill pumpkin. Rum may be served in a decanter on the side so guests may spike punch to taste and children can enjoy the same drink as their parents.

Hot Buttered Rum

1 pound butter
1 box dark brown sugar
1 box powdered sugar
1 quart best French vanilla
   ice cream (softened slightly)

1 teaspoon ground nutmeg
2 tablespoons ground cinnamon
Dark rum

Cream butter, brown sugar and powdered sugar. Add the ice cream and spices. Mix thoroughly. Store in freezer until ready to use. To serve, add one tablespoon mix to 1 cup boiling water and 1 jigger dark rum. Mix can be frozen so that you can have it on hand throughout the cold winter months!

Classic Wassail Bowl

3 quarts warm beer
1 cup sugar
1 teaspoon ground nutmeg

1 teaspoon ground ginger
3 cups cream sherry
Sliced lemon

Combine 1 quart of the beer and sugar in bowl, then stir in nutmeg and ginger. Add sherry and remaining 2 quarts of the beer. Float lemon slices on punch. Serve slightly warmer than room temperature. SERVES 30 PUNCH CUPS.

White House Eggnog

1 gallon commercial eggnog mix
2½ cups bourbon
1⅔ cups rum
1⅔ cups brandy

1 quart best vanilla ice cream,
  softened
Vanilla and nutmeg to taste

Mix eggnog, bourbon, rum and brandy. Pour over ice cream placed in a punch bowl and gently blend. Add vanilla to taste. Sprinkle top with nutmeg. Best if liquids, without ice cream, vanilla and nutmeg, are mixed one week in advance. SERVES 30.

Southern Comfort Punch

One fifth Southern Comfort
3 quarts lemon-lime soda
6 oz. fresh lemon juice

1 6-oz. can frozen orange juice
1 6-oz. can frozen lemonade

Chill ingredients. Mix in punch bowl, soda last. Add ice, orange and lemon slices. SERVES 30-35.

Pearita

1 can pears, pureed in a food
  processor or blender and frozen
1½ oz. tequila
½ oz. Triple Sec

1 oz. fresh lime juice
¼ cup finely crushed ice
1 fresh lime
Salt

Prepare pear puree by blending undrained pears thoroughly and freezing until firm. Combine ⅓ cup of the puree, tequila, Triple Sec, lime juice and ice in a blender and blend until frothy. Serve in glasses with rims coated with a cut lime and then dipped in salt. MAKES 2 SERVINGS.

Salads and Soups

uchello

Menu

Supper At Lee's Boyhood Home

Shenandoah Cheese Spread

Pumpkin and Tomato Bisque

Green Bean, Apple and Walnut Salad

Anne Marie's Cornbread

Southern Pecan Pie

Virginia Cider

In 1811, "Lighthorse Harry" Lee, the Revolutionary War hero and ex-governor of Virginia, brought his growing family of young Lees here to attend school in Alexandria. Living here from the age of four until he entered West Point, it was in this house that the 17-year-old Robert E. Lee is believed to have met the Marquis de Lafayette on his visit to America in 1824.

The Salad

1 14-oz. can artichoke hearts,
  drained and quartered
1 16-oz. can baby peas, drained
1 large red onion, thinly sliced
Fresh lettuce, any kind
Fresh spinach

½ cup crumbled Bleu cheese
1 11-oz. can Mandarin orange
  sections, drained
2 ripe avocados, pitted,
  peeled and sliced

DRESSING

¾ cup oil
¼ cup wine vinegar
½ teaspoon salt

¼ teaspoon sugar
¼ teaspoon pepper

Combine ingredients for dressing and marinate artichoke hearts, peas, and onion overnight. Before serving, put greens in salad bowl and add bleu cheese, fruit, avocados and marinated vegetables with dressing. Toss and serve. SERVES 6-8.

Portofino Salad

⅓ cup chopped sun-dried
  tomatoes packed in oil
4 large tomatoes, sliced
1 tablespoon balsamic vinegar
2½ tablespoons olive oil
⅓ cup sliced green olives

1 tablespoon drained capers
2 tablespoons chopped fresh basil
  or 1 teaspoon dried basil
Leafy lettuce
Salt and pepper, to taste

Drain sun-dried tomatoes and chop to make ⅓ cup. Arrange sliced tomatoes on a platter covered with an attractive leafy lettuce or arrange on individual salad plates. Whisk together vinegar and oil and drizzle over tomatoes. Sprinkle with salt and pepper. Top with sun-dried tomatoes, olives, capers and basil. NOTE: Can be made 1 hour ahead. SERVES 4.

Summer Tomato Salad

2 stalks celery, very finely
  chopped, tops included
½ green bell pepper, very finely
  chopped
¼ cup very finely chopped
  fresh basil

2 pounds ripe plum tomatoes
Coarse ground black pepper
  to taste
2 tablespoons cider vinegar
3 tablespoons olive oil

Mix finely diced celery, green pepper, basil and black pepper in a large bowl with oil and vinegar. Cut the tomatoes into bite-size chunks, approximately ½-inch in size, and toss with the vegetables in the bowl. Let the salad marinate in the refrigerator for 2 hours prior to serving, stirring occasionally. NOTE: For a different twist, add ½-pound of cooked pasta shells to make a robust pasta salad. ♥ *The Cardiovascular Services Program at Alexandria Hospital.*

Parsley Salad

Pita crisps, ready made
  or homemade
1 clove garlic, mashed
Butter
4 cups chopped parsley
  (bite-size pieces)

Scallions, chopped to taste
Sesame seeds
Lemon Vinaigrette
Parmesan cheese as garnish

To prepare pita crisps, slice pita in half horizontally. Melt butter with garlic and brush each half with mixture. Cut pita into ½-inch strips and toast in oven until crisp at 300 degrees. In a bowl, combine parsley, scallions, and sesame seeds. Coat with Lemon Vinaigrette. Top each serving with a few strips of pita crisps.

Fig and Prosciutto Salad

½ cup lowfat lemon yogurt
½ cup nonfat plain yogurt
1 tablespoon shredded fresh
  mint leaves

12 small or 6 large figs — no stems
4 thin slices prosciutto or lean ham

Combine yogurts and mint. Peel and cut figs into quarters. Cut ham in half and roll up. Divide yogurt and mint mixture onto the middle of each salad plate. Arrange ham and figs around yogurt. NOTE: Although a traditional Italian salad is made with prosciutto ham, substituting lean ham will substantially reduce the fat content. ❤ *The Cardiovascular Services Program at Alexandria Hospital.*

Green Bean, Apple and Walnut Salad

4 cups fresh green beans,
  ends snapped and chopped
  into 2-inch long pieces
4 cups tart, crunchy apples, skins
  left on and chopped into pieces

½ cup chopped walnuts
1 4-oz. package Bleu cheese, crumbled
2-3 tablespoons walnut or olive oil
Raspberry or red wine vinegar, to taste

Blanch green beans, being careful not to overcook, and cool in refrigerator. Add apples, walnuts and Bleu cheese. Add oil and vinegar to taste. Serve immediately. **SERVES 6-8.**

Black Bean Salad

1 16½-oz. can black beans, drained
½ red onion, chopped
1 can shoepeg corn, drained
1 4-oz. can artichokes, drained
1 ripe tomato, chopped

Fresh cilantro, to taste
Juice from 2 lemons
½ cup olive oil
Salt and pepper, to taste

Combine all ingredients and chill.

Jajik (Cucumber and Mint Salad)

4 cucumbers	1 cup low fat sour cream
Salt to taste	1 tablespoon olive oil
1 tablespoon white vinegar	1 tablespoon chopped fresh
1 clove garlic, finely sliced	mint leaves
1 teaspoon chopped fresh dill	

Peel cucumbers, quarter and slice thinly. Place cucumbers in a salad bowl and sprinkle with salt. Put the vinegar and garlic in a cup and soak for 10 minutes. Strain the vinegar but reserve for later use. In a separate bowl, blend dill, yogurt and the strained vinegar until smooth. Pour over the cucumbers and toss well. Sprinkle olive oil and chopped mint leaves on top of the salad. NOTE: This Middle Eastern salad is traditionally served cool but not refrigerated. **SERVES 6.**

Confetti Salad

1 cup diced carrots	3 radishes, sliced
1 cup diced zucchini	10 or more cherry tomatoes
1 cup cauliflowerets	Herb Wine Marinade
1 cup chopped broccoli	Romaine lettuce
½ cup diced green pepper	

In a large bowl combine all vegetables except lettuce. Add Herb Wine Marinade. Mix well. Cover and refrigerate for several hours. To serve, pile vegetables in center of serving bowl lined with crisp romaine. **SERVES 6 TO 8.**

HERB WINE MARINADE

¼ cup white wine	1 clove garlic, minced
1 cup sour cream	1 teaspoon sugar
½ teaspoon each oregano,	½ teaspoon salt
marjoram and basil	

Combine all ingredients and store in covered jar. NOTE: This is a nice, different salad for summer barbecues. **YIELD: 1 CUP.**

Broccoli Salad

1 large bunch of broccoli,
   finely chopped
¼ cup chopped red onion
½ cup raisins
½ cup sunflower seeds

¼ cup fried and crumbled bacon
1 cup mayonnaise
¼ cup sugar
1 tablespoon white wine vinegar

Mix all ingredients together except the bacon and sunflower seeds. Chill. Add the bacon and sunflower seeds just before serving.

Garden Patch Salad

1 16-oz. can tiny green peas,
   drained
1 12-oz. can tiny white shoepeg corn,
   drained
1 16-oz. can French cut green beans,
   drained
1 medium onion, chopped

¾ cup celery, finely chopped
Pimento (optional)
½ cup salad oil
½ cup wine vinegar
¾ cup sugar
1 teaspoon salt
½ teaspoon pepper

Toss the drained vegetables with onions, celery and pimento. Heat oil, vinegar, sugar, salt and pepper to boiling. Pour over vegetables. Chill. **SERVES 6-8.**

Celery Victor

2 or more stalks celery, quartered
   or halved widthwise with
   tops cut off and strings removed
2 cups water
½ - ¾ cup Port wine
4-5 beef bouillon cubes

Lettuce leaves
1 recipe Basic Vinaigrette
   Dressing
1 egg, hardboiled for garnish
Anchovy filets (optional)

Clean and prepare celery. Mix water, wine and bouillon cubes in a pan. Heat until cubes dissolve. Add celery and cook until just tender. Marinate at least 4 hours in vinaigrette dressing, turning occasionally. Serve on a bed of lettuce and top with sieved yolk of egg or chopped whole egg and anchovy garnish. NOTE: This recipe makes an elegant and unusual first course. **SERVES 2-4, DEPENDING ON AMOUNT OF CELERY.**

Indian Cabbage Salad

4 cups shredded green cabbage
½ cup shredded carrot

½ cup finely slivered green pepper

DRESSING:

¼ cup vinegar
4 tablespoons mayonnaise
1 tablespoon minced onion
2 teaspoons lemon juice

2 teaspoons sugar
½ teaspoon curry powder or more to taste
Dash of salt
Freshly ground pepper

In a bowl, toss cabbage, carrots and green pepper. Combine ingredients for dressing. Pour over vegetables and toss. Chill at least 2 hours. **SERVES 4-6.**

Green Pepper Coleslaw

2 medium heads of cabbage
2 green peppers

2 carrots

DRESSING:

1 small onion
¾ cup sugar
½ teaspoon celery seed
½ teaspoon dry mustard

1 teaspoon salt
6 tablespoons cider vinegar
1 cup salad oil

Shred cabbage and carrots. Mince seeded green peppers. To prepare dressing, begin by cutting onion into wedges and placing in a food processor. Process onion until very fine. Add remaining ingredients for dressing and blend until smooth. Toss with prepared vegetables. Chill. NOTE: Can be made ahead. It holds well and stays crisp. For color variation, use a combination of red and green peppers. **SERVES 8-10.**

Mardi Gras Salad for 100

When you really have a crowd, use these proportions to make your party perfect!

2 large or 3 small heads
  of iceberg lettuce
2 medium or large bunches
  of romaine
3 medium or large bunches
  of leaf lettuce

12 red peppers, julienned
8 Bermuda onions, thinly sliced
10 cucumbers, cut in half
  lengthwise and sliced
8 11-oz. cans Mandarin oranges

Core and wash heads of lettuce. Drain. Tear into pieces and put into kitchen-sized garbage bag. Cut ends off romaine and leaf lettuce bunches. Fill washing machine with cold water and put lettuce leaves in one at a time, submerging them. Close lid of machine and agitate 10 seconds or so. Remove leaves and place in two pillow cases. Tie with string. Place in dryer on "Air Dry" with 2-3 large towels and spin 15-30 seconds. Remove from cases and tear into pieces and put into kitchen sized garbage bags. Chill lettuce until serving time. When ready to serve, in two very large serving bowls or new trash can, combine lettuces, peppers, onions, Mandarin oranges, and cucumbers. Toss with ½ the dressing. Taste. Add more dressing if necessary.

SWEET AND SOUR SALAD DRESSING FOR 100

3 tablespoons salt
5 cups safflower oil
Crushed red pepper flakes
  and black pepper to taste

2¼ cups cider vinegar
2¼ cups sugar

Blend all ingredients in a large jar. Will keep indefinitely in the refrigerator.

Chicken Couscous Salad

3 whole chicken breasts, skinned
  and boned (or 6 breast halves)
2 14½-oz. cans chicken broth
1 10-oz. box couscous, quick cooking
1 tomato, chopped
3 green onions, chopped

¾ cup canned chick peas, drained
½ red bell pepper, julienned
  in 1-inch slices
½ cup dried currants
¼ cup chopped fresh parsley
½ cup toasted pine nuts

DRESSING

6 tablespoons fresh lemon juice
12 tablespoons olive oil
Salt and pepper to taste
¼ teaspoon ground cumin (optional)

¼ teaspoon curry powder (optional)
1 drop hot sauce
Pinch of garlic powder

Combine chicken and broth and simmer until chicken is tender. Reserve broth, bone chicken and tear meat coarsely into strips. Return broth to a boil and add couscous; mix with a fork and bring to new boil. Cover and let stand about 5 minutes. DO NOT OVERCOOK. Uncover and cool. Transfer couscous to bowl with chicken and add remaining ingredients. Blend dressing and add to couscous mixture. Mix in ½ cup toasted pine nuts. Refrigerate for at least 1 hour or serve at room temperature. Can be prepared one day ahead. NOTE: A nice accompaniment to marinated green beans and cherry tomatoes for a large crowd. SERVES 12, GENEROUSLY.

Lemon Chicken Salad

5 cups shredded red or
green cabbage or lettuce
2 cups cooked, cubed chicken breast
1 8-oz. can sliced water chestnuts,
drained
1 cup julienned carrot strips

1 cup Chinese pea pods,
blanched for 30 seconds
½ cup sliced radishes
½ cup sliced green onions
1 5-oz. can chow mein noodles

DRESSING

½ cup vegetable oil
3 tablespoons soy sauce
3 tablespoons fresh lemon juice
3 tablespoons rice vinegar
1 tablespoon brown sugar

1 tablespoon dry sherry or water
1 teaspoon garlic powder
½ teaspoon minced fresh ginger root
¼ teaspoon sesame oil

In a large salad bowl, combine all salad ingredients except chow mein noodles. In a small bowl, whisk all dressing ingredients until well blended. Pour dressing over salad, toss, and top with chow mein noodles. SERVES 6-8.

Ginger Chicken Salad

½ cup mayonnaise
¼ cup sour cream
1 tablespoon sugar
½ teaspoon grated lemon peel
1 tablespoon lemon juice
½ teaspoon ground ginger

¼ teaspoon salt
2 cups cubed, cooked chicken
1 cup seedless green grapes
1 cup diced celery
½ cup slivered almonds

In a mixing bowl, combine mayonnaise, sour cream, sugar, lemon peel, lemon juice, ginger and salt, stirring well. Add chicken, grapes, celery and almonds. Toss salad to coat well. Cover and chill several hours before serving. NOTE: Great company chicken salad. Can be doubled or tripled for a large crowd. SERVES 4.

Mango Chicken Salad

1 head Boston lettuce
1 head red leaf lettuce
1 bunch romaine
3 Granny Smith apples, chopped
¼ pound mushrooms, chopped

½ cup chopped pecans
½ small red onion, sliced thin
2 to 4 whole cooked
    chicken breasts, sliced diagonally

Combine all ingredients, toss with Mango Chutney dressing. SERVES 2-4.

MANGO CHUTNEY DRESSING

1 whole egg
2 egg yolks
1 tablespoon Dijon mustard
¼ cup blueberry vinegar
⅓ cup mango chutney

1 tablespoon soy sauce
Salt and pepper, to taste
1 cup peanut oil
1 cup corn oil

Combine all ingredients except oils in a food processor for 1 minute. With motor running, dribble oils in slow, steady stream. Refrigerate until ready to use. MAKES 2¼ CUPS.

Sesame Chicken Salad

1 pound boneless chicken breasts	½ teaspoon finely minced ginger root
White wine or lemon juice	2 teaspoons dark sesame oil
1 teaspoon soy sauce ("light"	Dash hot sauce
soy sauce may be substituted)	4 scallions, finely minced
Juice of 1 lime	1 tablespoon toasted sesame seed
1 clove garlic, mashed	Lettuce leaves

Arrange chicken in a glass pie dish, cover with 2 tablespoons white wine or lemon juice. Cover with vented plastic wrap and microwave on high for 5-6 minutes. Shred chicken into bite-size pieces. Whisk together soy sauce, lime juice, garlic, ginger, sesame oil and hot sauce. Mix chicken with sauce and stir to coat. Serve on a bed of lettuce; sprinkle sesame seeds and scallions on top. NOTE: Great for a summer meal! SERVES **4.**

Ensalada Con Pollo

2 corn tortillas	Oil and vinegar dressing
Vegetable oil	2 cups cubed cooked chicken,
1 cup sour cream	chilled
4 tablespoons chopped onion	6 cups romaine and head lettuce
1 garlic clove, mashed	mixed, torn into bite-sized pieces
in ½ teaspoon salt	Tomato slices
1 tablespoon chopped cilantro	4 pitted black olives
Pinch of sugar	

Cut tortillas into very thin, 1 inch long strips. Fry in hot oil until crisp and lightly browned. Drain and set aside. Mix sour cream, onion, garlic, cilantro and sugar. Add oil and vinegar dressing as needed to thin sour cream. Toss lettuce, half of chicken and half of tortilla strips in salad bowl with sour cream mixture. Turn out onto chilled salad plates and add remaining chicken and tortilla strips on top. Garnish with two tomato slices on side of each plate and one black olive on top. SERVES **4.**

Estelle's Curried Chicken Salad

½ cup mayonnaise
1 tablespoon curry powder
4 boneless whole chicken breasts,
  cooked and chopped
½ cup chopped celery

½ cup chopped green onion
⅓ cup mango chutney
  (or more to taste)
¼ cup currants

Mix curry powder with mayonnaise and mix together with other ingredients. NOTE:
You can add any other ingredients you wish, such as dried cherries. SERVES 8.

Smoked Salmon Salad

1 small bunch romaine,
  washed and sliced in strips
1 small red onion, sliced very thinly
½ English cucumber,
  sliced very thinly
1 green pepper,
  sliced into thin strips

1 red pepper, sliced into thin strips
3 oz. Feta cheese
1 3-oz. jar capers
6 oz. smoked salmon,
  cut in ½ x 1-inch strips
Lime Vinaigrette to taste, page __

Combine all salad ingredients and chill until ready to serve. Toss with Lime Vinaigrette.
4 GENEROUS SERVINGS.

Smoked Salmon and Dill Potato Salad

2½ pounds new potatoes,
  scrubbed and peeled
¼ cup minced dill weed
6 oz. smoked salmon slices,
  cut crosswise into short strips
1 medium shallot, peeled
1 egg

½ teaspoon salt
¼ teaspoon white pepper
1 teaspoon lemon juice
¾ cup oil
⅓ cup plain yogurt
¼ cup sour cream

Place potatoes in 4 quarts cold water and heat to boiling. Boil until tender, about 25 minutes. Quarter potatoes and set aside to cool. Chill thoroughly. Combine dill and salmon strips in a large mixing bowl. Set aside. Insert metal blade in a food processor container. With machine running, drop the shallot through food chute and process until minced. Add egg, salt, pepper and lemon juice. Process, adding oil within 45 seconds. Clean container side with a spatula, then process 5 seconds longer. Add yogurt and sour cream. Process 10 seconds. Add dressing to bowl with salmon and dill. Add potatoes and toss to thoroughly coat with dressing. Adjust seasoning and chill. Remove from refrigerator 30 minutes before serving. SERVES **6-8.**

Shrimp Rémoulade

¼ pound deveined medium shrimp	**1 tablespoon lemon juice**
or large shrimp cut in thirds,	**1 teaspoon minced fresh parsley**
boiled 5 minutes	**¼ teaspoon prepared horseradish**
½ stalk celery, minced	**⅛ teaspoon sugar, or more to taste**
½ green onion, minced	**Pinch tarragon**
1 heaping tablespoon	**Dash paprika**
Creole mustard	**Pinch salt**
3 tablespoons olive oil	**Dash black pepper**
2 tablespoons ketchup	**Lettuce leaves**
1½ tablespoons white vinegar	**1 avocado, thinly sliced (optional)**

Mix all ingredients in a medium glass bowl. Cover and marinate in the refrigerator for 24 hours. Serve on chilled salad plates covered with leafy lettuce. Thinly sliced avocado may be placed on top. NOTE: This makes an excellent first course served either on the bed of lettuce or in flour tortilla baskets. SERVES **2-4.**

Tortilla Baskets

7-inch flour tortillas	**Large muffin tins**

Brush tin cups with oil. Place one tortilla in each cup and pleat to fit. Bake at 350 degrees for about 5 minutes or until crisp but not brown. Fill baskets with salad as an attractive first course or luncheon dish.

Green Goddess Dressing

1 cup sour cream
1 cup mayonnaise
1 tablespoon fresh lemon juice
1 tablespoon wine vinegar

1 tablespoon anchovy paste
1 teaspoon chopped parsley
⅓ cup finely chopped onions
Salt, pepper to taste

Blend all ingredients together with a wire whisk. When well mixed, store in a covered container for up to two weeks. **MAKES ABOUT 2 CUPS.**

Tally Ho Dressing

1 cup oil
1 cup catsup
2 tablespoons vinegar

½ teaspoon garlic salt
1 dash salt
1 cup sugar

Combine all ingredients in a food processor until smooth and creamy. **MAKES ABOUT 2 CUPS.**

Poppy Seed Dressing

¾ cup sugar
1 teaspoon dry mustard
1 teaspoon salt
⅓ cup red wine vinegar

1½ teaspoons grated onion
1 cup corn oil
1½ teaspoons poppy seeds

In a food processor, blend first five ingredients. Gradually add the oil while processing. When blended, add poppy seed and stir to mix. Refrigerate in a glass jar. Shake to blend when ready to use. NOTE: This dressing keeps up to 2 weeks in the refrigerator. It is an excellent dressing for fruit, especially watermelon, cantaloupe, honeydew, green grapes, bananas, apples and strawberries. DO NOT USE PINEAPPLE. Just before serving, cut fruit into bite-size pieces. Great for buffets or serve as a summer luncheon. **MAKES APPROXIMATELY 1 ½ CUPS.**

Curried Salad Dressing

⅔ cup white wine vinegar
2 cups oil
1 small red onion, chopped
1 clove garlic, chopped
1 cup honey
1 egg

1 teaspoon ground cumin
1 teaspoon curry powder
2 teaspoons dry mustard
1 teaspoon paprika
5 teaspoons poppy seeds
½ teaspoon celery seed

Mix all ingredients together well. NOTE: An excellent accompaniment for a green salad which might include greens, black olives, sliced red onions and sliced tomatoes. After mixing salad and dressing, add croutons and chopped cashew nuts as garnish. **SERVES 4-6.**

Basic Vinaigrette

5 tablespoons good olive oil
2 tablespoons sherry vinegar

1 clove garlic, crushed slightly
Pinch of sugar

Whisk together all ingredients. Leave garlic clove in vinaigrette for no more than 10 minutes. Remove garlic and serve or store in refrigerator.

Tomato-Honey Vinaigrette

¼ cup sun-dried tomatoes,
   drained and chopped
2 teaspoons Dijon mustard
2 teaspoons honey

3 tablespoons balsamic
   or red wine vinegar
¼ cup olive oil

Combine all ingredients and whisk to blend well. **MAKES APPROXIMATELY ¾ CUP.**

Lemon or Lime Vinaigrette

1 small clove garlic,
  mashed into a paste
½ teaspoon salt
¼ teaspoon dry mustard
1 tablespoon red wine vinegar
1 tablespoon fresh lemon juice
  or ¾ tablespoon fresh lime juice

3 tablespoons olive oil
3 tablespoons vegetable oil
Fresh ground pepper to taste
1 tablespoon chopped
  fresh tarragon

Combine garlic, salt and dry mustard. With a wire whisk, blend in vinegar and lemon juice. Combine olive and vegetable oils and slowly whisk into vinegar mixture. When smooth and slightly thickened, add pepper and tarragon. NOTE: Excellent dressing for a pasta salad!

Lemon-Dill Dressing

2 tablespoons slivered almonds,
  toasted
⅔ cup almond oil or olive oil
¼ cup lemon juice
2 tablespoons chopped fresh dill
  or 1 teaspoon dried

1 tablespoon grated lemon peel
1 teaspoon Dijon mustard
¼ teaspoon pepper

Using a food processor or blender, process almonds until finely ground. Add remaining ingredients and blend until smooth. SERVES 6-8.

Mint Vinaigrette Dressing

¼ cup fresh lemon juice
½ teaspoon freshly ground pepper
¼ teaspoon chopped fresh
  mint leaves

¼ teaspoon oregano
1 coddled egg
1 cup olive oil

Pour lemon juice and seasonings into a bowl. Add coddled egg and beat vigorously. Add olive oil, whipping constantly until well blended. NOTE: A fabulous dressing to serve with romaine lettuce, tomatoes, green onions, Romano cheese, a bit of bacon and croutons. **MAKES ABOUT 1 ⅓ CUP.**

Dijon Mustard Dressing

1 egg, slightly beaten
¼ cup vegetable oil
Juice of one lemon
1 tablespoon grated Parmesan
2 tablespoons Dijon mustard

1 teaspoon sugar
1 teaspoon Worcestershire sauce
½ teaspoon salt
Dash of pepper

Combine ingredients in a jar. Tighten lid and shake until well-blended. Chill thoroughly. NOTE: Especially great with a spinach salad! **MAKES ABOUT ½ CUP.**

Asparagus Soup

1½ pounds fresh asparagus
1 quart chicken or veal stock
Salt and pepper, taste
¼ cup butter
2 tablespoons flour

1 cup whipping cream
2 tablespoons oil
4 slices white bread,
    crusts removed, diced

Wash asparagus, then trim ends. Cut stems in 1-inch lengths, reserving tips. Place stems in saucepan with stock and season to taste with salt and pepper. Cover and simmer until very tender, 20-30 minutes. Puree mixture in blender or food processor. Strain to remove fibers, pressing well to extract all juices.

Melt 2 tablespoons of the butter in saucepan. Whisk in flour and cook until foaming. Stir in reserved puree. Bring to a boil, whisking constantly until mixture thickens slightly. Add asparagus tips. Taste to adjust for seasonings. Simmer 5-8 minutes until asparagus tips are just tender. Stir cream into soup. Bring just to boil. Taste and adjust for seasoning. Soup can be stored, covered, in refrigerator up to 2 days.

To make croutons, heat oil and remaining 2 tablespoons butter in skillet until foaming. Add bread cubes. Sauté until golden brown, stirring constantly so croutons color evenly. Lift out with slotted spoon and drain on paper towels. When cool, wrap in foil. Croutons can be kept up to 2 days at room temperature. To finish, reheat soup on top of stove and warm croutons in foil in low oven. Pass croutons in separate bowl. **MAKES 6 SERVINGS.**

Chilled Avocado Soup

2 ripe avocados

2 13¾-oz. cans regular-strength
   chicken broth or more if needed

1 pint sour cream or drained yogurt
   or cottage cheese pureed
   in a food processor

2 tablespoons lemon juice

1 medium yellow onion, chopped

Salt and pepper, to taste

Puree everything but the salt and pepper in the food processor or blender. If too thick for your taste, add more chicken broth. Season to taste with salt and pepper and chill. Serve very cold.

Cold Cucumber Soup

3 cucumbers

2 oz. butter

1 sliced leek
   (or another ½ cucumber)

1 bay leaf

1 tablespoon flour

1 teaspoon salt

3 cups chicken stock

½ pint cream

1 tablespoon lemon juice

1 teaspoon finely chopped
   dill or mint

Salt and pepper to taste

¼ pint sour cream for serving

Peel 2 cucumbers and slice thinly. Sauté in butter in sauce pan with leek and bay leaf 20 minutes until tender (not brown). Stir in flour; add chicken stock and salt; cover and simmer 30 minutes. Cool and puree in blender. Chill. Peel remaining cucumber, remove seeds and grate the flesh of the cucumber, and stir into the puree with the cream, lemon juice, dill or mint and seasonings Chill at least 30 minutes. Garnish each bowl of soup with 1 teaspoon sour cream. **SERVES 4-6.**

Soup Verde

⅓ cup sliced green onions

2 cups diced uncooked potatoes

3 oz. spinach leaves, stems
   removed and torn in small pieces

5 tablespoons unsalted butter
1 teaspoon salt
2 cups chicken stock
3 oz. arugula, stems removed
  and torn in small pieces

4 oz. each lettuce and spinach,
  torn in small pieces
Salt and white pepper
Crème Fraîche or sour cream
Chives, chopped

Sauté the green onions for 5 minutes, until wilted, in melted butter. Add potatoes, salt and 1 cup of the chicken stock. Simmer for 10 minutes, covered. Add torn greens. Simmer for another 10 minutes or until potatoes are tender. Puree the vegetables in a food processor; taste for seasoning, add the remainder of the chicken stock, and simmer a few minutes more. Serve either hot or at room temperature. Garnish with a dab of crème fraîche or sour cream and a sprinkling of chopped chives on top. **SERVES 6.**

Summer Soup

4 ripe cantaloupes, 3 of which are
  peeled, seeded and cut into pieces
1 fifth dry champagne

¼ cup chopped fresh mint
Mint springs, for garnish

In food processor, puree the cantaloupe pieces in manageable batches. Add champagne as necessary to thin to make a soup consistency. Cut remaining cantaloupe in half, seed, and scoop out with a melon baller. Add melon balls to the soup along with the mint. **SERVES 6-8.**

Apple and Honey Soup

1 pound cooking apples
1 pound onions
1 teaspoon curry powder
1 tablespoon honey

1 tablespoon chicken bouillon
  granules
Salt and pepper

Pare, core and quarter apples. Peel and quarter onions. Cover with water in a saucepan and add curry and bouillon. Bring to a boil and cook for 10 minutes. Place in a blender or food processor and process to liquid form. Add honey and salt and pepper. Reheat and serve. **SERVES 4-6.**

Garden Tarragon Soup

1 pound zucchini, washed
   and diced (unpeeled)
1 cup diced carrots
1 medium onion, chopped
1 clove garlic, minced
2 tablespoons butter
1 13¾-oz. can of chicken broth

1 broth can milk
1 teaspoon dried tarragon
   (or less for milder taste)
½ teaspoon salt
⅛ teaspoon freshly ground pepper
Parsley, chopped

In a large stock pot, sauté zucchini, carrots, onions and garlic in butter over medium heat until onions are tender. Add chicken broth, milk, tarragon, salt and pepper. Simmer for 30 minutes. Using a blender or food processor, puree the mixture a few cups at a time. Serve warm and garnish with a bit of chopped parsley if desired. NOTE: This soup may be made ahead and reheated slowly. Do not allow to boil. SERVES 4.

Cream of Pimento Soup

2 pimentos, chopped
3 tablespoons butter
1 small onion, chopped
3 tablespoons flour
1½ cups chicken broth

1½ cups milk (may use
   half and half for a richer taste)
¾ cup grated Cheddar cheese
Salt and pepper, to taste

Sauté pimentos and onion in butter until tender but not brown. Blend in flour and gradually add broth and milk. Cook, stirring until thickened. Add cheese and stir until melted. Season with salt and pepper. SERVES 4.

Curry Soup

1 large onion, chopped
2 carrots, chopped
2 large tomatoes, chopped
   (peel if desired)

2 tablespoons flour
2-4 teaspoons mild curry powder
4 cups beef stock
¾ pound ground beef

3 celery stalks, chopped
1 apple, pared, cored and chopped
2 tablespoons butter

1 cup cooked rice
Salt and pepper
Parsley, chopped

In a large, heavy saucepan, melt butter and sauté vegetables until golden. Add flour and curry. Stir and cook for 1 minute. Add beef stock and salt and pepper to taste. Bring to a boil, reduce heat, and simmer, covered, for 1 ½ hours. While soup is simmering, brown ground beef in skillet and drain off all fat. When vegetable mixture is ready, puree the mixture in a blender or food processor. Return to pot, add beef and cooked rice. Cook over medium heat for 10 minutes. Check seasonings. Serve with a garnish of chopped parsley on top.

NOTE: This recipe may be frozen and reheated slowly. Serve this soup with chutney as a garnish, if desired. **SERVES 6.**

Fresh Mushroom Bisque

2 cups thinly sliced green onions
4 oz. butter
3 tablespoons flour
3 13¾-oz. cans chicken stock
½ pound fresh mushrooms,
    washed and finely chopped
1 cup heavy cream

¼ cup dry sherry
Salt and freshly ground pepper
    to taste
¼ pound fresh mushrooms,
    washed and thinly sliced,
    to be used at serving time

In a large, heavy saucepan, melt butter and stir in green onions. Cover and simmer over a low heat for about 20 minutes until onions are soft but not browned. Add the flour and cook, stirring, for one minute. Slowly pour in the stock and bring the mixture to a boil. Add the ½ pound mushrooms, reduce heat, and simmer, partially covered, for about 10 minutes. Using a processor, food mill or blender, puree the mixture. Return to the saucepan and stir in the cream and sherry. Taste and add salt and pepper as needed. May be made ahead to this point.

When ready to serve, place the ¼ pound of mushrooms in the bottom of a soup tureen or divide among individual serving bowls and pour the hot soup over them. Serve immediately. **SERVES 6-8.**

Potato Leek Soup

4 cups peeled and coarsely
  chopped potatoes
3 cups thinly sliced leeks (the white
  portion plus 2 inches of the green)
2 13¾-oz. cans chicken stock

1 clove garlic, peeled
1 tablespoon each salt and pepper
½ cup heavy cream
3 tablespoons chopped chives
3 tablespoons chopped parsley

Simmer potatoes, leeks, stock and garlic partially covered in water for 40-50 minutes or until vegetables are tender. Force soup through a food mill or process until pureed and return to pan. Taste and season. Stir in cream. Freeze if desired at this point. Before serving, bring to a simmer and garnish with fresh parsley and/or chives. NOTE: A great recipe to make ahead, freeze, thaw and reheat for a cold winter's night! **SERVES 6.**

Pumpkin Soup

7 tablespoons butter
6 green onions, chopped
1 onion, sliced
3 cups pumpkin puree,
  homemade or canned
6 cups chicken stock

½ teaspoon salt
3 tablespoons flour
1 cup light cream
Croutons
Lightly salted whipped cream

Melt 4 tablespoons of the butter in a large saucepan. Sauté the green onions and onion until soft and golden. Add the pumpkin, chicken stock and salt. Bring to a boil, stirring, then simmer 10 minutes. Blend mixture in a blender or food processor. Return soup to pan. Knead flour with 2 tablespoons of the butter and gradually add to the soup. Bring to a boil, beating with a whisk while it thickens. Add the cream and remaining tablespoon of butter. Garnish with croutons and whipped cream. **SERVES 8.**

Pumpkin and Tomato Bisque

4 tablespoons butter
  or vegetable oil
2 large onions, chopped

1 tablespoon maple syrup or honey
4 cups fresh pumpkin or butternut
  squash puree or canned pumpkin

4 cups chicken or vegetable stock   Salt and pepper to taste
White wine for thinning, if necessary   Garnish of finely chopped tomatoes
1 28-oz. can whole tomatoes with   (optional)
   their juices

In a 10-inch skillet, melt the butter or heat the oil over medium-low heat. Add the onions and sauté slowly, stirring often, until they are limp but not brown (about 6-7 minutes). Stir in 3 cups of the stock and let simmer, partially covered, about 15 minutes. Pour the tomatoes with their juices into a food processor. Add the maple syrup or honey to the tomatoes and puree. Add the pumpkin and puree again. Strain the onions from the stock, reserving the stock. Add the onions to the processor. Puree again and, if an extra smooth soup is desired, put mixture through a fine sieve. Add the tomato-pumpkin puree to the reserved stock. Add extra stock or white wine if too thick. Season to taste with salt and pepper. Reheat and serve very hot.

NOTE: A fabulous soup for a cold winter's night. Serve with bread and salad for a perfect meal! **SERVES 6-8**

Borscht

2 10¾-oz. cans consommé   1 tablespoon lemon juice
1 16-oz. can shredded beets,   3 bay leaves
   drained   1 tablespoon sugar
3 carrots, pared and shredded   Dash each of dried dill weed,
1 large onion, chopped fine   dried thyme and freshly ground
2 cups shredded cabbage   pepper
1 28-oz. can tomatoes, chopped   1 cup sour cream (optional)
2 tablespoons vinegar

Combine ingredients in a large pan. Simmer 20-25 minutes, covered. Remove bay leaves from soup. Process briefly in food processor to puree. Return to pan and reheat, or chill and serve cold. Garnish with a dollop of sour cream if desired.

NOTE: This soup will please everyone because the taste of beets is barely noticeable. Can be made ahead. **SERVES 6.**

New Year's Day Bean Soup

¼ cup of each of the following
  dried legumes:
  Black-eyed peas
  Kidney beans
  Lima beans
  Pinto beans
  Lentils
  Navy beans
  Split green beans
  Great northern beans

2 tablespoons salt
½ pound lean ham, coarsely chopped
1 28-oz. can tomatoes, chopped
2 onions, diced large
2 tablespoons fresh lemon juice
3 teaspoons chili powder
Black pepper to taste

Cover beans in salted water and soak overnight. Drain. In a large soup pot, combine drained beans and 2 quarts water. Simmer for 3 hours. Add remaining ingredients. Simmer for 30 minutes more. **SERVES 6.** ♥ *The Cardiovascular Service at Alexandria Hospital*

She-Crab Soup

1 stick sweet butter (¼ pound)
1 small onion, chopped fine
2 leeks, chopped fine,
  white part only
1 heaping tablespoon minced
  shallots
1 teaspoon minced garlic
2 teaspoons salt
1 teaspoon ground black pepper
1 teaspoon paprika

½ teaspoon cayenne pepper
¼ teaspoon ground thyme
¼ teaspoon ground oregano
4 heaping tablespoons
  white flour
½ gallon whole milk
1 quart heavy whipping cream
¼ cup Harvey's Bristol Cream
  sherry
1 pound backfin or lump crabmeat

Melt the butter in a large sauce pan. Add the onions, leeks, and shallots and sauté until onions are translucent; do not brown them. Add the garlic and the rest of the spices and mix thoroughly. Add flour and mix until all the liquid is incorporated. Cook over low heat for a few minutes. Transfer this roux to a large double boiler; gradually whisk milk into the roux until thoroughly mixed. Cook until the soup begins to bubble, stirring often. Slowly add the heavy whipping cream and heat until it begins to boil again. Remove from the heat and add the cream sherry and crabmeat. Heat slowly. **SERVES 8-10.** *The Warehouse Bar and Grill Restaurant, 214 King Street*

Chesapeake She-Crab Soup

3 cups table cream der

1 cup milk

1 10½-oz. can cream of celery soup

1 stick butter (¼ pound)

½ teaspoon Worcestershire sauce

½ teaspoon Old Bay seasoning

¼ teaspoon crushed garlic or garlic powder

Tabasco (optional)

Salt (optional)

¼ teaspoon pepper

1 pound crabmeat

½ cup sherry

Place first eight ingredients in a 3-quart saucepan over medium heat until butter is melted; stir until all ingredients are combined. DO NOT BRING TO A BOIL. Taste and adjust seasonings if desired. Add more Old Bay seasoning, a dash of Tabasco and salt to taste. Add crabmeat and sherry. If soup is too thick add more sherry or milk. Heat thoroughly without boiling and serve. **AS A SOUP COURSE THIS SERVES 6-8. AS A MAIN COURSE, SERVES 4.**

Cajun She-Crab Soup

3 onions, diced

5 shallots, diced

1 bunch scallions, diced

1 pound unsalted butter

1 gallon milk

1 quart half and half

1 quart whipping cream

½ tablespoon crab base or chicken base

2 pounds backfin crab meat

⅓ cup Cajun spices

Fresh parsley for garnish

Sauté onions, shallots and scallions in butter until clear. Add milk, half and half and whipping cream. Stirring constantly, heat slowly until just below boiling point. Do not allow to boil. Add crab or chicken base, crabmeat and Cajun spices. Heat until warm. Serve garnished with sprigs of fresh parsley. **MAKES APPROXIMATELY 2 GALLONS.** *Two-Nineteen Restaurant, 219 King Street*

Virginia's Best Clam Chowder

50 hard clams
4 onions, diced finely
½ pound salt pork

8 large potatoes
Salt to taste
Black pepper to taste

Clean clams and shuck. While shucking, reserve any liquid from the clams. Cut the salt pork in ¼-inch squares. In a skillet, fry until brown. Add the onions and cook for 5 minutes or until clear. Cut potatoes in one-inch squares. In a soup pot, mix the onions and potatoes. Add reserved clam juice and enough water to cover all the potatoes. Simmer potatoes until tender. Cut the clams into 6 to 8 pieces each. Add to the soup base and cook about 10 minutes. Season with salt and pepper.

Florida Pascoe's Shrimp Chowder

½ cup chopped onion
2 tablespoons butter or margarine
1½ cups water
1 lb medium-size shrimp, peeled, de-
    veined and cut into bite-sized pieces
3 cups frozen hash brown potatoes

1½ teaspoons salt
½ teaspoon pepper
4 cups milk
½ cup half and half
1 cup shredded Cheddar cheese
¼ cup chopped parsley

In a large saucepan, sauté onions in butter over medium heat for 5-7 minutes until tender but not brown. Add water and bring to a boil. Add shrimp and cook 3-5 minutes, until no longer translucent in the center. Remove the shrimp with a slotted spoon. (Don't worry if a few chopped onions find their way onto your spoon. It all goes back into the pan in the end.) Add potatoes, salt and pepper to the saucepan. Simmer 4-6 minutes until potatoes are tender. Add milk and half and half. Bring just to a boil, stirring occasionally. Remove from heat and stir in cheese and parsley. Let stand 2 minutes until cheese melts. Stir in shrimp and serve. SERVES 4.

Shrimp and Crab Gumbo

2 pounds raw peeled
    and deveined shrimp
3 slices bacon

Dash Worcestershire sauce
Pinch thyme
1 bay leaf

½ cup diced smoked ham
2 tablespoons flour
2 cups finely chopped onions
1 cup finely chopped celery
½ cup finely chopped green pepper
½ teaspoon grated lemon peel
½ lemon
1 head garlic, finely chopped
2 drops hot pepper sauce

Salt and pepper, to taste
3 cups water
1 pound fresh okra,
   or 1 10-oz. package frozen okra
2 tablespoons bacon grease
½ pound crab meat
¼ cup chopped parsley
¼ cup sliced green onion tops
Cooked rice

If shrimp is frozen, let thaw and dry with paper towels to absorb all moisture. Cook bacon in a large saucepan. Drain and crumble. Reserve bacon drippings. Add ham to bacon grease and cook until browned. Remove. Add flour to pan drippings and cook over low heat, stirring constantly, until flour is cooked, making a dark roux. Add onions and cook slowly until well-browned and onions are reduced to a pulp. Add celery, green pepper and lemon peel. Trim ½ lemon of white membrane, chop lemon, and add to onion mixture. Add garlic, hot pepper sauce, Worcestershire, thyme, bay leaf, salt, pepper and water. Add reserved bacon and ham. Cook, simmering, for about 45 minutes. While soup is cooking, clean and trim okra if fresh. Slice and cook in bacon grease, stirring to prevent browning, until okra is tender. Add okra to mixture after 45 minutes and continue to cook for about 20 minutes. Add shrimp and crab meat. Bring mixture to a boil and cook for 5 minutes or just until shrimp is cooked. Add chopped parsley and green onion tops. Serve with cooked rice in soup plates. **SERVES 8.**

Crab Gazpacho

1 clove garlic, minced
⅓ cup chopped onion
½ cup diced celery
½ cup minced green bell pepper
½ cup minced red bell pepper
¾ cup diced cucumber
1¼ cups peeled, seeded and
   diced tomatoes
2 tablespoons shredded fresh basil

1½ tablespoons minced fresh parsley
1 teaspoon minced fresh thyme
1½ tablespoons cider vinegar
2 teaspoons Worcestershire sauce
4 cups spicy tomato juice, chilled
1¾ cups fresh crab, picked and
   rinsed with cold water
Salt and freshly ground black pepper,
   to taste

Combine all ingredients except crab, salt and pepper. Cover and refrigerate for 8 hours or more. Before serving, add crabmeat and season with salt and pepper. NOTE: This soup must be made ahead. Serve with toasted French or sourdough bread. **SERVES 4-6.**

Eggs, Cheese, Pasta
& SPECIAL SAUCES

Menu

Brunch Before The Scottish Games

Portofino Salad

Smoked Salmon and Dill Potato Salad

Chicken Medallions

Pasties

Scottish Shortbread

Lemon Torte

Summer Sangria

 The Scottish Games, a festival with traditional Highland fiddling, harp and athletic competitions, dog trials, dancing, pipers, crafts and even an antique car show, is held every summer on the 270 year-old campus of Episcopal High School. One of the oldest such events in America, the Games are host to an annual "Gathering of the Clans" who travel here from around the country to celebrate their heritage.

Virginia Apple Hotcakes

2 eggs, slightly beaten
½ cup flour
½ cup milk
¼ teaspoon salt
1 tablespoon margarine or butter
¼ cup margarine or butter

6 cups peeled apple slices
¼ cup sugar (if using tart apples)
½ teaspoon cinnamon
Strawberry or other preserves
  (optional)

Heat ovenproof skillet in a 450 degree oven until very hot. While heating, combine eggs, flour, milk and salt and beat until smooth. Remove skillet from oven and coat with 1 tablespoon butter and immediately pour in batter. Bake on lowest rack in oven at 450 degrees for 10 minutes. Reduce heat to 350 degrees and bake another 10 minutes. Pancake will puff and look like a bowl. While baking pancake, melt ¼ cup butter in another skillet over low heat. Add the apples, sugar if needed, and cinnamon. Cook until apples are tender. When pancake is ready, slit open and fill with apple mixture. Top with preserves. Serve immediately. **SERVES 4-6.**

Apple Dutch

¼ cup plus 1 tablespoon
  all-purpose flour
½ teaspoon baking powder
⅛ teaspoon salt
3 eggs, separated
2 tablespoons sugar, divided
  in half

¼ cup skim milk
1 tablespoon plus 1½ teaspoons
  lemon juice
1 tart apple, cored and cut
  into thin wedges
¼ teaspoon ground cinnamon

Combine flour, baking powder and salt and set aside. Beat egg whites to soft peaks. Gradually add 1 tablespoon sugar, beating until stiff peaks form. Set aside. Combine and mix together egg yolks and milk. Add yolk mixture to the flour mix, stirring just to moisten dry ingredients. Fold reserved egg whites into flour mixture. Stir in lemon juice. Place a 10-inch ovenproof skillet coated with vegetable oil spray in a 375 degree oven for 10 minutes. Pour egg mixture into the hot skillet. Arrange apple slices in a circle on top of the egg mixture. Combine 1 tablespoon sugar and cinnamon; sprinkle over apples. Bake at 375 degrees for 15 minutes. **SERVES 4-6.**

Flannel Cakes

4 cups flour
1 teaspoon salt
¼ cup lukewarm water
   (105-115 degrees)
1 package active dry yeast
3½ cups milk

3 tablespoons sugar
3 eggs, beaten
2 tablespoons butter, melted
Melted butter and maple syrup
   to serve

On the evening before serving, sift together the flour and salt into a bowl and set aside. Dissolve the yeast in the water for about 10 minutes until foamy. Combine the milk and sugar, place in a saucepan and scald. Stir to dissolve sugar. Remove from the heat, pour into a mixing bowl, and stir continually until lukewarm. Add the yeast and beat in the flour mixture to make a dough. Cover with a towel and put in a warm place to rise overnight.

The next morning beat together the eggs and butter and then beat into the dough. Using a hot griddle, cook the cakes as you would regular pancakes. Serve with melted butter and syrup. NOTE: These are delicious colonial-style pancakes which folklore says were named for the flannel towels used to cover the bowls. MAKES ABOUT 2 DOZEN 3-INCH CAKES.

Tidewater Breakfast

16 slices white bread, thinly sliced
8 slices Canadian bacon
8 oz. sharp Cheddar cheese, grated
8 eggs, lightly beaten
3½ cups milk
½ teaspoon salt
½ teaspoon pepper
1 teaspoon dry mustard
½ cup chopped green pepper

1 or 2 teaspoons Worcestershire
   sauce
Dash cayenne pepper
¼ cup butter, melted
Optional additions:
   1 cup crab meat, well picked
   ½ cup onion, finely chopped
   ½ cup mushrooms, finely chopped

Butter a 9x13 baking dish and line with one half of the bread. On each slice of bread, place a round of bacon and ⅛ of the cheese. Top with another layer of bread. Mix eggs and milk with remaining ingredients, except the butter. Pour over the bread. Cover with foil and refrigerate overnight. One hour before baking, remove from refrigerator, uncover and pour melted butter over top. Bake for 1 hour at 350 degrees. SERVES 8.

Cinnamon Pancakes

¼ cup flour
2 teaspoons baking powder
¼ teaspoon nutmeg
¼ teaspoon cinnamon
¼ teaspoon salt

2 tablespoons vegetable oil
2 tablespoons dark brown sugar
½ teaspoon vanilla
1 egg
1 ⅓ cups buttermilk

Mix dry ingredients. Blend together oil, brown sugar, vanilla, egg and buttermilk and add to dry ingredients. Let sit for a couple of minutes. Cook pancakes on a hot, well-greased griddle. NOTE: Half and half or a combination of buttermilk and half and half can be substituted. Any milk, such as whole, 2% or skim can also be used. The richer the milk, the more flavorful the pancake. This recipe can be doubled or tripled as necessary. Batter can be made ahead and refrigerated until ready to cook. SERVES 4.

Belgian Waffles

Egg substitute to equal 2 eggs
1 tablespoon sugar
¼ cup butter or margarine, melted
1 cup skim milk
1 teaspoon vanilla extract

2 cups flour
2 teaspoons baking powder
½ teaspoon salt (optional)
4 egg whites

Beat egg substitute and sugar in bowl until light. Add cooled melted butter, milk and vanilla extract. Add flour, baking powder and salt and beat well. Beat egg whites until stiff and gently fold into the batter. Bake in a waffle iron. MAKES 10 4½-INCH SQUARE WAFFLES.

Eggs in a Jacket

4 large potatoes
1 oz. butter

Salt and pepper to taste
4 medium-size eggs

Scrub potatoes and place on cookie sheet which has been lightly greased. Bake at 400 degrees for 1 ½ hours or until soft. Remove from the oven and cut a slice from the top of each potato. Do not turn off oven. Carefully remove potato from the shells so as not to pierce the skin. Mix potato with the butter and seasonings and return to the shell. Make a well in the potato center and break an egg into each well. Return to the oven for another 10 minutes or so to set egg. NOTE: This makes an excellent supper for a winter's night when served with a green salad. SERVES 4.

Basic Omelette for Two

4 eggs	**⅛ teaspoon pepper**
¼ cup milk or water	**1 tablespoon butter or margarine**
½ teaspoon salt	**Filling (see below)**

In a bowl, beat the eggs until frothy and light. Add milk, salt and pepper and beat again. Melt butter in an 8-inch omelette pan over medium heat. Make sure butter coats entire bottom of pan. Pour in the egg mixture and cook until the edges begin to set. Do not stir. Lift up a portion of the egg with a spatula and allow uncooked egg to run underneath. Work your way around the omelette until all uncooked egg has been allowed to run underneath. You may tilt the pan if necessary. Cook until the liquid has set and the top is creamy. Add any filling you desire and fold half of the omelette over the other half and serve.

FILLING VARIATIONS FOR TWO:

½ cup shredded sharp Cheddar cheese

¼ cup finely diced cooked ham

½ cup thawed frozen fruit such as raspberries or strawberries. (When ready to serve, top with a bit of sour cream and a sprinkle of powdered sugar)

½ cup sliced mushrooms, sautéed

Bacon, crumbled and combined with ½ cup finely chopped tomatoes

Hot pepper jelly or marmalade

Bacon and Eggs Mornay

1 pound bacon	2 tablespoons dry mustard
¼ cup diced onion	Dash of Worcestershire sauce
¼ cup diced green pepper	1 cup shredded sharp cheese
¼ cup flour	⅔ cup peeled and chopped tomato
1 ½ teaspoons salt	8 hard cooked eggs, diced
½ teaspoon paprika	6 English muffins or
2 cups milk	patty shells for serving

Preheat oven to 350 degrees. Fry bacon until crisp, saving 3 tablespoons of the drippings. Break all but 4 strips of bacon into 1-inch lengths. Sauté onion and pepper in bacon drippings until soft. Blend in flour, salt and paprika. Add milk and cook, stirring constantly, until thickened. Add mustard, cheese, tomato and Worcestershire sauce. Stir and heat until cheese is melted. Add eggs and broken bacon. Pour into greased 9x13 casserole and bake for 20-30 minutes or until bubbly. Garnish with bacon strips. Can be made ahead and baked just prior to serving. SERVES 4-6.

Spicy Vegetable Cheese Omelette

2 tablespoons olive oil	8 asparagus spears, chopped
¾ cup medium chopped red pepper	1½ teaspoons garlic powder
¼ cup medium chopped red onion	1½ cups shredded Monterey Jack
1 ¾ cups chopped fresh broccoli	with jalapeño cheese
8 mushrooms, sliced	6 large eggs

In a 10-inch skillet, heat olive oil and sauté the vegetables until tender. Stir in garlic powder. Remove from pan and set aside. Keeping pan warm, beat the eggs and pour into the pan. Do not scramble. Add the shredded cheese and cook evenly until pancake is formed. Fold sautéed vegetables into the pancake. Slice in half and serve. SERVES 3.

Zucchini Quiche

1 deep-dish pie shell, prebaked	3 eggs, beaten
½ pound mushrooms, sliced	1 teaspoon dill
3 medium zucchini, sliced	⅛ teaspoon pepper

1 clove garlic, minced
1 onion, chopped
3 tablespoons butter or margarine

1 teaspoon parsley
1 large tomato cut in chunks
2 cups cubed Monterey Jack cheese

Sauté mushrooms, zucchini, garlic and onion in margarine or butter. Drain and place in prebaked pie shell. Beat the eggs, parsley and seasonings together Pour over the zucchini mixture. Distribute the tomato and cheese chunks on top. Bake in a 325 degree preheated oven for 45-50 minutes. Freezes well. **SERVES 6.**

Cheese Soufflé Superior

Butter for soufflé dish
1½ cups grated Swiss or
  Gruyère cheese (about 6-oz.)
2-3 tablespoons freshly grated
  Parmesan cheese
1¾ cups milk
6 tablespoons butter
5½ tablespoons flour

½ teaspoon freshly grated nutmeg
1 teaspoon salt
Large pinch cayenne pepper
¼ teaspoon freshly ground
  black pepper
1½ tablespoons Dijon mustard
6 egg yolks
7 egg whites

Preheat oven to 400 degrees. Using a 2-quart soufflé dish, butter bottom and sides and sprinkle with grated cheeses. Shake off the excess onto a piece of waxed paper and set aside for later use.

Bring the milk almost to a boil, gradually, in a saucepan. In another pan, melt the butter and add the flour. Stir to form a roux and cook, stirring constantly, for about 3 minutes so that flour is cooked thoroughly but not brown. Remove milk from stove and add roux all at once, using a whisk to stir vigorously. Put pan back on stove and cook for another minute or two, stirring constantly, until smooth and thick. Remove from stove and season with spices and mustard. Add yolks to the pan, one at a time, stirring after each addition. Add reserved cheeses and check seasonings for taste. If you wish to delay making the soufflé, cover with waxed paper or plastic wrap so that a skin will not form.

When ready to bake, whip the egg whites until stiff but not dry. Using a whisk, vigorously stir ¼ of the egg whites into cheese mixture. Then pour the cheese mixture over the remaining ¾ of the egg whites and fold in the mixture. Spoon into the prepared soufflé dish and smooth the top with a spatula. Run your finger or thumb around the rim near the mixture. Place the soufflé on the lowest oven rack and bake for 35-40 minutes or until done. Serve at once. **SERVES 4.**

Dilled Onion Soufflé

Butter for pan
2 tablespoons butter
1 medium onion, minced
½ teaspoon dried dillweed
¼ teaspoon salt

2 tablespoons flour
¾ cup milk
3 eggs, separated
2 tablespoons freshly grated
  Parmesan cheese

Heat oven to 375 degrees. Butter a 4-cup soufflé dish lightly. Melt butter in a saucepan. Sauté onion in butter until golden and tender. Add dillweed, salt and flour and cook for about 2 minutes more. Using a whisk, slowly pour in milk and stir constantly until thickened. Remove pan from stove and add each egg yolk separately, beating after each addition. Whip the egg whites until firm but not dry. Fold into egg yolk mixture. Pour into buttered mold and top with grated Parmesan. Bake at 375 degrees for 15-18 minutes or until brown and puffy. Serve immediately. NOTE: This is wonderful as an accompaniment to fish. **SERVES 4.**

Spinach Soufflé

¼ cup margarine
1 tablespoon grated onion
5 tablespoons flour
1 cup milk
1 cup grated Swiss cheese
  (or combination of grated Swiss
  and Cheddar)

1 package frozen chopped spinach,
  thawed and drained
Salt, pepper and celery salt
  to taste
3 eggs, separated

Preheat oven to 350 degrees. In a large skillet, melt margarine; add salt, pepper, celery salt and onions and sauté for 2 minutes. Add flour. Add milk and stir until thick and smooth. Add spinach. Add cheese and mix. Turn off heat. Separate eggs. Beat yolks lightly and add to spinach mixture. Beat egg whites until stiff and fold into spinach mixture. Pour into a greased soufflé dish and bake for 45 minutes. Can be doubled easily. **Serves 4.**

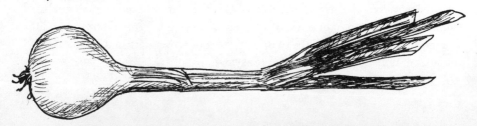

Cappellini with Oil and Garlic Sauce

⅓ cup + 1 tablespoon olive oil
1 small onion, chopped
2 cloves garlic, chopped
3 tablespoons minced fresh parsley
⅛ teaspoon crushed red pepper flakes
  (or cayenne pepper, for a
  sharper flavor)

¼ cup pine nuts
⅓ - ½ cup sun-dried tomatoes,
  drained and chopped
8-9 oz. cappellini (angel hair pasta),
  uncooked

Heat olive oil over low heat in a small saucepan. Add onion and sauté until softened but not brown, about 5 minutes. Stir in garlic, parsley and red pepper and cook for 1 minute longer. Add dried tomatoes and pine nuts and keep warm over low heat. Cook pasta according to package directions. Drain pasta in a colander. Transfer pasta to a large, warm bowl and add sauce. Toss to coat. NOTE: To serve cold, substitute 1 tablespoon oil with 1 tablespoon balsamic vinegar. SERVES 4-5.

Mozzarella Baskets

1 loaf firm French bread,
  thickly sliced
Mozzarella cheese cut in
  ¼-inch slices
3 eggs, beaten

1 teaspoon salt
Vegetable oil
Anchovy Butter
Basic Tomato Sauce

Using a cookie cutter of your chosen shape, cut two pieces of bread per person. Place a slice of mozzarella between the two pieces of bread. When ready to serve, beat the eggs with the salt. Soak the sandwiches in the egg and let stand about 15 minutes. Heat ½-inch of oil in a skillet to about 360 degrees. Fry the sandwiches on each side until they are crisp and golden. Serve topped with a spoonful of the Basic Tomato Sauce and Anchovy Butter on the side. SERVES 8.

Anchovy Butter

1 anchovy filet, mashed   2 oz. sweet butter
  (or ¼ teaspoon anchovy paste)

Blend the filet and butter and cook over a low heat until the butter is melted. Serve warm.

Pesto Sauce

½ cup finely chopped basil leaves   Pinch of salt
¼ cup finely chopped walnuts   ¾ cup olive oil
  or pine nuts   ¼ cup freshly grated Parmesan
2-3 cloves of garlic, minced   or Romano cheese
Juice of 1 lemon

Using a food processor, blend together all ingredients except the cheese. For a thinner sauce, add more olive oil. Stir in the cheese. The pesto sauce will keep for several months refrigerated. Pour a thin layer of olive oil on top and seal in a tight jar.

Basic Tomato Sauce

1 carrot, minced   4 parsley sprigs, snipped
1 stalk celery, minced   1 tablespoon snipped fresh basil
1 onion, finely chopped   or ½ teaspoon dried
4 tablespoons olive oil   Salt and pepper
4 cups (32 oz.) Italian plum
  tomatoes, fresh or canned

Cook the carrot, celery and onion in the olive oil until barely tender. If the tomatoes are canned, chop them coarsely; if fresh, peel, seed and chop. Add tomatoes, parsley and basil. Salt and pepper, to taste. Simmer, covered, for 30 minutes. Uncover and simmer another 15 minutes or until tomatoes are reduced to pulp. It can be run through a blender or food processor at this point if you wish a smoother sauce. This sauce will keep for a week in the refrigerator and for months if frozen. **MAKES ABOUT 1 PINT.**

Linguine with Broccoli

1 large bunch of broccoli	½ teaspoon black pepper
3 quarts water	⅔ cup dry white wine
2 tablespoons salt	1 pound fresh linguine
3 tablespoons olive oil	1 cup fresh Parmesan cheese, grated
3 tablespoons butter	Salt and pepper to taste
7 medium garlic cloves, minced	

Trim the broccoli into flowerets so that each has about 2 inches of the stem left. Cut flowerets in ½-inch wide pieces. Bring water and salt to boil in a large pot. Add broccoli to boiling water and cook until just tender. Melt the butter in a medium saucepan and add the oil, garlic and black pepper. Sauté the garlic until light brown in color over a medium heat. Do not overcook. Turn heat to medium high and immediately add wine. Bring to boil and reduce heat to simmer for three minutes. Remove from stove and set aside. Upon serving, add broccoli to wine mixture and gently reheat. Boil pasta until *al dente* and drain. Add pasta and broccoli to a warm large mixing bowl. Add Parmesan cheese and toss gently. Correct seasonings if necessary. **SERVES 6 AS A FIRST COURSE.**

Linguine Genovese

2 cups loosely packed fresh basil leaves (about 1 ½ cups ground)	1 cup olive oil
	2 pounds linguine
4 cloves garlic	Parmesan cheese, grated, to taste
¼ cup pine nuts	Black pepper, to taste

In food processor or grinder, finely grind basil, garlic, pine nuts and oil. Place linguine in boiling, salted water and cook until *al dente* (still slightly firm, 7-10 minutes) or to your taste. Place pesto sauce in a large serving bowl. Drain cooked linguine and place in serving bowl with pesto. Toss linguine, pesto, Parmesan cheese and black pepper. NOTE: This recipe is from Genoa, so serve it on Columbus Day! Basil is said to be good for digestion. This makes an excellent first course when half portions are served. **SERVES 8.** *Geranio Restaurant, 722 King Street*

Tomato and Asparagus Penne

6 tablespoons olive oil	½ cup dry white wine
1 leek, well washed, dried and minced	1 tablespoon chopped fresh tarragon
1 red bell pepper, seeded and minced	4 tablespoons chopped fresh basil
4 cloves garlic, minced	Salt and pepper to taste
2 carrots, peeled and minced	1½ pounds penne pasta
2 large ripe tomatoes, seeded and diced	1½ pounds thin, fresh asparagus
	1 large egg
1½ large cans whole tomatoes, drained (42 oz.)	2 large egg yolks
	1 cup heavy cream
	2 cups freshly grated Parmesan cheese

Using 4 tablespoons of the olive oil, sauté the leek, bell pepper, garlic and carrots for about 10 minutes. Stir in the fresh tomatoes and sauté about 2 minutes more. Add the canned tomatoes and break up with the back of a spoon. Add wine, tarragon and half the basil. Add salt and pepper to taste. Simmer, uncovered, for 45 minutes. Stir occasionally. Cook pasta in boiling water until *al dente*. Meanwhile snap the tough ends off the asparagus and slice diagonally the remaining stalks into 2-inch pieces. Sauté in the remaining 2 tablespoon of olive oil over high heat until just tender. Set aside.

When pasta is about finished, place egg yolks, cream and egg in a small bowl and whisk together. Add asparagus and remainder of the basil to tomato sauce and heat thoroughly. Drain pasta and place in warmed large bowl. Add tomato sauce and toss. Quickly stir in the eggs and about 1 cup of the Parmesan cheese. Toss and serve immediately. Serve with remaining Parmesan on the side. NOTE: This is excellent reheated in the microwave. SERVES 6.

Fettuccine with Pistachio Sauce

¾ pound roasted and salted pistachio nuts	2 cloves garlic, crushed
¼ cup olive oil	Salt and pepper to taste
¾ cup cream	1 pound fettuccine

Remove pistachio shells, saving the nut meats. Crush enough to break meat, but not finely. In a heavy skillet, add crushed nut meats and garlic to olive oil; sauté over medium heat for 5 minutes. Add cream, salt and pepper and continue to cook, reducing the mixture slightly. Boil the fettuccine until *al dente* or according to your taste. Toss the sauce with the pasta and serve. **SERVES 4 AS A FIRST PLATE OR "PRIMO PIATTO."**

Chicken Fettuccine Quattro Formaggi

1 portion fresh fettuccine	5 oz. cream sauce
¼ cup diced Mozzarella	1 tablespoon sun-dried tomatoes
¼ cup diced Fontina cheese	¾ cup cooked chicken, diced
2 tablespoons diced Gorgonzola	1 tablespoon chopped scallion
cheese	1 tablespoon pine nuts,
2 tablespoons Parmesan cheese	lightly toasted

Place the cheeses, cream sauce, sun-dried tomatoes and chicken in a saucepan and heat until hot but not boiling. Simultaneously, cook the fettuccine in boiling salted water. Drain the fettuccine well and toss with the hot cheese sauce to gently mix. Place on a serving plate or in a bowl and garnish with chopped scallions and toasted pine nuts. **SERVES 1.** *Ecco Cafe, 220 North Lee Street*

Pasta Primavera

2 carrots, sliced	½ teaspoon marjoram
½ pound broccoli	½-1 box petit pois, defrosted
1 onion, diced	½ box cherry tomatoes, halved
1 clove garlic, minced	¼ cup white wine
4 tablespoons butter	14 oz. pasta, cooked *al dente*
½ pound mushrooms,	Salt and pepper to taste
thickly sliced	Parmesan cheese, freshly grated
½ teaspoon basil	

Steam carrots until barely fork tender. Drain. Cut broccoli into flowerets and slice stems about ½-inch thick. Steam until barely tender. Drain. Meanwhile sauté onion and garlic in butter until limp. Add mushrooms, basil and marjoram and sauté another minute or two. If necessary add a bit more butter. Add petit pois, tomatoes, wine, carrots and broccoli. Cook another minute or two and add drained pasta and salt and pepper to taste. Serve with freshly grated Parmesan cheese. NOTE: Cream can be added to the wine sauce for a thicker sauce. **SERVES 4.**

Sweet and Sour Pasta

2 cups pasta of a variety
  of shapes, uncooked
½ purple onion, chopped fine
¼ cup finely chopped green
  or red bell pepper
1 stalk celery, chopped fine
1 small carrot, diced
2 tablespoons finely chopped
  fresh chives
1 tablespoon finely chopped
  fresh parsley

¼ cup olive oil
1 tablespoon white wine vinegar
1 teaspoon sugar
¼ cup mayonnaise
¼ cup sour cream
1 teaspoon salt
Freshly ground black pepper
Parsley or pepper strips
  for decoration

In a medium pot, cook the pasta for 5-6 minutes or until *al dente* and drain. Transfer pasta to a large bowl and add the onion, green or red pepper, celery, carrot, chives and parsley. Set aside. In a medium bowl, combine the olive oil, vinegar, sugar, mayonnaise, sour cream, salt, and pepper. Use a whisk to beat until very creamy. Pour over pasta and mix well. Cover and refrigerate a few hours. Remove the salad from the refrigerator 30 minutes before serving. Decorate with parsley or pepper strips before serving. NOTE: Low fat mayonnaise and sour cream can be used to make this a low calorie meal. SERVES 4-6.

Tortellini Rosé

4 oz. heavy cream
2 tablespoons butter
2 tablespoons finely grated
  Romano cheese
2 tablespoons pancetta or bacon
2 tablespoons sun-dried tomatoes

Salt and pepper, to taste
12 oz. tri-colored tortellini,
  filled with Ricotta and Gorgonzola
2 teaspoons pesto sauce
Freshly grated Romano

Sauté all ingredients except tortellini, pesto and Romano in a medium saucepan or skillet, making a creamy tomato sauce. At the same time, cook tortellini, until *al dente* or to your liking. Toss sauce with pasta. Serve on a plate with 1 teaspoon of pesto in the center and a sprinkling of Romano. *Radio Free Italy, 5 Cameron Street*

Tortellini and Chicken Salad

1 pound cheese tortellini
1½ cups pesto sauce
3 cups shredded cooked chicken
⅓ cup parsley

⅓ cup chopped chives
½ small Bermuda onion, chopped
8 oz. plain yogurt
¼ cup olive oil if needed

Cook tortellini for 7 minutes or until *al dente*. Add pesto and chill for 4 hours. Add chicken, parsley, chives, onion and yogurt. Chill until ready to serve. Only add oil if needed to thin. NOTE: A great summer dish for a picnic. SERVES 6.

Rosemary Pasta Salad with Chicken

4 whole chicken breasts poached
  in chicken stock 20 minutes
  and shredded
1 pound pasta, such as rotini

2 zucchini, sliced ⅛-inch thick
½ cup chopped scallions
½ cup minced parsley
1½ cups shredded lettuce

DRESSING:

2 cups safflower oil
1 cup lemon juice
2 tablespoons garlic salt
3 tablespoons sugar

3½ tablespoons dry mustard
¼ oz. fresh rosemary, minced
2½ teaspoons pepper
Salt to taste

Prepare dressing by mixing all ingredients except the oil. Slowly beat in the oil with a whisk, drizzling oil into the bowl in a steady stream. Cook pasta in boiling water with oil and salt. Drain. Put in large bowl. Add chicken and toss with 4/5 of the rosemary dressing. Chill 24 hours. When ready to serve, toss chicken and pasta mixture with zucchini, scallions, parsley and lettuce and remaining dressing. NOTE: Other fresh vegetables can be blanched the day ahead and added to the pasta such as asparagus tips, snow peas, carrots, pepper strips and mushrooms. SERVES 16-20.

Fettuccine with Spinach

2 tablespoons olive oil
3 large cloves garlic, crushed
1 medium onion, diced
2 10-oz. packages frozen,
 chopped spinach, thawed

1 cup chicken broth or white wine
1 pound cooked fettuccine
½ cup crumbled Feta cheese
 (or more, to taste)

Sauté garlic and onion in olive oil. Add spinach and broth (or wine) and bring to a boil. Toss with hot fettuccine. Serve with small amounts of Feta cheese on top. **SERVES 2.**
♥ *The Cardiovascular Service Program at Alexandria Hospital*

Baked Ziti

¾ pound small ziti
3 sweet, hot Italian sausages
 (or Italian turkey sausage)
1 cup chopped onion
3 garlic cloves, minced
2 tablespoons olive oil
2 tablespoons minced parsley
2 16-oz. cans crushed or stewed
 tomatoes

Pepper to taste
½ cup Parmesan cheese
1 pint Ricotta or low fat
 cottage cheese grated
1 egg, beaten
1 cup grated Mozzarella cheese,
 low fat or regular
Grated nutmeg, to taste

Cook ziti for 8 minutes. Drain and cool. Remove sausage from casings, break up and sauté with onion and garlic in the olive oil. Add parsley, tomatoes and pepper and cook 25 minutes over low heat. Mix Parmesan, egg, Ricotta and nutmeg. Add ziti. Spray a 9x13 pan with a vegetable spray and add a little sauce. Add ziti and rest of the sauce. Sprinkle Mozzarella on top. Cover lightly with foil and bake at 350 degrees for 25 minutes. Remove foil and bake another 15 minutes. Let stand before serving. **Serves 6.**

Basque Country Spaghetti with Shrimp

½ pound thin spaghetti
4 tablespoons butter or margarine
4 tablespoons olive oil
4 large garlic cloves, chopped
20 medium shrimp,
  peeled and deveined
¼ teaspoon salt

½ teaspoon freshly ground
  black pepper
3 tablespoons minced fresh
  parsley
¼ cup freshly grated Parmesan
  cheese

In a large saucepan bring 3 quarts of water to a boil. Add spaghetti and cook until tender but still firm. Meanwhile, heat butter and olive oil over medium heat in a large skillet. Add garlic, cooking until golden; discard garlic pieces. Add shrimp, salt, pepper and 2 tablespoons of the parsley to the skillet and cook for 1-3 minutes until shrimp turns pink. Remove skillet from heat. Drain spaghetti and add to skillet. Add Parmesan cheese. Place in a warmed serving bowl and sprinkle with remaining 1 tablespoon parsley. Serve immediately. SERVES 4

Shrimp Scampi with Linguine

½ cup olive oil
3 tablespoons parsley
2 tablespoons fresh lemon juice
1 teaspoon salt
½ teaspoon pepper

4 cloves garlic, minced
1½ pounds large shelled shrimp
1 pound linguine
Parmesan cheese, freshly grated
Parsley, chopped for garnish

Combine olive oil with parsley, lemon juice, salt, pepper and garlic. Pour over the shrimp to marinate at least 30 minutes prior to serving. When ready to serve, cook linguine until *al dente* or to your taste. While cooking, preheat oven to broil. Place shrimp and sauce in a 9x13 pan. Broil shrimp and sauce until shrimp is pink. Mix with cooked pasta and sprinkle with Parmesan cheese and parsley on top. SERVES 8-10.

Red Snapper Pasta with Sauce

2 tablespoons olive oil
1½ pounds red snapper filets
  cut into approximately
  1-inch size pieces
1 large onion, grated or pureed
  in the food processor
½ pound mushrooms, sliced
1 small can of tomato paste
1 tablespoon flour

Juice of 1 lemon
2-3 cups skim milk
¼ teaspoon ground nutmeg
1 pound cooked fettucine
  or other pasta of your choice
Parsley, chopped for garnish
Parmesan cheese, freshly grated,
  for garnish

In a skillet, heat the olive oil and sauté the pieces of red snapper over low heat. The snapper will exude a lot of juice and most of this will not evaporate. When the snapper is firm but not browned, remove from the skillet and add the onion and mushrooms; simmer until the mushrooms are cooked, about 10 minutes. Turn off the heat, add the tomato paste and stir until the onion, tomato paste and mushrooms are well mixed; add the lemon juice and stir well. Sprinkle flour over the mixture and stir until well blended. Slowly add two cups of skim milk, stirring throughout to make a smooth mixture.

Once this is complete, return skillet to the stove and simmer over low heat until the mixture begins to thicken. Depending on the consistency of the mixture, you may need to add more milk to make a sauce the consistency of heavy cream. Add the nutmeg and return the snapper to the sauce until it is heated, about 5 minutes.

Toss with your favorite pasta and sprinkle with chopped parsley and grated Parmesan cheese to taste. **SERVES 4.** ♥ *The Cardiovascular Service Program at Alexandria Hospital*

Warm Cucumber-Rosemary Sauce

1¼ cups peeled, seeded and
  coarsely chopped cucumbers
  (about 2 medium)
⅓ cup diced sweet red pepper
1 tablespoon sugar
½ teaspoon salt

¼ teaspoon crushed rosemary
⅛ teaspoon ground ginger
Dash white pepper
3 tablespoons lime juice
2 tablespoons water

Place cucumbers in a small pan with the remaining ingredients. Bring to a boil, reduce heat and simmer, covered, until cucumbers are softened. Stir occasionally. It should take about 3 minutes. Serve warm with fish or chicken. **MAKES ABOUT 1½ CUPS.**

Tomato Sauce with Rosemary

3 cups chopped fresh tomatoes
¾ teaspoon grated orange peel
½ teaspoon salt
½ teaspoon garlic powder

¼ teaspoon crushed rosemary
Dash cayenne pepper
2 tablespoons water

Place all ingredients in a small saucepan and bring to a boil. Reduce heat and simmer, covered. Stir occasionally until tomatoes are soft, about 3 to 5 minutes. Serve cold or warm with chicken, lamb, beef, pork or seafood. **MAKES 2½ CUPS.**

Chasseur Sauce

About 6 medium mushrooms
3 tablespoons butter
2 tablespoons finely chopped onion
1 tablespoon flour
¼ cup beef broth

¾ cup water or reserved
mushroom juices from
Individual Beef Wellingtons
½ cup dry red wine

Sauté mushrooms and onion in butter about 3 minutes. Add flour to the broth and blend before adding to mushrooms and onions. Add wine and mushroom juices or water. Bring to a boil and reduce heat. Sauce will be slightly thickened. Serve with Beef Wellington. This sauce can be made ahead and reheated at the last moment. **MAKES ABOUT 1½ CUPS.**

Shenandoah Pork Sauce

¾ cup apple butter
⅓ cup Dijon mustard

1 cup apple cider or apple juice
Pinch of sage

Combine all ingredients and mix well. Slather pork well with mixture before baking.

Sauce Paloise

¼ cup wine vinegar
¼ cup dry white wine
  or vermouth
1 tablespoon minced shallot
  or green onion
3 tablespoons minced fresh
  mint leaves

Pinch of salt
Pinch of freshly ground pepper
3 egg yolks
2 tablespoons cold butter
½ cup butter, melted

Combine vinegar, wine, shallots, tablespoon of the mint leaves, salt and pepper in a small saucepan. Bring to a boil over medium heat and cook until the liquid is reduced to 2 tablespoons. Cool. Strain into another saucepan. Beat the egg yolks until thick and creamy. Stir in the vinegar mixture and beat thoroughly. Add 1 tablespoon cold butter and thicken over very low heat, beating constantly. Beat in another tablespoon of cold butter then add ½ cup of melted butter, drop by drop, beating all the time. When all the butter has been added and the sauce has thickened to the consistency of Hollandaise, take off the heat and beat in 2 tablespoons of the fresh mint leaves. Serve warm with chicken or with hot or cold roast lamb. **MAKES ABOUT ½ CUP.**

Pancho Sauce for Hamburgers

¼ cup horseradish sauce
½ cup catsup
1 teaspoon vinegar
1 teaspoon Worcestershire sauce

3 drops Tabasco sauce
¼ teaspoon ground ginger
1 teaspoon dry mustard
1 tablespoon pineapple sauce

Combine all ingredients and mix well. **MAKES 1 CUP.**

Barbecue Sauce

1 cup catsup
½ cup cola
½ cup water
2 tablespoons butter

4 tablespoons Worcestershire sauce
2 tablespoons apple cider vinegar
2 tablespoons brown sugar
8 drops Tabasco

Place all ingredients in a sauce pan and mix well. Bring to a boil. Simmer for a while. The longer it simmers, the thicker it will be. Serve on chicken, spare ribs and on sandwiches of any meat. Keep refrigerated indefinitely. **MAKES 2 CUPS.**

Beef Marinade

1½ cups vegetable oil
¾ cup soy sauce
¼ cup Worcestershire sauce
2 tablespoons dry mustard
2¼ teaspoons salt
½ tablespoon freshly ground
  pepper

½ cup red wine or garlic-flavored
  vinegar
1½ teaspoons dried parsley flakes
2 cloves garlic, crushed
⅓ cup fresh lemon juice

Mix all ingredients well. Store in refrigerator for 1 week or freeze indefinitely. Soak meat 4-5 hours. **MAKES ABOUT 3½ CUPS.**

Lamb Marinade

¾ cup hot water
⅓ cup soy sauce
¼ cup honey

2 tablespoons olive oil
2 tablespoons fresh lemon juice
4 cloves garlic, crushed

Combine all ingredients and mix well. Marinate lamb for no less than two hours. This is an excellent marinade for shish kabob. **MAKES 1¼ CUPS.**

Raspberry Sauce for Duck

6 tablespoons raspberry preserves
  with no additives
2 tablespoons red wine vinegar

½ teaspoon horseradish
½ teaspoon minced garlic

Combine all ingredients in a saucepan and simmer 3-4 minutes. Serve with cold duck slices garnished with fresh raspberries.

Lime Butter for Vegetables

½ cup butter or margarine, softened
1 tablespoon snipped fresh savory (or
  1 teaspoon dried) or crushed thyme

1 teaspoon finely shredded lime peel

Combine all ingredients. Store, covered, in refrigerator. Serve with corn on the cob or other fresh, cooked vegetables. **MAKES ½ CUP.**

Vegetable Marinade

¼ cup balsamic vinegar
¾ cup olive oil

1 clove garlic, crushed
Salt and pepper, to taste

Dice or slice vegetables as you desire. Peel eggplant if you use it. Marinate vegetables about 1 hour or more, stirring occasionally. Grill vegetables in a basket and use sauce for basting while cooking. **MAKES 1 CUP.**

Crème Fraîche

1 cup heavy cream
1 teaspoon buttermilk

1 teaspoon plain yogurt with active
  enzymes, such as Dannon or Colombo

In a saucepan, scald the cream. Remove from heat and let cream cool to 100 degrees. Use a thermometer to test. Stir in the yogurt and buttermilk until well mixed. Pour into a container, cover and keep in a warm place, about 80 to 90 degrees, overnight or until it has thickened. Chill until ready to use, no more than 7-10 days. MAKES 1 CUP.

Parsley Sauce

1 cup milk
1 tablespoon cornstarch
2 tablespoons margarine

⅛ teaspoon pepper
¼ cup chopped parsley
1½ tablespoons lemon juice

Mix ¼ cup of the milk with the cornstarch in a small saucepan until smooth. Add remaining milk, margarine and pepper. Cook over medium heat, stirring constantly, until mixture comes to a boil. Boil for one minute. Remove from heat. Stir in parsley and lemon juice. NOTE: An excellent accompaniment to Crab Croquettes. YIELDS 1 CUP.

Flavored Oils

Flavored oils have been used for centuries and are as versatile as your imagination. Brush vegetables for roasting, dip in crusty bread for a flavor treat or use to marinate meats.
   2 cups good quality oil, such as olive, canola or sunflower
   1 cup herbs of your choosing

Combine oil and herbs in a processor and puree. Pour into a jar and allow to sit for two days, shaking occasionally. On the third day, allow the herbs to settle to the bottom of the jar. Carefully ladle out the oil and strain thoroughly through a coffee filter. Be sure to strain until the oil is clear but not colored. If cloudy, strain again. Keeps 2-3 weeks.

Try the following combinations:
   Oregano oil for salad dressings
   Dill oil for seafood
   Red pepper flakes and garlic for chicken and seafood
   Thyme, garlic and peppercorns for vegetables and pork
   Basil for chicken, seafood, pasta and vegetables

Accompaniments

Menu

Vegetarian Luncheon
After A Morning At The Farmer's Market

Borscht   PAGE 50

The Salad   PAGE 30

Goat Cheese Quesadillas   PAGE 17

Fettuccine with Pistachio Sauce   PAGE 68

Zuppa Inglese   PAGE 197

Bermuda Bloody Marys   PAGE 25

For more than two centuries Alexandrians have gathered at Market Square in the heart of Old Town, to meet friends, buy produce and select fresh-cut flowers. To catch the best of the country's oldest market in continuous operation, come early on a Saturday morning.

Stuffed Artichokes

4 fresh artichokes
¼ cup butter or margarine
4 tablespoons celery, minced
4 tablespoons onion, minced
1 cup prepared bread crumbs,
  finely cut

½ cup Romano cheese,
  freshly grated
1 clove garlic, crushed
Olive oil

Prepare artichokes. Using kitchen shears, remove tough bottom row of leaves and trim upper leaves by one fourth. Cut off stems. Wash and drain. Melt butter in a small frying pan and sauté celery and onion until soft. Combine bread crumbs, cheese, and garlic in a medium sized bowl. Add butter, celery and onion mixture. Push stuffing between artichoke leaves. Drizzle a small amount of olive oil over each artichoke. Using a heavy pot large enough to hold artichokes, cover bottom of pan with 1 inch of water. Place artichokes in pot, cover, and simmer for one hour. Add small amounts of water throughout cooking, if necessary. **SERVES 4.**

Walnut and Cheese Artichokes

1 artichoke, washed, stem
  removed and trimmed
  ½ inch from tips
¼ cup bulgur wheat
¼ cup boiling water

¼ cup walnuts, chopped finely
¼ cup sharp Cheddar cheese,
  shredded
Fresh oregano, minced

Place wheat in a mixing bowl and cover with boiling water. Cover with plastic wrap and let stand about 20 minutes or until the water is almost all absorbed. Pour off any excess water and add walnuts, cheese and oregano to taste to the wheat. Stuff the mixture into the spaces between the artichoke leaves. Hold it over mixing bowl as you do this. Place a rack in a large pot and add enough water to just cover the rack. Put artichoke on the rack, cover pot and steam over a low heat for about 30 to 45 minutes or until leaves pull away easily. **MAKES 1 SERVING.**

Asparagus Chantilly

1 pound asparagus
½ cup whipping cream, whipped
Fresh lemon juice

Salt and pepper to taste
Paprika

Cook asparagus until just tender, drain and arrange on a round platter with the points into the center. Whip the cream, season with salt, pepper and a little lemon juice and spoon onto middle of platter. Sprinkle a bit of paprika over whipped cream. Serve as a beautiful buffet dish. Quantities can be adjusted to suit the size of your crowd.

Warm Sesame Asparagus

2 pounds asparagus
1 small shallot, peeled and chopped
¼ cup olive oil
2 tablespoons rice wine vinegar
1 tablespoon orange juice

1 teaspoon Dijon mustard
¼ teaspoon Oriental sesame oil
¼ teaspoon salt
1 hard cooked egg white, chopped

Wrap asparagus air tight in plastic wrap. Place on a paper plate and microwave on high for 3-8 minutes (depending on wattage) until tender. Combine remaining ingredients except chopped egg white in a small bowl. Cover and microwave on high one minute. Unwrap asparagus, place on serving plate, cover with dressing and sprinkle egg white on top.

Gail's Ginger Carrots

24 carrots, cut in 1-inch lengths
4 tablespoons butter (½ stick)
½ cup brown sugar

1½ teaspoons grated fresh ginger
Dash of salt

Cook carrots in just enough water to cover in a pot with a tight lid. When carrots are tender, drain and return to the pan. Add butter, sugar, ginger and salt. Mix well. Cook over low heat for 5 minutes, turning often. Transfer to heated serving dish. **SERVES 12.**

Moroccan Carrots

2½-3 pounds carrots,
  peeled and cut in ½-inch
  diagonal slices
1 cup olive oil
1 cup red wine vinegar
1 cup or more fresh parsley,
  finely chopped

8-10 cloves garlic, finely chopped
2 tablespoons ground cumin
2 tablespoons ground sweet paprika
1 teaspoon salt, if desired
½ teaspoon freshly ground pepper

Steam carrot slices until tender but still firm. Whisk together oil and vinegar; add other ingredients. Pour sauce over carrots while still warm and toss. Serve hot or cold. SERVES 8.

Celery Root

1 celery root
Butter

Salt and pepper to taste
Fresh parsley, chopped

Using a stiff brush, clean the celery root well. The crevices could be filled with dirt! When ready to prepare, peel the root and slice thin. Sauté in plenty of butter until tender and just about to become golden. Remove from heat, add salt, pepper and toss with plenty of chopped parsley. Complements duck or goose extremely well but is good with almost everything.

Sautéed Corn

2 tablespoons olive oil
2 tablespoons unsalted butter
1 small onion, chopped
2 cups fresh corn kernels,
  about 8 ears of corn

¾ cup chopped green pepper
2 teaspoons white wine vinegar
Salt and pepper to taste
1 teaspoon chopped fresh dill

Heat the oil and butter in a skillet. Stir in onion and cook slowly for 5 minutes. Raise the heat to moderately high and add corn and sauté 1 minute, stirring. Add the green pepper and sauté 1-2 minutes longer. Stir in vinegar, salt, pepper and dill. Accompanies grilled chicken or fish nicely. **SERVES 4.**

Corn Casserole

¼ **cup butter or margarine**	¼ **teaspoon salt**
¼ **cup flour**	¼ **teaspoon pepper**
¼ **cup sugar**	**2 medium eggs, slightly beaten**
2 16-oz. cans creamed corn	

Preheat oven to 350 degrees. Melt butter in a 2-quart casserole dish until bubbly but not brown. While butter is melting, mix flour, sugar, salt and pepper in a medium-sized mixing bowl. Stir eggs into dry ingredients until mixture is smooth. Add creamed corn to batter and mix well. Pour corn mixture into hot casserole dish and bake, uncovered, for approximately 1 hour. NOTE: This recipe may be doubled or tripled but the amount of butter need not be increased proportionately. **SERVES 6.**

Swiss Corn Pudding

6 ears fresh corn	**1 cup milk**
6 slices bacon	**4 egg yolks**
¼ **cup all-purpose flour**	**4 oz. shredded, processed Swiss cheese**
¼ **teaspoon salt**	**4 egg whites**

Cut kernels from cob. You should then have about 2 cups cut corn. Cook corn, covered, in a small amount of boiling, salted water for 6-8 minutes until done. Drain and set aside. In a skillet, cook bacon until crisp. Drain, reserving ¼ cup drippings. Crumble bacon and set aside. In a saucepan, blend flour, salt and pepper into reserved drippings. Add milk, cook and stir until thickened and bubbly. Remove from heat. Beat egg yolks until thick and lemon-colored. Blend a moderate amount of hot mixture into egg yolks; return to saucepan. Cook, stirring rapidly until blended. Stir in cheese until melted. Stir in corn and bacon. Remove from heat. Beat egg whites until they form stiff peaks. Fold hot mixture into egg whites. Turn into ungreased 1 ½-quart soufflé dish. Bake in 350 degree preheated oven for 30-40 minutes or until knife inserted off-center comes out clean. Garnish with bacon curl, if desired. NOTE: One 9-oz. package of frozen corn may be substituted when fresh is not available. **SERVES 4-6.**

Hunt Country Corn Pudding

3 eggs
⅔ cup sugar
2 cups milk

1 tablespoon melted butter
Salt and pepper to taste
2 cups fresh corn kernels

Beat eggs thoroughly. Add sugar, butter, salt, pepper and milk. Add corn last. Turn into a buttered 1 ½-quart baking dish. Bake in a 375 degree preheated oven for 30-35 minutes. SERVES 4.

Braised Escarole

1 large head, about 1½ pounds,
   escarole or curly chicory
3 tablespoons olive oil

3 cloves garlic, crushed
3 anchovy filets, chopped
Salt and pepper to taste

Remove outer leaves and trim stem of escarole. Cut it in 6 wedges and wash thoroughly. Mix oil, garlic and anchovies in a shallow baking dish. Add escarole wedges and turn so they are thoroughly coated with the oil. Sprinkle with salt and pepper and press a piece of tin foil over escarole — not dish. Bake in a 350 degree oven 35-40 minutes until escarole is very tender. Remove foil occasionally while baking and baste with anchovy-garlic oil. Remember to place foil back on escarole. Escarole can be folded to form a neat package when tender and served as such. SERVES 6.

Green Beans with Feta Cheese

1½ pounds fresh green beans
¾ cup olive oil
½ cup fresh mint
¼ cup white wine vinegar
¾ teaspoon salt

½ teaspoon minced garlic
¼ teaspoon fresh ground pepper
1 cup walnuts, toasted and chopped
1 cup diced green onion
1 cup Feta cheese, broken in pieces

Cook beans until slightly tender. Run under cold water, drain and cool in a shallow serving dish. Combine oil, mint, vinegar, salt, garlic and pepper in a food processor.

Process until smooth. Sprinkle walnuts, onion and cheese over beans. Pour dressing over beans (you may not need all). Chill and serve. SERVES **6-8.**

Green Bean Bundles

2 pounds fresh whole green beans, preferably extra long 6-8 slices of bacon cut in half, proscuitto or Smithfield ham cut in strips	½ cup butter or margarine, melted 1 cup brown sugar, dark or light

Preheat oven to 350 degrees. Make bundles of green beans, at least eight to ten beans per bundle, and wrap with meat strips. Use toothpicks to secure meat around bundles if necessary. Place bundles close together, with seam side down, in a shallow baking dish. In a small mixing bowl, stir the brown sugar and butter together until smooth. Pour over bundles. Bake at least 30 minutes or until bacon crisps. Plan on two bundles per person. SERVES **6.**

Prosciutto and Peas

1 small red onion, minced 4 tablespoons unsalted butter 4 cups fresh peas, shelled 1 tablespoon sugar 4 oz. proscuitto, thinly sliced and cut into thin strips or finely minced Smithfield Ham	1 cup chicken stock Salt to taste Fresh ground pepper to taste 3 tablespoons chopped fresh parsley

Melt the butter in a saucepan and add the onions. Cook until just softened, about 5 minutes, stirring occasionally. Add the peas, sugar and stock and simmer, covered, until the peas are just tender, about 5 minutes. Add the proscuitto and cook another minute. With a slotted spoon, remove peas and proscuitto to a warm serving bowl. Heat remaining liquid on high heat and reduce until it is a syrupy but thin glaze. Pour over peas and season with salt and pepper to taste. Sprinkle with parsley and serve. SERVES **6-8.**

Spinach Horseradish

2 envelopes unflavored gelatin	1½ teaspoons hot horseradish
¼ cup water	1 10-oz. package frozen,
½ teaspoon salt	chopped spinach, thawed
2 tablespoons lemon juice	and well-drained
1 cup mayonnaise	¼ pound crisp fried bacon, chopped
1 10-oz. can beef consommé	4 hard-boiled eggs, finely chopped
¼ cup chopped green onion	

Dissolve gelatin in water. Add salt, lemon juice and mayonnaise to the dissolved gelatin. Add consommé, onion and horseradish; stir well to mix. Gradually add spinach, bacon and eggs. Pour into a 1½-quart mold. Serve with mayonnaise mixed with a small amount of horseradish as an accompaniment to ham. SERVES 8.

Pecan Crisp Squash

2 acorn squash, about 1 pound each,	⅓ cup melted butter or margarine
cut in half lengthwise,	3 tablespoons brown sugar
seeds and membranes removed	½ teaspoon salt
⅔ cup buttery-type cracker crumbs	¼ teaspoon nutmeg
⅓ cup coarsely chopped pecans	

Place squash, cut side down, in an 8-inch square glass pan and cover with waxed paper. Microwave on high for 6 minutes. Meanwhile combine crumbs, butter, sugar, salt and nutmeg. When cooked, turn squash right side up, fill cavities with the mixture, and microwave another 6-8 minutes until squash is tender. Remove waxed paper and let stand 5 minutes before serving. SERVES 4.

Autumn Acorn Squash

4 acorn squash	¼ cup brown sugar
2 tart apples, cored,	¼ cup raisins or cranberries
peeled and chopped	2 tablespoons butter, melted
⅓ cup chopped walnuts	¼ cup maple syrup

Preheat oven to 400 degrees. Cut tops off squash and scrape out seeds and membranes. Place face down in a shallow baking dish. Add ¼ cup water and bake until squash is tender, about one hour. Combine remaining ingredients in a saucepan, heat and mix well. Stuff cooked squash with mixture. Reheat in oven 5 minutes.

To microwave, prepare squash and place in shallow glass dish. Cover with wax paper and cook for 15-20 minutes at high power until tender. Test your microwave. If the power is too low, you may only be able to do two at a time. Prepare remaining ingredients as directed above and stuff squash. Cook in microwave 10 minutes, rotating dish after 5 minutes.

Squash and Carrot Purée

4 pounds carrots	**½ cup butter**
2 medium butternut squash	**1 teaspoon nutmeg, freshly grated**
2 cups water	**½ teaspoon white pepper**
1 cup light cream or half and half	

Peel and shred carrots. Blanch in one cup of water for 1 minute in the microwave. Drain. Peel, half and remove seeds from squash. Cut into 1-inch cubes or smaller. Place squash in a saucepan and cover with one cup or more of water. Bring to a boil and simmer until very tender, about 30-40 minutes. Drain liquid and purée both squash and carrots in a processor. Transfer to a large bowl and pour butter over and beat well. Beat in rest of ingredients. Best served hot so reheat in microwave if necessary. **SERVES 24.**

Squash Napoli

1 small onion or more, chopped	**2 zucchini, sliced but not peeled**
1 tablespoon or more olive oil	**¼ teaspoon oregano**
1 tomato, chopped	**Salt and pepper to taste**

Sauté onion in oil until clear but not brown in a saucepan. Add zucchini, tomato and spices. Cover and simmer on low heat, shaking the pan occasionally to keep vegetables from sticking, for 35-40 minutes or until tender. **SERVES 4.**

Scalloped Tomatoes and Artichoke Hearts

1 2-pound 3-oz. can whole
   plum tomatoes
1 14-oz. can artichoke hearts
½ cup finely chopped onion
2 tablespoons finely chopped
   shallots

6 tablespoons butter
½ teaspoon dried basil
2 tablespoons sugar
Salt and pepper to taste

Preheat oven to 325 degrees. Grease a shallow earthenware or other casserole. Drain tomatoes and artichokes well. Rinse artichokes in water and quarter or half, depending on size. Leave tomatoes whole. Sauté onions and shallots in butter in a saucepan until tender. Add tomatoes, artichokes and basil. Heat 2-3 minutes, stirring gently. Season with sugar, salt and pepper. Turn into a greased casserole and bake at 325 degrees for 10-15 minutes until vegetables are heated through. This can be made a day ahead but not put in oven until 10-15 minutes before serving. NOTE: This is excellent when served over angel hair pasta. When serving over pasta, retain a little liquid from the tomatoes to thin the mixture. SERVES 4-6.

Zucchini Mexicana

3 large zucchini
2½ cups grated Monterey Jack
6 tablespoons diced green chiles
¼ cup chopped pine nuts

3 tablespoons chopped green onions
1 small can sliced black olives
Seasoned salt

Parboil washed but not pared zucchini in salted water for 3 minutes. Remove, cool, chop off ends and slice in half lengthwise. Partially hollow out the zucchini halves and salt them lightly if desired. Mix together the cheese, chiles, pine nuts, green onions and olives. Fill zucchini hollows to heaping. Sprinkle with a little seasoned salt and place on a greased baking sheet. Bake at 350 degrees for 20 minutes. Serve as a main or first course. SERVES 6.

Grated Zucchini

6 medium zucchini, washed
  and coarsely grated
½ teaspoon salt
3 green onions, chopped

Juice of half a lemon
⅛ teaspoon freshly ground pepper
3 tablespoons butter

Place grated zucchini in a colander and add the salt. Let sit for one half hour. Press out the zucchini so all the liquid is released and mix the zucchini with all the ingredients except the butter. Melt the butter in a large skillet, add zucchini and cook, stirring, about 5 minutes. It should be tender but still a little crisp. **Serves 6.**

Zucchini-Carrot Vinaigrette

6 medium zucchini (6-inches long)
½ teaspoon salt
4-6 young carrots (6 inches long)
¼ teaspoon salt
¼ teaspoon sugar
1 recipe Lemon Vinaigrette
Lettuce or chicory leaves

2 tablespoons finely chopped
  fresh parsley
2 tablespoons finely chopped
  green onions
1 teaspoon coarsely grated lemon peel
Cherry tomatoes

Julienne zucchini and carrots after cleaning. Be sure to pare carrots and cut ends off zucchini. Blanch zucchini in ½ cup boiling water with ½ teaspoon salt for no more than 3 minutes. Drain. Place carrots in a saucepan. Add ½ inch boiling water, ¼ teaspoon salt and ¼ teaspoon sugar. Cook 5-6 minutes. Drain. Place vegetables in a shallow dish and sprinkle a couple of tablespoons of Lemon Vinaigrette over all. Refrigerate overnight, covered. When ready to serve, line a glass bowl with lettuce leaves. With a slotted spoon, transfer vegetables to the bowl. Top with parsley, onions and lemon peel. Dress with more vinaigrette and line edge of bowl with cherry tomatoes. **Serves 12.**

Roasted Vegetables

Vegetables, washed and cut   **Flavored Oil**
in desired pieces

Place a variety of vegetables such as zucchini, summer squash, eggplant, potatoes, sweet onions and peppers in a roasting pan. Brush vegetables on all sides with a flavored oil. Roast at 500 degrees for 15 minutes until vegetables are crisp and caramelized on the outside.

Grilled Vegetables

Vegetables   **Vegetable Marinade**

Slice a variety of cleaned vegetables as for roasting. Do not use broccoli. Marinate the vegetables at least one hour. Place in a basket, such as a fish basket, and grill over a medium-high heat for 20 minutes.

Black Bean and Chile Cassoulet

1 pound black beans
10 cups vegetable or chicken broth
¼ pound salt pork
2-4 cloves garlic, minced
1 carrot, diced
1 onion, diced
2 tablespoons flour
2 tablespoons tomato purée
2 tablespoons olive oil
2 jalapeño chiles, seeded and diced
1 pound lean pork, diced
  or 3 sausages

1-2½ teaspoons chopped
  fresh thyme
1 bay leaf
1 teaspoon minced fresh rosemary
Salt and pepper
1 cup fine bread crumbs
¼ cup finely chopped cilantro
Sour cream or crème fraîche
  for garnish
Cilantro sprigs

Pour broth in a large pot. Add beans, salt pork, garlic, carrot and onion. Bring to boil. Boil 2 minutes. Remove from heat, cover and let stand 1 hour to soften beans. When soft, bring back to a boil. Turn heat to low and simmer 1 hour. Remove salt pork and beans. Strain bean liquid into a bowl and stir in flour and tomato purée. In the pan, heat olive oil, add chiles and sauté until tender. Remove and set aside. Add pork or sausages and cook until browned on all sides. (If using sausage, remove from casings and slice sausage into ½-inch pieces.) Put meat in pan. Add bean liquid, chiles, thyme, bay leaf, rosemary and salt and pepper to taste. Simmer 1 hour until beans are very soft.

Cover bottom of a casserole with half the beans. Add pork mixture to beans in casserole. Cover pork with rest of beans and liquid. Mix bread crumbs and cilantro and top casserole with about ¼ of the mixture. Can be made ahead to this point. Cover and bake at 350 degrees about 1 hour. Remove cover, sprinkle with remaining crumbs and bake 10 minutes longer. Serve with sour cream and cilantro sprigs. **SERVES 6.**

Southern Baked Beans

4 slices bacon	¾ cup ketchup
1 cup diced Spanish onion	1 cup dark brown sugar, packed
1 large clove garlic, mashed	1 teaspoon dry mustard
16-oz. can oven baked beans	1 tablespoon chili powder
½ cup maple syrup	2 drops hot sauce

Preheat oven to 325 degrees. Cook bacon until crisp and when cool, cut or break in pieces. Add onion and garlic to bacon grease and cook until onion is transparent but not brown. Combine all ingredients, including bacon grease. Pour into an ungreased 2-quart baking dish. Bake uncovered at 325 degrees for 2½-3 hours.

Curried Kidney Beans

2 onions, chopped	2 tablespoons white cider vinegar
2 green peppers, chopped	Salt and pepper to taste
2 green apples, chopped	2 28-oz. cans crushed tomatoes
3 teaspoons curry powder	4 15-oz. cans kidney beans,
¼ pound butter or margarine	slightly drained
1¾ cups brown sugar	Freshly grated Parmesan cheese

Melt butter and sauté onions, peppers, apples and curry powder until tender. Combine tomatoes with sautéed onion mixture, kidney beans, brown sugar, vinegar, salt and pepper in a casserole. Bake at 350 degrees for 30 minutes. Sprinkle with Parmesan before serving. NOTE: This can be prepared ahead and baked 30 minutes before serving. **SERVES 12.**

Hopping John

1 pound black-eyed peas	1 cup rice
¾ pound cubed, parboiled	2½ quarts boiling water
salt pork or fatty bacon	Salt
½ teaspoon salt	White pepper
1 large bay leaf	1 20-oz. can Italian plum tomatoes
1 medium onion, chopped	1 teaspoon basil
8 peppercorns, freshly ground	

Wash peas. Cover with 2 inches cold water. Add pork, salt, bay leaf, onion and peppercorns. Cook until beans are tender. Add more boiling water if necessary. Meanwhile, cook rice until tender and season with salt and pepper. While rice is cooking, heat tomatoes with basil. Serve rice and black-eyed peas separately; pour peas over a mound of rice and surround with tomatoes. SERVES 6.

Lentils with Spinach and Rice

1 medium yellow onion, chopped	½ cup uncooked rice,
2 cloves garlic, mashed	long grain or brown
2 teaspoons olive oil	1 10-oz. package frozen
1 cup dried lentils, washed	chopped spinach, thawed
4 cups chicken broth,	Salt, pepper, hot sauce to taste
boiling water or a combination	

In a 3-quart saucepan, sauté onion and garlic in olive oil until soft and translucent. Add washed lentils and coat with oil, garlic and onions. Add boiling water or chicken broth. Reduce heat to low, cover and simmer about 20 minutes until lentils are al dente. If using brown rice, add with lentils and simmer about 35 minutes. If using long grain rice, stir and bring to a boil again; reduce heat to low, cover and let simmer 15 minutes. Add spinach and additional water or broth if necessary. Continue cooking 5-15 minutes until it reaches desired consistency. Add a few splashes of hot sauce to spice up dish. Remember, it will be spicier the next day! NOTE: This can be made ahead and freezes well. SERVES 8.

Wild Rice Pignoli

5 cups of water
1 cup brown rice
1 cup wild rice
2 tablespoons freshly squeezed
   orange juice
2 tablespoons grated orange peel

¼ cup dried currants
¼ cup olive oil
¾ cup toasted pine nuts
4 tablespoons chopped parsley
Salt and freshly ground pepper, to taste
Parmesan cheese, freshly grated

Prepare rices in separate saucepans with lids. Pour 3 cups of water in one pan, bring to boil, add wild rice and cook, covered, for 25 minutes. Drain and place in a large bowl. Put 2 cups of water in other saucepan and bring to boil. Add brown rice, cover, reduce heat and cook 15 minutes. Combine rices. Add orange juice, peel, currants, oil, parsley and salt and pepper to taste. Place in ovenproof casserole and cover with foil until ready to use. Do not refrigerate. Preheat oven to 350 degrees. Heat rice, covered, for 20 minutes. Sprinkle with Parmesan before serving. **SERVES 6-8.**

Risotto all'Empolese con Carciofi

600 grams of rice
   (Uncle Ben's, parboiled converted)
6 fresh artichokes
   (baby artichokes preferable)
50 grams unsalted butter
One small onion or shallots

2 cubes vegetable bouillon
6 tablespoons olive oil
1 wine glass dry white wine
Parmigian cheese, grated
Salt and pepper to taste

In a pot filled with two liters of water, place the bouillon, pinch of salt and 2 artichokes (after removing outer leaves and tips). Boil until tender. Chop the onion. Place a clay pot on the burner with the olive oil and, after two seconds, add the chopped onion and cook for about 5 minutes. Add the rest of the artichokes which you have previously cleaned and thinly sliced. Cook the artichokes for about 10 minutes. Add the rice and stir using a wooden spoon. Toast the rice until it sticks to the pot, then add one glass of very dry white wine and let evaporate. When the rice sticks to the pot again, slowly add the vegetable and artichoke bouillon a little bit at a time and keep stirring until the rice is cooked and bouillon is absorbed. Rice should be moist. Once the rice is cooked, add the butter and Parmigian cheese and stir for two minutes before serving. **SERVES 10.**
Landini Brothers Restaurant, 115 King Street

Risotto alla Milanese

4-5 tablespoons of butter
1 small onion, chopped very finely
12 oz. risotto
⅔ cup dry white wine

1 quart chicken stock, warmed
Pinch of saffron
Parmesan cheese, freshly grated

Melt 2-3 tablespoons of the butter in a heavy skillet. Add onions and cook until golden, but not brown. Add risotto and stir well so grains are covered in butter. Add wine and cook over moderate heat until absorbed. Add chicken stock, ¾ cup at a time and stir. Add more stock as rice absorbs moisture. Toward the end of cooking, stir continually to keep from sticking. When rice is tender and mixture creamy but not sticky (about 20-30 minutes), add a pinch of saffron and stir to color dish. Add 2 tablespoons butter and two tablespoons Parmesan and mix well. Pass more butter and Parmesan on the side. SERVES 4-6.

Mushroom Risotto

1 oz. dried mushrooms,
   such as morels
11 cups chicken stock
8 tablespoons unsalted butter
1 medium yellow onion, diced
12 oz. button mushrooms,
   cleaned and sliced
2 cups Italian rice
2 tablespoons chopped fresh
   rosemary or 2 teaspoons dried

1 teaspoon dried thyme
Salt and freshly ground pepper,
   to taste
¾ teaspoon saffron
¼ cup freshly grated Parmesan
   cheese
½ cup chopped parsley

Wash dried mushrooms under cold water, gently. In saucepan, add 1 cup chicken stock and bring to boil. Add dried mushrooms, reduce heat and simmer for 2 minutes. Remove from heat and set aside for 30 minutes. Drain mushrooms. In a heavy pan, melt butter and add onions and sliced mushrooms. Gently sauté, about 8-10 minutes, until onions are tender. Add rice, rosemary and thyme. Stirring constantly, sauté for 3 minutes. Bring rest of stock to a boil. Add one cup of stock to casserole. Stir. Continue adding boiling stock as it is absorbed. Stir after each addition. After 15 minutes, add drained dried mushrooms and saffron. Gradually add rest of stock and cook until rice is tender, about 10-15 minutes, and liquid is absorbed. Remove from heat and stir in Parmesan and parsley. **SERVES 8.**

Minnesota Wild Rice

1 pound uncooked wild rice
1 cup butter
1 pound mushrooms, sliced
4 tablespoons minced onion

¼ teaspoon minced garlic
3 cups chicken broth
Salt and pepper to taste

Soak wild rice in a large kettle, covered with hot water, overnight. Rinse and drain several times the next morning. Set aside. Melt butter and add mushrooms, onions and garlic. Cook 5 minutes, stirring often. Add broth. Divide rice equally into two, greased, 1 ½-quart casserole dishes. Salt and pepper to taste. Equally divide liquid mixture into both casseroles. Cover and bake in a 325 degree oven for one hour. Uncover and continue baking 20-25 minutes. NOTE: Keep leftover rice refrigerated. Add chicken or turkey for a delicious main course. **SERVES 12-16.**

Savory Cheese Rice

½ cup rice
1 cup milk
1 egg
⅓ cup salad oil
½ cup chopped parsley

1 teaspoon salt
1 cup freshly grated Parmesan
   cheese
¼ cup chopped onion
½ cup chopped green pepper

Cook rice. Let cool. Add rest of ingredients and mix well. Put in a buttered casserole dish. Let sit one hour. Bake 40 minutes in a 300 degree oven. **SERVES 2-3.**

Red Potatoes and Asparagus

4-6 small red potatoes,
  about 1-inch in diameter
¼ pound asparagus

1 tablespoon butter
¼ teaspoon sugar
Salt and pepper to taste

Scrub unpeeled potatoes and cut in quarters. Put in a 1-quart microwave casserole. Add about ¼-inch water. Microwave on high, covered, for about 4-6 minutes or until potatoes are barely tender. While cooking, remove tough ends of asparagus, wash, and cut tender parts in ½-inch pieces. Drain potatoes. Add asparagus, butter and sugar. Salt and pepper. Microwave on high, covered, until asparagus is tender but crisp. Let stand 2 minutes before serving. **SERVES 2.**

Cheddared New Potatoes

1 pound small new potatoes
1½ cups plain yogurt
½ cup green onions, chopped
½ cup tomato, peeled and chopped

1 teaspoon dried oregano
2 cups Cheddar cheese, shredded
Pepper to taste
Parsley, chopped

Scrub potatoes and boil until tender. Split in halves and place in shallow baking dish, cut side up. Combine yogurt, green onions, tomatoes and oregano. Mix well and pour over potatoes. Sprinkle with cheese. Season to taste with salt and pepper and garnish with parsley. Serve immediately. **SERVES 4.**

Portofino Potatoes

2½ pounds baking potatoes,
  peeled and quartered
1 egg yolk
½ cup grated Parmesan
1 teaspoon grated lemon rind

½ teaspoon freshly grated nutmeg
¾ pound Mortadella,
  cut into ½-inch cubes
¼ cup mild Cheddar, grated
Pepper to taste

Place potatoes in a pot and cover with water. Bring to a boil and cook for 30 minutes or until tender. Strain, peel and mash well. Combine potatoes with the egg yolk, Parmesan, lemon rind, nutmeg and pepper and mix quickly. Add the Mortadella. Place mixture into a greased 9-inch pie plate. Sprinkle grated cheese on top. Bake at 350 degrees for 30 minutes. Let cool slightly and cut into wedges. **SERVES 6.**

Grilled Potatoes Parmesan

3 large baking potatoes
Onion salt
Celery salt
Freshly ground black pepper

⅓ cup Parmesan cheese,
freshly grated
⅓ cup butter, cut in slices

Scrub potatoes, do not peel, and cut in ¼-inch lengthwise slices. Spread slices out on a 20-inch length of 18-inch wide foil. Dash liberally with onion salt, celery salt and pepper. Sprinkle with Parmesan and dot butter between each slice before overlapping foil. Bring edges of foil together, leaving a little space for expansion of steam, and seal well with a double fold. Place wrapped potatoes on grill. Cook over coals 30-45 minutes or until done, turning package several times. Can also be baked in an oven at 350 degrees for 1 hour. **SERVES 4.**

Roasted Rosemary Potato Slices

2 tablespoons melted butter
2 Russet potatoes,
  about 1¼ pounds, scrubbed
1 teaspoon Kosher salt

½ teaspoon dried rosemary,
  crumbled
Black pepper to taste

Into an 8-inch baking dish, pour half the butter. Make sure it covers the entire bottom. Slice potatoes ¼-inch thick and layer in baking dish. Sprinkle potatoes with salt, rosemary and pepper. Pour the remaining butter over them. Bake at 425 degrees, turning each row once with spatula, for 45 minutes to an hour or until they are crisp. Sprinkle potatoes with additional salt, if desired, before serving. **SERVES 2.**

Cheesy Garlic Potatoes

4 large potatoes, peeled
4 cloves garlic, minced
6 tablespoons butter
  or margarine

⅔ cup Parmesan cheese,
  freshly grated
Salt and freshly ground pepper
  to taste

Cut potatoes in half lengthwise. Slice ⅛-inch thick. Place in bowl. Melt butter in pan. Add garlic and cook for about a minute over medium heat. Add garlic butter to potatoes. Add ⅓ cup Parmesan, salt and pepper. Mix to coat potatoes well. Pour into a buttered 8x8 baking pan. Top with remaining cheese. Bake, uncovered, at 400 degrees about 35-40 minutes. **SERVES 4.**

Sweet Potatoes with Apples and Roasted Chestnuts

3 pounds sweet potatoes,
  pricked with fork and baked
  at 400 degrees for 1 hour
  or until tender
3 cups Golden Delicious apples,
  peeled, and cut lengthwise
  into eighths
¼ cup fresh lemon juice

1 cup roasted chestnuts,
  peeled and quartered
½ cup butter or margarine
½ cup firmly packed light
  brown sugar
½ cup honey
½ teaspoon cinnamon
¼ teaspoon ground ginger

Toss apples with lemon juice. Set aside. Peel cooled sweet potatoes and slice diagonally into ¼-inch slices. Arrange with the apples in a buttered 9x13 baking dish. Top with chestnuts. Combine butter, sugar, honey and spices in a saucepan and cook over moderate heat, stirring until sugar dissolves. Spoon the mixture over the sweet potatoes and apples. Bake at 400 degrees, basting occasionally, for 30 minutes or until apples are tender. Put under broiler for 4 minutes to brown top. **SERVES 8-10.**

ROASTED CHESTNUTS

Buy Italian chestnuts (dark brown shells). Make a ½-inch slice on the top and bottom of each chestnut. Steam in old pie plates on top of stove over medium-high heat, sprinkling with water every 3-5 minutes and turning with tongs. Keep covered with inverted pie plate or foil in between sprinklings. Cook 15-20 minutes until tender. Chestnuts may be cooked and frozen for later use.

Port City Sweet Potatoes

3 medium sweet potatoes or yams
⅔ cup light brown sugar
1 teaspoon salt
3 tablespoons butter or margarine

3 bananas, peeled and sliced
⅓ cup orange juice
¼ cup shredded coconut

Cook sweet potatoes in boiling water to cover about 25 minutes or until tender but firm. Cool, pare, and cut into ¼-inch slices. Arrange layer of potatoes in a buttered 1-quart casserole. Sprinkle with sugar mixed with salt. Dot with butter. Top with layer of bananas. Repeat layers. Pour orange juice over layers. Sprinkle with coconut. Bake 20 minutes in 350 degree preheated oven or until top is lightly browned. **SERVES 6.**

Pecan Sweet Potatoes

3 pounds sweet potatoes
¾ cup orange juice
2 large eggs
2 tablespoons butter, melted
2 tablespoons sugar
1½ teaspoons ground cinnamon
½ teaspoon ground nutmeg

Salt and pepper, to taste
½ cup all-purpose flour
¼ cup plus 2 tablespoons
   firmly packed golden brown sugar
½ teaspoon ground cinnamon
¼ cup butter, room temperature
½ cup chopped pecans

For sweet potatoes, preheat the oven to 350 degrees. Place potatoes in oven rack and bake until all potatoes are tender, about 1 hour. Do not turn off oven. Butter or spray with vegetable oil an 8 x 8 x 2 square glass baking dish. Scrape sweet potato pulp from skins into a large mixing bowl. Discard sweet potato skins. Using an electric mixer or food processor, mash sweet potatoes. Add orange juice, egg, melted butter, sugar, cinnamon and nutmeg. Season with salt and pepper. Spoon potatoes into baking dish. In another bowl, combine flour, brown sugar and ½ teaspoon cinnamon. Add ¼ cup butter and cut in until mixture resembles coarse crumbs. Mix in chopped pecans. Sprinkle pecan topping over sweet potatoes. Bake until potatoes are hot and pecan topping is dry, about 30 minutes. Serve warm. **SERVES 6.**

Fried Sage Leaves

Bunch of fresh sage leaves
  or young spinach leaves

Oil for frying
Flour

Clean and pat dry sage leaves. Dust lightly with flour. Heat 1-inch of oil in skillet. Drop sage leaves into hot oil and cook a few seconds until crisp. Remove immediately with a slotted spoon. Drain on paper towels.

Fried Parsley

Follow instructions for Fried Sage Leaves, substituting parsley, for an unusual accompaniment for main courses.

Fried Shitaki Mushrooms

Accompany a special dish with shitaki mushrooms. Wash and slice the mushrooms paper thin. Dust with flour. Flash fry in oil and serve.

Duxelles

2 tablespoons butter
1 cup chopped onions
1 cup chopped mushrooms

¼ cup chopped parsley
¼ teaspoon salt
1½ teaspoons fresh lemon juice

Place butter and onions in a ½-quart microwave casserole. Microwave at high 1½-2 minutes, until onions are tender. Add mushrooms and stir to blend well. Microwave on high another 1½-2 minutes, until cooked through. Add parsley, salt and lemon juice. Microwave on high 1½-2 minutes more. Freeze in a plastic bag or store in a jar in the refrigerator. NOTE: Duxelles can be prepared ahead and kept, refrigerated, for several weeks. These dried mushrooms are a wonderful flavoring for the following recipe or as a flavoring for stuffings. **MAKES ABOUT 1½ CUPS.**

Onions and Duxelles

2 to 3 large onions
2 to 3 tablespoons butter, melted

2 to 3 tablespoons Worcestershire sauce
1 recipe Duxelles

Cut onions in halves crosswise and fit into 2-quart microwave dish. Sprinkle with melted butter and Worcestershire sauce. Cover with lid or plastic wrap. Microwave on high 7-11 minutes or until tender. Let stand 5 minutes. Spoon hot Duxelles over onions and let stand several minutes more before serving. **Makes 4-6 servings.**

Mirepoix
(Herbed Carrots and Onions)

2 tablespoons butter
1 cup chopped onions
1 cup chopped carrots
¼ cup chopped parsley

¼ teaspoon dried thyme
½ teaspoon salt
1 bay leaf

Combine all ingredients in a microwave 1½-quart dish. Microwave on high for 10-13 minutes, stirring every 5 minutes. Remove bay leaf before serving. Excellent with asparagus or pork. **Makes about 1½cups.**

Celery Mirepoix

3 cups celery, diagonally sliced
2 tablespoons water

1 tablespoon butter
1 recipe Mirepoix

Place celery slices, water and butter in 2-quart microwave dish. Cover and microwave on high 7-11 minutes, stirring every 3 minutes or until just tender but crisp. Immediately add Mirepoix and stir. Let stand several minutes before serving. **Serves 4-6.**

Mushroom Dressing

3 cups toasted bread cubes
¾ to 1 cup Parmesan cheese,
   freshly grated
½ cup chopped green onions
½ cup diced celery
5 cups fresh mushrooms,
   chopped (about 1¼ pounds)

3 tablespoons butter or margarine
2 tablespoons lemon juice
2 cups milk
4 eggs
1 teaspoon salt
1 teaspoon thyme

Combine bread cubes, cheese and green onions in a bowl. Set aside. Sauté celery and mushrooms in butter over medium heat for 5 minutes. Add lemon juice. Continue stirring and cooking until juice evaporates. Stir vegetables into bread mixture and spoon into a 5-6 cup baking dish. Beat together the milk, eggs, salt and thyme. Pour over all and mix well. Set casserole in a pan of hot water and bake, uncovered, in a slow 325 degree oven for 45 minutes or until custard is set and top is crusty and brown. NOTE: This dressing is wonderful with roast beef and tastes even better when made ahead and reheated. SERVES 8-10.

Cranberry Bake

3 cups chopped apples
2 cups fresh cranberries
6 pats butter
½ cup oats

½ cup brown sugar
½ cup chopped pecans
1 teaspoon cinnamon
½ teaspoon nutmeg

Preheat oven to 325 degrees. Place fruit in a 3-quart buttered casserole. Combine dry ingredients, place in casserole and top with pats of butter. Decorate with pecan halves. Cook, covered, for 45 minutes at 325 degrees. SERVES 6-8.

Cranberry Applesauce

2 cups cranberries
2 cups apples, cored and quartered,
   skins on

¾ cups water
1 cup sugar

Cook ingredients slowly until the fruit is soft. Put through a food mill, add 1 cup sugar and cook and stir until sugar is dissolved. Cool and refrigerate. Serve with chicken or turkey.

Fried Apples

6 tablespoons butter
1 teaspoon ground cinnamon
¼ teaspoon ground nutmeg
¼ teaspoon ground mace

⅛ teaspoon ground cloves
8 apples, peeled, cored,
 and sliced
Apple cider as needed

Melt butter in a deep skillet. Add spices and mix well. Add apples and cook over medium heat, turning often, about 3-5 minutes. Cover apples with cider and bring to boil. Reduce heat and simmer until apples are tender, about 20 minutes. Serve hot or cold. **SERVES 6.**

Apple-Raisin Coulis

1 cup golden raisins
½ cup Burgundy
¼ pound unsalted butter
¼ cup fresh lemon juice

6 medium Golden Delicious apples,
 peeled, cored and coarsely chopped
½ cup sugar

In a small bowl, soften raisins in Burgundy about 2 hours. Melt butter in a large saucepan. Add lemon juice and apples. Cook over medium heat until apples are soft, stirring occasionally. Stir in the sugar and cook over medium heat until apples and sugar caramelize slightly. Add raisin mixture and cook 5 minutes longer until thickened. **MAKES 3 CUPS.**

Red Raspberry Gelée

1 10-oz. package frozen
  red raspberries, thawed
2 3-oz. packages raspberry
  gelatin

2 cups boiling water
1 pint vanilla ice cream
1 6-oz. can frozen pink
  lemonade concentrate, thawed

Drain raspberries and reserve syrup. Dissolve gelatin in boiling water; add ice cream and stir until melted. Stir in lemonade and reserve syrup. Chill until thickened. Add raspberries; turn into a 6-8 cup mold and chill until firm. SERVES **12.**

Spiced Peach Bombé

1 30-oz. can sliced peaches,
  reserve juice
¼ cup vinegar
12 cloves
3 sticks cinnamon

1 6-oz. package orange
  gelatin
3¾ cups liquid (drained
  peach juice and water)

Boil vinegar, reserved peach juice and spices. Cook 10 minutes; remove spices. Add gelatin. Cool until slightly thickened; add peaches. Pour into 1 ½-quart mold. Refrigerate. SERVES **6-8.**

Scalloped Pineapple

1 stick butter or margarine
¾ cup sugar
4 eggs
1 20-oz. can pineapple chunks,
  drained
1½ teaspoons fresh
  lemon juice

¼ teaspoon fresh nutmeg,
  grated
5 slices of white or wheat bread,
  cubed

Cream together butter and sugar. Add 4 eggs and beat well. Fold in pineapple chunks, lemon juice and nutmeg. Fold in bread. Butter a 1½-quart baking dish. Pour mixture into dish. Bake at 350 degrees for 50 minutes. Serve hot.

Cucumber Relish

3 pounds hot house cucumbers, seeded and diced
5 garlic cloves, minced
2 red jalapeños, sliced and seeded
2 bunches scallions, sliced
1 tablespoon minced ginger

1 bunch cilantro, chopped
1 cup sugar
2 cups rice wine vinegar
1 tablespoon salt
1⅓ cups water
1 star anise, sliced

Place cucumbers in a bowl. Bring all other ingredients to a boil and pour over cucumbers. Chill and serve on a side with grilled seafood, salads and shellfish. *The Blue Point Grill, Franklin Street at South Washington*

Madeira Jelly

1 cup water
3 envelopes unflavored gelatin
1½ cups Madeira
1½ cups orange juice

6 tablespoons lemon juice
¾ cup sugar
1 cup whipping cream, stiffly whipped

Place water in a small saucepan. Sprinkle gelatin on top. Let stand until softened, about 5 minutes. Mix Madeira, orange and lemon juices in bowl. Stir in sugar until dissolved. Melt gelatin over low heat then stir into fruit juices. Put bowl over a pan of ice and chill until very cold and starts to set. Stir often. Pour into a 5-cup mold, cover and chill at least 5 hours. Can be made two days ahead and refrigerated until ready to use. When serving, unmold onto a platter at least two hours before serving. Serve with whipped cream on the side or decorate with whipped cream forced through a pastry bag. NOTE: Serve as a side dish with beef or chicken. **SERVES 6.**

Breads

1760

Menu

The Bread And Butter Ball

As recorded by George Washington in an engaging entry in his diary, the "Bread and Butter Ball" was hosted by Mr. Carlyle, Dr. Laurie and Mr. Wilson in 1760 at the Royal George on the northwest corner of Cameron and Royal Streets. Mr. Washington notes that pocket handkerchiefs served as napkins and tablecloths and "no apologies were made for either."

Virginia Apple Bread

½ cup shortening
1 cup sugar
1 egg
2 cups flour
1 teaspoon baking soda
⅔ teaspoon ground nutmeg

½ teaspoon ground cloves
1 teaspoon cinnamon
½ teaspoon salt
2 cups pared, chopped apples
1 cup chopped nuts
Confectioners sugar (optional)

Cream together shortening and sugar. Add egg and beat well. Sift together dry ingredients, add to creamed mixture, then stir in the apples and nuts. Pour into a 9-inch greased loaf pan. Bake at 350 degrees for 1 hour. Let cool sightly and sprinkle the top with confectioners sugar, if desired. Freezes well. NOTE: This recipe is best when made with apples that are a little past their prime. It may be doubled and can be served toasted for breakfast or with fruit as a dessert.

Anne Marie's Corn Bread

1 cup flour
1 cup yellow cornmeal
1 cup milk or buttermilk
½ teaspoon salt
4 teaspoons baking powder

½ cup sugar
½ cup oil
1 beaten egg
1 can cream style corn (8.5 oz.)
2 tablespoons butter to grease pan

Grease 8 x 8 inch pan. Preheat oven to 350 degrees. Combine all dry ingredients. Add liquid ingredients and stir until just moistened. Pour into the greased pan. Bake for 45 minutes. Serve warm. NOTE: Do not increase pan size — it will be too moist. SERVES 8.

Lemon Blueberry Bread

¾ cup sugar
¼ cup butter, softened
1 zest of lemon, chopped
2½ teaspoons baking powder

¾ cup milk
2 eggs, beaten
2 cups flour
½ cup fresh or frozen blueberries

Cream the butter and sugar together until light and fluffy. Add the beaten eggs and the lemon zest. Beat well. Sift all but 2 tablespoons of the flour with the baking powder and salt. Add the dry mixture alternating with the milk to creamed mixture until they are both incorporated. Beat until smooth after each addition. Combine the remaining 2 tablespoons of flour with the blueberries and fold into the batter. If using frozen berries, thaw them first and drain well. Pour into a well-greased loaf pan. Bake for 1 hour at 350 degrees. NOTE: Coating the berries with flour will keep them from falling to the bottom of the batter while cooking. Serve lightly toasted and with butter for an afternoon tea or a special breakfast! MAKES 1 LOAF.

Strawberry Bread

3 cups flour
1 teaspoon salt
1 tablespoon cinnamon
1 teaspoon baking soda
1¼ cups sugar
3 eggs, beaten

1¼ cups cooking oil
1 16-oz. package fresh or frozen
   whole strawberries, slightly
   thawed and drained and
   coarsely chopped
1¼ cups chopped pecans

Combine all dry ingredients in a large bowl. Make a well in the center. Add eggs and oil. Stir until moistened. Stir in strawberries and pecans. Put mixture in 2 lightly greased loaf pans. Bake at 350 degrees for one hour or until done. MAKES 2 LOAF PANS OR 48 MINI-MUFFINS. Serve with strawberry cream cheese.

Zucchini Bread

3 eggs
1 cup oil
2 cups sugar
2 teaspoons vanilla
3 cups flour
1 teaspoon salt
3 teaspoons cinnamon

1 teaspoon lemon rind
2 cups zucchini, unpeeled
   and finely grated
½ teaspoon baking powder
1 teaspoon soda
½ cup chopped nuts

Beat eggs thoroughly. Add next 3 ingredients and mix well. Add dry ingredients, including nuts and zucchini, and mix well. Grease loaf pans and pour in batter. Bake at 350 degrees for 1 hour. MAKES EITHER 3 SMALL LOAVES OR 2 LARGE LOAVES.

Holiday Walnut Bread

3 cups all-purpose flour
¾ to 1 cup granulated sugar
½ to 1 teaspoon salt
4 teaspoons baking powder
¾ cup shortening

1¼ to 1½ cups chopped
 walnuts
1½ cups milk
1 egg, beaten
1 teaspoon vanilla

Mix flour, sugar, baking powder and salt. Cut in shortening. Add milk, egg and vanilla. Stir in 1 cup of the walnuts. Mix until ingredients are blended. Grease and flour a 9 x 5-inch loaf pan. Pour mixture into pan. Sprinkle with chopped walnuts (¼-½ cup). Bake 60-70 minutes at 350 degrees. NOTE: This bread may be frozen and enjoyed at a later date! MAKES 1 LOAF.

Chesapeake Gingerbread

½ cup sugar
½ cup butter
2 eggs
1 cup dark molasses
1 cup boiling water
1½ teaspoons baking soda

½ teaspoon ground ginger
½ teaspoon salt
¼ teaspoon ground cloves
1 teaspoon ground cinnamon
2½ cups flour

Cream together the butter and sugar until smooth and light. Add the eggs and beat until light. Mix together the water and molasses and add to the creamed mixture. Sift together all the dry ingredients and add to the creamed mixture and beat until smooth. Pour into a greased and floured square baking pan. Bake 40-45 minutes in a 350 degree preheated oven. NOTE: Whipped cream makes a wonderful topping for this bread. Gingerbread may be served warm or cold.

English Muffin Loaf Bread

6 cups unbleached flour
2 packages active dry yeast

2 cups milk, or skim milk
½ cup water

1 tablespoon sugar	Cornmeal
2 teaspoons salt	Cinnamon, dried fruit (cut up),
¼ teaspoon baking powder	raisins, if desired. Add to taste.

Preheat oven to 400 degrees. Mix 3 cups flour with yeast, sugar, salt and baking powder. Heat milk and water until very warm (can be done in the microwave). Add to the flour mixture. Stir until well blended. Add 3 cups of flour to mixture, one cup at a time, stirring after each addition until well mixed. Sprinkle 2 greased loaf pans with cornmeal. Spoon dough (it will be soft and sticky) equally into the two pans. Sprinkle top of loaves with cornmeal. Cover loosely with greased waxed paper (a vegetable spray works well). Let rise in a warm place for 45 minutes or until to tops of pans. Remove waxed paper. Bake 25 minutes in a 400 degree oven. Turn out immediately and cool on racks. NOTE: This keeps in the refrigerator for one week or can be frozen. Serve immediately after baking or, if you wish to serve at a later date, it is best when toasted. Serve with apple butter, jams or just buttered. If "Better for Bread" flour is used, you will have an even nicer bread. Increase the water by ¼ cup. In this case, your yield will only be one loaf. MAKES 2 LOAVES.

Veteflator

2 packages dry yeast	1 tablespoon butter
¼ teaspoon ginger	½ teaspoon salt
1 teaspoon sugar	½ cup sugar
¼ cup warm water	1 egg (¾ in dough, ¼ reserved)
1 cup milk	3½ to 4 cups flour

Dissolve yeast in warm water with ginger and one teaspoon sugar. (Ginger chemically reacts with yeast; let it bubble about 15 minutes; it makes bread moist.) Melt butter and add milk; cool until lukewarm. Mix all ingredients with half of flour until smooth and elastic, adding more flour gradually, saving about 1 cup of the flour. Sprinkle dough with small amount of flour. Cover with a towel and let rise in a warm place until double in bulk, approximately 50-60 minutes. Punch down dough and turn onto floured board. Knead until smooth, adding small amounts of flour gradually, if necessary. Divide dough into two parts to make two braids. Cut each portion into three equal parts. Shape parts into strands, 12 inches long. Braid. Place on greased sheet. Cover and let rise until double, about 45 minutes. Brush with beaten egg. Bake in 375 degree oven for 20 minutes. MAKES 2 BRAIDED LOAVES.

Special Breakfast Popovers

1 cup all-purpose flour	2 tablespoons honey
½ teaspoon salt	1 tablespoon melted butter
¾ cup milk	2 large eggs

Sift flour and salt together. Add the milk, honey and melted butter. Stir to blend. Beat in the eggs. Fill greased 2 or 2½-inch muffin tins just under half full. Bake 25-30 minutes at 425 degrees (watch carefully) or until sides are rigid and the top and sides of the popovers are brown. Do not open the oven until you think they are done or the popovers will fall and not rise again. If popovers are preferred dry inside, slit each with a sharp knife and bake 5 minutes longer. Serve with honey butter. NOTE: For regular popovers, omit the honey and butter.

Aebleskivers

1½ cups sifted flour	2 eggs, beaten
1 teaspoon baking powder	2 cups buttermilk
½ teaspoon baking soda	2 Golden Delicious apples,
¼ teaspoon salt	pared, cored and shredded
2 teaspoons sugar (optional)	

Sift together dry ingredients. Add eggs, milk and apples. Beat mixture until smooth. Heat an aebleskiver pan. Put 1 teaspoon of butter into each section. Half-fill each section with batter. Cook until light brown on a low heat. Sprinkle some apple on top. Turn and brown other side. Be sure to cook on a low heat in order to cook thoroughly. Garnish with cinnamon sugar if desired. NOTE: Aebleskiver pans are available at most kitchen stores and make a special breakfast treat.

French Bread with Herbs and Cheese

½ cup butter or margarine	1 (1 pound) loaf French bread
1 teaspoon oregano	12 oz. Mozzarella cheese, sliced
½ teaspoon minced garlic	¼ cup grated Parmesan cheese

Melt butter with oregano and garlic. Slice bread thickly, cutting not quite all the way through so that the loaf still holds together. Brush butter mixture on both sides of each slice and insert sliced Mozzarella between slices. Sprinkle with grated Parmesan cheese. Place in shallow pan lined with foil. Bake at 375 degrees about 20 minutes or until bread in heated through and cheese is melted. **MAKES 1 LOAF.**

Herb Bread (for your bread machine)

1⅓ cups water	1 teaspoon dill seed
1 egg	2 teaspoons dillweed
¾ cup chopped onions	2 teaspoon dried parsley
1 teaspoon sugar	3 cups bread flour
1 teaspoon salt	1½ teaspoons yeast
1 teaspoon anise seed	

To bread machine, add water and egg, onions, sugar, salt, anise seed, dill seed, dillweed and parsley. Add flour. Make a well in the flour and add yeast. Bake on regular setting, not rapid, according to your machine. Do not use delayed setting because of the egg. Allow to cool a few minutes and serve warm with butter to accompany beef stew or a fish entree. **MAKES 1 LOAF.**

Irish Soda Bread

4 cups all-purpose flour	1 cup seedless raisins
¼ cup sugar	1⅓ cups buttermilk
1 teaspoon salt	1 egg
1 teaspoon baking powder	1 teaspoon baking soda
¼ cup butter	

Preheat oven to 375 degrees. Mix flour, sugar, salt and baking powder. Cut in butter until it resembles coarse cornmeal. Stir in raisins. Combine buttermilk, egg and soda. Add to flour mixture until just moistened. Bake in greased 1-quart pan until golden, about 45-50 minutes in a 375 degree oven. **MAKES 1 LOAF.**

Sour Dough Bread

STARTER:

¾ cup sugar
3 tablespoons instant potato flakes

1 package yeast
1 cup warm water

Melt yeast in warm water and mix with remaining ingredients. Store in refrigerator 3-6 days. Take out of refrigerator and feed with a mixture of the starter ingredients without the yeast. Mix in feed well and leave out of refrigerator 8-12 hours. Remove one cup of starter to make bread. If you are not making bread, throw one cup of starter away when feeding. Repeat feeding process every 3-5 days.

TO BAKE BREAD:

1 cup starter
2 tablespoons sugar
½ cup corn oil

1 teaspoon salt
1½ cups warm water
6 cups bread flour

In a large bowl, make a stiff batter of the above ingredients. Grease another large bowl. Put the dough in the greased bowl and turn over so the oiled side will be on top. Cover lightly. Let stand overnight. The next morning punch down. Divide dough into two parts and knead each part on a floured board a few times (8-10). Put into two bread pans. Allow the dough to rise in a warm spot. It will rise very slowly. After it rises, to about double in size, bake at 350 degrees for 35 minutes. After 5 minutes, remove from pan and allow to cool on a rack.

Sally Lunn Bread

1 package dry yeast
¼ cup lukewarm water
1 teaspoon sugar
6 tablespoons butter
6 tablespoons lard or shortening
1 cup milk

4 cups flour
⅓ cup sugar
2 teaspoons salt
4 eggs
Melted butter

Dissolve yeast in warm water; add sugar and set aside. Warm butter, lard and milk until all is melted; let stand until lukewarm (105-100 degrees). Sift together flour, sugar and salt. Combine milk and yeast mixtures in a large bowl. Beat eggs thoroughly and add to yeast and milk mixture. Beat well. Add flour and beat well. Set bowl in a pan of hot water to rise. Leave a wooden spoon in the batter and cover with a towel. Every 20 minutes beat dough down, then put it back in the hot water, cover and let rise again. It will rise after every beating. Do this at least 3 hours. (This beating is very important to achieve a nice texture). After last beating put dough in a well-greased bundt or tube pan, cover with towel and let rise again (about 1½ hours). Bake at 325 degrees for 45-60 minutes. Baste with melted butter during the last 10 minutes of baking. Freezes beautifully if wrapped in foil. Remove from the freezer 1 hour before serving and heat in a 350 degree oven for 20-30 minutes in the foil. **SERVES 15.**

Bishop's Bread

1½ cups glazed diced fruits
½ cup chopped nuts, preferably
   pecans or almonds
2 cups flour
1½ teaspoons baking powder
1 teaspoon salt
½ teaspoon baking soda
1 cup sugar
½ teaspoon each cinnamon,
  allspice, cardamom and
  freshly grated nutmeg

1 cup orange juice
1 egg
½ teaspoon each vanilla and
  almond extracts
¼ cup butter or margarine,
  softened (for glaze)

Flour fruit and nuts with 2 tablespoons of the flour. Mix remaining flour with all other dry ingredients. Cut in butter with a pastry blender or knives. Add to fruit and nuts. Beat the egg and add to the orange juice and extracts combined. Stir egg and juice mixture into dry mixture. Pour into 2 medium loaf pans, well-greased and floured. Bake at 350 degrees 45-60 minutes until golden and toothpick tests clean. Glaze with butter when removed from oven. Cool in pans 20-30 minutes on wire racks before removing from pans. NOTE: This recipe can easily be doubled. You can use any size loaf pan. Miniature pans make excellent gifts. Just remember to fill the pans only ⅔ full. **MAKES TWO MEDIUM LOAVES.**

Monterey Dilled Pumpernickel

1 3-oz. package cream cheese,
  softened
⅓ cup Monterey Jack cheese,
  finely shredded

2 tablespoons snipped parsley
½ teaspoon dried dill weed
½ of a 16-oz. loaf pumpernickel
  bread, cut in ½-inch slices

In a bowl, combine cream cheese, Jack cheese, parsley and dill; spread on one side of each bread slice. Reassemble the loaf. Wrap loaf loosely in heavy duty foil. Place on edge of grill. Grill over slow coals 15-20 minutes, turning frequently. May be placed in oven at 250 degrees instead.

Pepperoni-Double Cheese Hospitality Bread

2¼ cups warm water
  (105-115 degrees)
1 tablespoon sugar
1 tablespoon salt
2 packages yeast
1 teaspoon melted margarine
6-6½ cups bread flour

1¼ pounds (24 slices) Provolone
¾ pound (1½) cups pepperoni
8 oz. Mozzarella, shredded
1 medium egg, beaten
1 tablespoon poppy seeds
1 tablespoon sesame seeds

In a large bowl, mix the water, sugar, salt, margarine and yeast; add 2 cups of the flour. Blend well until moistened. Mix for two minutes. Stir in an additional 3-3½ cups flour until dough pulls cleanly away from the sides of the bowl. On a floured surface, knead in remaining ½-1 cup of flour until dough is smooth and elastic, about 8-10 minutes. Place dough in a large greased bowl; cover loosely with plastic wrap and cloth towel. Let rise in a warm place (80-85 degrees) until light and doubled in size, about an hour.

When doubled, grease a large cookie sheet. Punch down dough several times to remove all air bubbles. Allow to rest on counter covered with inverted bowl for 15 minutes. Divide dough in half. Roll each half into a 14 x 10 rectangle. Place Provolone, then pepperoni on dough. Fill gaps and top with Mozzarella. Starting with longest side, roll up; pinch edges firmly to seal. Place seam side down on cookie sheet; taper edges to a point. With a sharp knife, make five ¼-inch deep diagonal slashes on top of each loaf. Cover; let rise in warm place until doubled, about an hour. Heat oven to 375 degrees. Bake 25 minutes.

While bread is baking, beat egg in a small bowl. Remove bread from oven. Brush with egg. Sprinkle sesame and poppy seeds on top. Return to oven and bake for an additional 5-10 minutes or until loaves sound hollow when lightly tapped. Immediately remove from cookie sheet and cool on wire racks. NOTE: Slice into ½-¾ inch pieces and serve on a hot platter. Use as an appetizer or with salad and wine for a complete meal. Bread loaf tins are desirable and if you are not using a "non-stick" cookie sheet, it helps to cover the baking sheet with corn meal. MAKES 2 LOAVES.

Hardtack

Add flour, with unbleached wheat, to a mixture of water and salt. Mix until a sturdy dough is produced. Roll the dough about ¼-inch thick and cut into squares measuring approximately 3 inch x 3 inch. Prick each square with holes (16 holes was standard). Bake hardtack squares 45-90 minutes at 325 degrees, making sure all moisture is removed from the mixture before taking out of oven. *{Extract from the section, "Field and Barrack Cooking for the Army," Soyer's Cookbook, 1861.}*

Delta Hushpuppies

Vegetable oil
1¾ cups white or yellow
  corn meal
1¼ cups all-purpose flour
1 tablespoon baking powder
3 tablespoons sugar
1 teaspoon salt

1 teaspoon pepper
½ teaspoon cayenne pepper
1 large onion, minced
  (or 1 bunch scallions, chopped)
1 egg, slightly beaten
2 cups buttermilk

In deep fat fryer, heat 2-3 inches of oil over medium heat (370 degrees). Meanwhile, combine all dry ingredients in a deep bowl. Stir in onion pieces until coated. Add egg and buttermilk. Beat until mixed. Drop by rounded teaspoonsful into hot oil. Do not try to fry too many at one time. Hushpuppies should cook on one side and turn over to cook on the other. Remove with a slotted spoon when golden brown all over. Drain on paper towels and keep warm. SERVES 8-10.

Optional additions: If desired, 1 cup of creamed corn may be added with the egg and buttermilk; however, the amount of buttermilk should be reduced by ½ cup. Chopped red or green peppers may be added with the onions.

NOTE: Hushpuppies are a natural accompaniment to fried fish. Traditionally, they were made with the corn meal left over from coating the fish and were fried in the same oil.

Marmalade Muffins

1 egg, beaten
¼ cup orange juice
2 tablespoons sugar
1 tablespoon salad oil

1 cup Bisquick
¼ cup English orange marmalade,
   such as Dundee

Preheat oven to 400 degrees. Combine egg, juice, sugar and oil. Add Bisquick and beat 30 seconds. Stir in marmalade. Fill greased muffin tin ⅔ full and bake 15-20 minutes. **MAKES 6 LARGE MUFFINS.**

Glorious Morning Muffins

1¼ cups sugar
2¼ cups flour
1 tablespoon cinnamon
2 teaspoons baking soda
½ teaspoon salt
½ cup walnuts
½ cup raisins

½ cup shredded coconut
2 cups grated carrots, about 4 large
1 apple, grated
8 oz. can crushed pineapple, drained
3 eggs
1 cup vegetable oil
1 teaspoon vanilla

Sift together the sugar, flour, cinnamon, baking soda and salt into a large bowl. Combine and add the nuts, carrots and fruit. Whisk the eggs with the oil and vanilla in a separate bowl. Add eggs to the dry ingredients and mix well. Preheat oven to 350 degrees. Line a muffin tin with muffin papers. Fill each cup to the brim. Bake in a preheated 350 degree oven for 35 minutes or until a toothpick inserted into the center of a muffin is withdrawn clean. Cool the muffins in the pan for 10 minutes then remove and finish cooling on a rack. Make muffins 24 hours in advance of serving so muffins can develop flavor. Freezes beautifully! **MAKES 16 MUFFINS.**

Pecan Corn Muffins

⅔ cup flour
⅔ cup yellow cornmeal
⅔ cup ground pecans
½ cup sugar
¾ teaspoon baking powder

½ teaspoon baking soda
2 eggs, beaten
½ cup buttermilk or sour milk
⅓ cup butter or margarine, melted
⅓ cup chopped pecans (optional)

Grease muffin cups, spray with a vegetable spray or line with paper baking cups. In a medium mixing bowl stir together flour, cornmeal, ground pecans, sugar, baking powder and baking soda. Make a well in the center of these dry ingredients. Mix together eggs, buttermilk and butter. Add all at once to flour mixture. Stir just until moistened. (Batter should be lumpy.) Gently fold in chopped pecans. Fill prepared muffin cups 3/4 full. Bake at 375 degrees 18-20 minutes until golden. Remove from tins. Serve warm. NOTE: If made in madeleine pan or mini-muffin pan bake at 350 degrees for 15 minutes. **MAKES 12 MUFFINS.**

Maple Spice Muffins

2 eggs, beaten
1 8-oz. carton plain yogurt
1 cup maple syrup
½ cup brown sugar
½ cup oil
1½ cups whole wheat flour
1¼ cups flour

½ cup quick oatmeal
2 teaspoons baking powder
2 teaspoons cinnamon
1 teaspoon baking soda
½ teaspoon ground cloves
1 cup chopped walnuts
1 banana, chopped (⅔ cup)

Heat oven to 400 degrees. Combine eggs, yogurt and maple syrup. Beat in brown sugar and oil. Stir together flours, oatmeal, baking powder, baking soda and spices. Add dry ingredients, nuts and banana to wet mixture. Stir until just mixed. Spoon into greased or paper lined muffin cups. Fill ⅔ full. Bake at 400 degrees for 15-20 minutes. While warm, drizzle with more maple syrup. Serve warm. **MAKES 30 MUFFINS.**

Hungarian Butter Horns

4 cups flour
½ teaspoon salt
1 teaspoon vanilla
1 package dry yeast

2½ sticks butter
3 egg yolks
½ cup sour cream

FILLING

3 egg whites
1 cup sugar
¼ pound ground nuts

1 teaspoon vanilla
Powdered sugar for dusting

Sift together flour, salt and yeast. Cut butter into flour mixture. Add beaten egg yolks, sour cream and vanilla. Mix with hands. Shape in ball and wrap and chill while you are making the filling or overnight. Beat egg whites until stiff. Add a cup of sugar gradually. Fold in nuts and vanilla. Then cover pastry board with powdered sugar. Divide dough into 8 equal parts and roll each out the size of a pie pan. Cut in 8 wedges. Spread about 1 teaspoon of filling on each wedge and roll toward the center as for a crescent roll. Place on a greased cookie sheet with point side down so that these do not lose their shape while baking. Bake for 15-18 minutes at 375 degrees. When horns have cooled off, sprinkle with powdered sugar for a final touch! NOTE: Although these are time consuming to make, they are well worth the effort and can be made ahead and frozen. MAKES 64 BUTTER HORNS.

Gingerbread Muffins

2½ cups flour
1 cup light molasses
1 cup buttermilk
1 cup pecans, chopped
½ cup sugar
½ cup shortening

1½ teaspoons baking soda
1 teaspoon ground cinnamon
1 teaspoon salt
1 teaspoon ground ginger
¼ teaspoon ground nutmeg
1 egg

Grease and flour 24 muffin tin cups. Preheat oven to 375 degrees. Measure all ingredients into a large bowl. With a mixer set at low speed, beat until blended. Increase speed to medium and beat for 2 minutes. Fill muffin cups halfway. Bake for 20-25 minutes. Cool in pans on wire rack for 10 minutes. Remove from pans. MAKES 24.

Virginia Country Oven Toast

1 large or 2 medium loaves
   French bread cut in 1-inch slices
8 large eggs
2 cups milk
2 cups half and half

2 teaspoons vanilla
½ teaspoon nutmeg
½ teaspoon cinnamon
½ teaspoon mace

TOPPING:

¾ cup butter, softened
1⅓ cups brown sugar
3 tablespoons dark corn syrup

1⅓ cups coarsely chopped
   walnuts or pecans

Heavily butter a 13 x 9 x 2 inch baking pan. Fill with bread to within ½ inch of top.
Set aside. In a blender mix eggs, cream, milk, vanilla and spices. Pour this over bread
slices. Refrigerate overnight, covered. Make topping by combining all ingredients and
set aside until baking toast. Spread topping on toast. Bake at 350 degrees for 50 minutes
until puffed and golden. Shield top with foil if it begins to brown too rapidly. Serve
with or without syrup. **MAKES 8-10 SERVINGS.**

Rollins Dog Biscuits

3½ cups all purpose flour
2 cups whole wheat flour
1 cup cornmeal
1 cup rye flour
2 cups cracked wheat
½ cup nonfat dry milk

1 tablespoon salt
1 package dry yeast, dissolved
   in ¼ cup warm water
1 pint chicken stock, warmed
   (or appropriate substitute)
1 egg, beaten with 1 tablespoon milk

Combine dry ingredients and add the dissolved yeast and chicken stock. Knead into a
stiff dough and roll the dough into ¼-inch sheets. Cut with cookie cutters. Bake in a
300 degree oven for 45 minutes, then leave them in the oven with no heat overnight.
By morning they will be "bone-dry." NOTE: These are even safe for children!

Meats

Menu

Christmas Walk Dinner Before The Ceilidh

Crab Mousse with Crackers PAGE 22

Apple Honey Soup PAGE 47

Pork Normandy PAGE 138

Pecan Sweet Potatoes PAGE 101

Sesame Asparagus PAGE 83

Lemon Vinaigrette on Mixed Greens PAGE 44

Raspberry Chartreuse Bombé PAGE 217

The Ceilidh, (pronounced *kay-lee*) or Scottish gala, is the traditional finale to Alexandria's annual Scottish Christmas Walk. Sponsored by the Junior Friends of the Campagna Center, the Ceilidh often has taken place at the Torpedo Factory Art Center. This event marks the opening of the Christmas season in Alexandria.

Jim Brady's Prize-Winning Texas Chili

2 pounds round steak
1 pound fresh pork
3 tablespoons fat
3 medium onions, chopped
4 cloves garlic, minced
1 tablespoon oregano
1 tablespoon red wine vinegar
1 2.4-oz. box hot chili powder
1 tablespoon masa flour
1 28-oz. can Italian tomatoes,
   drained

2 bay leaves
1 tablespoon salt
1 tablespoon cumin
1 tablespoon brown sugar
1 4-oz. can jalapeño peppers,
   seeded (add more if extra spicy
   flavor desired)
1 pint ripe olives, sliced
Cheddar cheese, shredded

Cut meat into cubes. Brown in hot fat, then add chili powder and stir. In another skillet, sauté onions and garlic with jalapeño peppers until golden. Add to meat, the tomatoes, onions, garlic and masa flour. Cook for 20 minutes. Add remainder of spices, vinegar and brown sugar. Add olives last. Cook slowly for several hours. Serve with shredded Cheddar cheese on top. This is very spicy!

Chili with Ginger and Kidney Beans

1 pound lean hamburger or chili meat
2 tablespoons peanut oil
1 yellow onion, chopped
3 cloves garlic, crushed
2-3 tablespoons chili powder

1½ tablespoons whole cumin seeds
1 tablespoon Worcestershire sauce
1 28-oz. can puréed tomatoes
1 16-oz. can kidney beans
2-3 tablespoons ground ginger

In Dutch oven, brown beef in oil with onion, garlic and chili powder; drain. Add remaining ingredients. Simmer for 90 minutes. This recipe is best when served the following day. NOTE: Try turkey as a healthy substitution for the beef in this recipe!
Jim Cole, a special friend of Alexandria Hospital

Roquefort Stuffed Flank Steak

1 flank steak (2-3 pounds)	3 oz. Roquefort cheese, crumbled
Beef Marinade	Salt and pepper
2 tablespoons chopped scallions	4 or 5 slices bacon (optional)
1 clove garlic, finely chopped	Small skewers or toothpicks
2 tablespoons chopped parsley	

Pound flank steak until thin and marinate for 24 hours in Beef Marinade, turning occasionally. When ready to grill, combine scallions, garlic, parsley, Roquefort, salt and pepper in a small bowl. Place steak on a flat surface and spread with Roquefort mixture. Starting at small end of steak, roll up jelly-roll fashion. Cut into 4 slices. Wrap a slice of bacon around each piece, if desired. Secure with toothpicks. Grill for 10 minutes on each side over medium-hot coals. NOTE: Can be made ahead and frozen after cooking. Reheat in microwave. SERVES 4.

Twig's Favorite Flank Steak

1 flank steak (3-4 pounds)

MARINADE

⅓ cup oil	2 cloves garlic, minced (or 1 teaspoon
⅓ cup soy sauce	garlic powder)
1 tablespoon ground ginger	1 teaspoon sugar
⅓ cup dry wine or gin, vodka or sherry	

Combine marinade ingredients in long shallow dish just large enough to contain steak. Marinate steak for 4-5 hours, turning occasionally. When the rest of the dinner is nearly ready, place steak in oven broiler close to heat and cook for approximately 7 minutes on one side and 5 minutes on the other. Transfer steak to carving board and slice in a thin, cross-grain manner. NOTE: This is one steak that can be cooked well done and still taste good. The cutting produces ample juices, excellent for dunking crusty bread. SERVES 6-8.

Individual Beef Wellingtons

1 4-pound whole filet of beef	¼ teaspoon thyme
Bacon or suet to cover filet	¼ teaspoon sage
1 teaspoon salt	1 bay leaf
½ cup olive oil	10 peppercorns
½ cup sliced onions	2 cups dry vermouth
½ cup sliced carrots	½ cup Cognac
½ cup sliced celery	

Sprinkle beef with salt, place in casserole with tightly-fitting lid. In separate pan, cook vegetables and herbs in oil until tender. Spread vegetables over beef and add vermouth and Cognac. Cover and refrigerate for 1-3 days, turning occasionally.

Preliminary Baking: Remove meat from vegetable marinade; scrape off vegetables and discard. Reserve marinade for preparing Madeira Sauce. Preheat oven to 425 degrees. Place bacon or suet on top of fillet and roast for 15 minutes. Let cool or refrigerate until ready to use.

PASTRY

6 cups flour	2 eggs, well beaten
1 tablespoon salt	2 tablespoons vinegar
1 cup butter	⅔ cup cold water
1½ cups shortening	

Mix flour and salt. Cut in butter and shortening. Combine eggs, vinegar and water. Mix with flour until dough is formed. Divide pastry into 10 equal balls. Refrigerate until 1 hour before using. (If you wish fancy decorations on top, make an extra half-recipe of pastry.)

MUSHROOM FILLING

3 lbs mushrooms, finely chopped	¾ cup Madeira
3 tablespoons butter	Salt and pepper
⅔ cup minced shallots	8 oz. foie gras (optional)

Twist mushrooms in the corner of a linen towel over a small bowl, to extract as much juice as possible. Reserve juice for preparing Madeira Sauce. Sauté mushrooms with shallots in butter for 10 minutes. Add Madeira; boil until liquid has evaporated. Salt and pepper to taste. Beat in foie gras if desired; refrigerate.

To ASSEMBLE: Slice meat into 10 equal pieces. Roll out each ball of pastry into a 10-inch circle. Spread small amount of mushroom mixture in the center of dough. Place filet on top and pat more mushroom mixture on top and sides. Wrap dough around filet. Seal bottom. Place seam-side down and make a small opening in top center for steam to escape. (You may decorate around opening with pastry cutouts.) Refrigerate overnight or freeze. Wrap in freezer wrap before freezing. Defrost in refrigerator for 6 hours before baking.

FINAL BAKING: Preheat oven to 425 degrees. When ready to bake, brush each pastry with egg glaze (2 eggs beaten with 2 tablespoons water). Insert meat thermometer into filet through center opening of pastry. Bake for 25-30 minutes or until meat thermometer registers 140 degrees. Let stand for 20 minutes in a warm place. Serve with Madeira Sauce. Also excellent with Chausseur Sauce. **SERVES 10.**

MADEIRA SAUCE

Reserved marinade	1 tablespoon tomato paste
Reserved mushroom juices	2 tablespoons cornstarch
2 cups beef bouillon	½ cup Madeira

Simmer marinade, mushroom juice, bouillon and tomato paste for one hour or until reduced to 2 cups. Strain, season and thicken with cornstarch blended with Madeira. Pass sauce separately.

Braddock Bourguignon

1 cup chopped onions	½ cup red wine
1 clove garlic, chopped	2 tablespoons catsup
½ teaspoon oregano	2 tablespoons vinegar
3 tablespoons olive oil	2 cups water
3 pounds beef, preferably sirloin,	Sour cream, optional
cut into 1-inch cubes	Chopped onions, optional
½ cup soy sauce (or less,	Chopped tomatoes, optional
depending on taste)	Chopped green peppers, optional

Sauté onions and garlic in oil. Add meat and brown. Combine remaining ingredients and put all into a large Dutch oven. Simmer for at least 2 hours or up to 6 hours. (Sauce will be thin; do not thicken.) Serve over rice. If desired, top with sour cream, chopped onions, chopped tomatoes and chopped green peppers. NOTE: Stew can be prepared in the morning and reheated. **SERVES 6.**

Grilled Corned Beef

1 corned beef (size depends on how many servings you wish)	Bay leaf
	Peppercorns
Water	Garlic, chopped

Cover corned beef in water in a heavy Dutch oven. Add bay leaf, peppercorns and garlic. Boil 1 hour for every pound of meat.

SAUCE:

3 tablespoons Dijon mustard	2 tablespoons vinegar
½ cup brown sugar	¼ teaspoon garlic powder
⅛ teaspoon hot sauce	

Mix together ingredients for sauce. (It should be thick, like a barbecue sauce. If too thin, add more brown sugar.) Place cooked corned beef on the grill and baste with the sauce. Grill for 45 minutes, turning and basting often. The end result should be a thickly-coated corned beef. It can be cooked in advance and refrigerated until needed.

Beef Tenderloin with Horseradish

1 5-pound whole beef tenderloin, trimmed of all fat	1 tablespoon marjoram
	Whipping cream
3 garlic cloves or more, minced	Horseradish
¼ cup butter, melted	

Preheat oven to 400-425 degrees. After all fat has been trimmed from the meat, tuck under thin end of tenderloin and place in a shallow roasting pan. Brush with mixture of melted butter, garlic and herbs. Place in oven and cook for 35 minutes. Remove from pan, place on a cutting board and let stand for 20 minutes to absorb juices. Slice thinly. Meanwhile, whip the cream and add horseradish to taste. Serve sauce in a separate bowl. SERVES **8-10.**

Roasted Garlic Beef Tenderloin

2 garlic heads
2 tablespoons olive oil, divided
1 tablespoon chopped fresh parsley
1 tablespoon chopped fresh thyme
(or ½ teaspoon dried)

1 teaspoon salt
½ teaspoon freshly ground black pepper
1 2-pound beef tenderloin roast,
center cut

MARINADE

½ cup olive oil
3 tablespoons freshly squeezed
lemon juice
1 tablespoon finely chopped
fresh basil
1 tablespoon finely chopped
fresh parsley
1 teaspoon finely chopped
fresh thyme (or ½ teaspoon dried)

1½ teaspoons Dijon mustard
1 tablespoon tiny capers
1 clove garlic, finely minced
Salt and freshly ground pepper
to taste
Basil leaves for garnish

Preheat oven to 425 degrees. Peel garlic heads but leave whole. Place on a square of foil and drizzle with 1 tablespoon of the olive oil. Wrap tightly and set aside. Mix remaining tablespoon of the olive oil with herbs and seasonings until well blended. Rub mixture over meat and place meat on rack in shallow roasting pan. Put the foil-wrapped garlic in one corner of the roasting pan. Roast for 25-35 minutes or until meat thermometer registers 135 degrees. This roast is best served rare. When cooked, remove meat and garlic from pan and allow to cool. Refrigerate until chilled. When roast is cold, slice into ¼-inch slices. Meanwhile, prepare marinade by combining all ingredients in a jar and shaking until well blended. Arrange meat slices in a large serving dish. Remove garlic from foil and separate leaves. Sprinkle over meat and pour marinade over all. Refrigerate meat again for at least 3 hours or up to 12 hours. Garnish with basil leaves. Serves 4 to 8.

Pasties

5 cups flour
1½ cups shortening
1¾ teaspoons salt

1½ teaspoons baking powder
1 cup water

FILLING:

1½ pounds sirloin, diced
¾ pound pork steak, diced
3 potatoes, diced
3 onions, sliced

Salt and pepper to taste
Butter
4 tablespoons sauce, any flavor

Preheat oven to 450 degrees. Combine dry ingredients, cut in shortening, add water and stir until dough forms into a ball. Divide into 8. Roll out each ball of pastry into a circle. In center of each pastry round, place a layer of diced potatoes, then meat, then onions. Season and dot with butter. Spoon a small amount of sauce on top. Fold crust as for a turnover and seal edges. Make 2 small slits in the top. Bake at 450 degrees for 10 minutes and reduce heat to 375 degrees. Bake an additional 50 minutes. NOTE: These can be frozen before baking. The pasties are quite large and are great served cold at picnics. For a crowd, smaller pasties may be prepared by dividing dough into 12 portions rather than 8. Proceed with recipe as directed. **SERVES 8.**

Stuffed Cabbage Rolls

1 large head of cabbage,
  cored and washed
4 tablespoons butter
2 large onions, chopped
1 clove garlic, mashed
1 pound ground round steak
1 cup cooked white rice

¾ teaspoon allspice
1 28-oz. can tomatoes
1 8-oz. can tomato sauce
1 6-oz. can tomato paste
1 teaspoon salt
1 teaspoon dried thyme
Sour cream, optional

In a large kettle, steam cabbage for 10 minutes or until leaves are tender and will peel away from head. Cool. Separate leaves and carefully pat dry with paper towels. Preheat oven to 350 degrees. Meanwhile, melt butter in a large skillet and sauté onions with garlic until onions are tender and golden. Remove half of the onions from the skillet and add to ground beef in a mixing bowl. Add rice and allspice to ground beef mixture, combining gently. In skillet, mix tomatoes, tomato paste and tomato sauce with the remaining onions. Season with salt and thyme. Cook over very low heat for 15 minutes, stirring occasionally. Place a portion of the rice/beef mixture on a large cabbage leaf and fold to enclose. Place seam-side down in a baking dish. Continue until all beef mixture is used. Cover cabbage rolls with tomato sauce. Bake uncovered for 1 hour. Garnish with sour cream, if desired. **SERVES 8.**

Veal Scaloppine

½-pound scaloppine of veal,
  cut into ¼-inch thick slices
3 tablespoons or more flour
Salt and freshly ground pepper

2 tablespoons unsalted butter
2 tablespoons olive oil
¼ cup Marsala wine

Unless the scaloppine are very small, cut them into 3x3-inch pieces. Place between sheets of waxed paper and pound lightly with mallet to flatten. Mix flour, salt and pepper. Dredge scaloppine in seasoned flour. Heat butter and oil in a large, heavy skillet until very hot and add meat in one layer. Cook until golden brown on both sides. It should take 4-6 minutes. Transfer scaloppine to 2 warmed plates. Add wine to skillet and stir to dissolve all particles in the pan. Cook a few more moments to reduce wine slightly, and ladle the wine sauce over each serving. **SERVES 2.**

Eggplant and Veal Sauté

1 medium eggplant
Salt
1½ pounds boneless veal,
  thinly sliced

⅓ cup olive oil
1 recipe Tomato Sauce
Parsley, chopped

Remove stem from eggplant. Do not peel. Slice crosswise in ½-inch slices, then ½-inch strips. Place strips on paper towels and sprinkle, liberally, with salt. Let stand for 20 minutes to remove moisture. Blot moisture with towels. Cut veal in bite-sized pieces. Heat olive oil in pan. Add eggplant strips and sauté until brown and tender. Remove from heat. Quickly sauté veal. Return eggplant to pan and stir in Tomato Sauce. Heat thoroughly and sprinkle with parsley. **SERVES 4-6.**

TOMATO SAUCE

1 medium onion, chopped
2 cloves garlic, chopped fine
3 tablespoons olive oil
2 tomatoes, peeled and chopped
1 tablespoon tomato paste

1 teaspoon basil
¼ teaspoon rosemary
¼ teaspoon salt
¼ teaspoon black pepper
¼ cup dry white wine

Sauté onion and garlic in oil until tender. Add tomatoes, tomato paste, basil, rosemary, salt, pepper and wine. Bring to a boil, lower heat and cook, uncovered, until thickened.

Veal Alfredo Gambrel

12 oz. fresh spinach fettucine
4 small carrots
4 small onions
8 tablespoons butter
4 cloves garlic, minced
¾ teaspoon pepper

1 pound of veal cutlets
8 oz. prosciutto ham,
   very thinly sliced
1¼ cups half and half cream
8 tablespoons freshly grated
   Parmesan cheese

Cook fettucine al dente in oiled and salted water. Drain and set aside. Pare carrots and cut into thin strips. Cut ends off onions, peel, lay on one end and cut into sixths. Pull wedges apart. Set onions aside. Pound veal slightly and pat dry. Melt butter in a large, heavy skillet. Add carrots, garlic, and pepper; cook for 2 minutes. When butter begins to bubble, add veal to skillet and brown meat on both sides. Remove veal from pan and set aside. Add onions and prosciutto to carrots in pan and cook, tossing mixture, for 1-2 minutes. Add the half and half and 4 tablespoons of the cheese to skillet. Cook until liquid is reduced and cream begins to thicken. Toss pasta and veal into the mixture and heat until warm. Cover skillet and keep on very low heat until ready to serve. Garnish with remaining cheese just before serving. SERVES 4.

Veal Piccatta

1½ pounds of veal cutlets
⅓ cup flour

¼ cup dry white wine or vermouth
Salt and pepper to taste

4 tablespoons butter	**1 lemon, thinly sliced**
¼ cup olive oil	**Chopped parsley**
Juice of 2 lemons	

Dredge cutlets very lightly in flour. Heat butter and oil in a frying pan until quite hot, but not smoking. Quickly sauté cutlets on both sides until golden brown. Add the lemon juice and white wine; reduce the heat and simmer for 5 minutes. Season to taste. Serve immediately, garnished with the lemon slices and parsley. NOTE: If more sauce is preferred, after veal is sautéed, remove from pan. Add ½ cup chicken bouillon, lemon juice, 1 cup white wine and ½ teaspoon salt. Cook one minute. Return veal to sauce. Cook 2 to 3 minutes until bubbly. Sprinkle with freshly ground pepper. Garnish as directed. SERVES **4-6.**

Smithfield Ham

TRADITIONAL BOILED METHOD: Cut off hock, wash and scrub ham well with brush to remove any mold. Soak overnight. Place ham skin-side down in ham boiler and cover with cold water. Bring to a boil on top of stove and simmer for 20 minutes per pound or until paddle bone loosens. Remove ham from water. (One quart of apple cider and ¼ cup of brown sugar may be added to the water during final hour of cooking time.)

NIGHT OVEN METHOD (FOR HAMS 12-13 POUNDS): Prepare ham for cooking as above. Preheat oven to 375 degrees. Place ham in boiler skin-side up with 5 cups of water. Cover and place in oven. Turn temperature to 500 degrees for 10 minutes. Turn off oven for 3 hours and then again to 500 degrees for 15 minutes. Turn off and leave in oven overnight.

GLAZE: Remove skin and partially trim fat while ham is still warm. Moisten ¾ cup brown sugar with pickle or orange juice. Stir in 1 teaspoon ground cloves. Pat mixture over ham. Place in 350 degree oven until glaze has set.

To serve, slice very thin. May be served warm or cold and is excellent for Ham Biscuits. To store, wrap well and refrigerate. The cooking methods shown here may be used for any aged and cured ham.

NOTE: The Smithfield Ham is the result of the diet of the hog, the long cut of the ham, the ancient curing process, and the lengthy aging period. Only hams meeting these specifications and cured within the town limits of Smithfield, Virginia (less than two square miles), can be commercially labeled as Smithfield Hams.

Cassis Roasted Pork

1 6 to 7-pound pork roast
10 bay leaves
Coarse salt

Peppercorns
1 cup ice water
1 cup Crème de Cassis

Preheat oven to 500 degrees. Cut slits in the roast at even intervals all over on the fatty side. Fill the slits with pieces of bay leaf and 2-3 peppercorns. Put the roast on a rack in a roasting pan. Pour coarse salt over the top of the roast. It should be applied heavily. Put in the oven for 5 minutes. Lower heat to 350 degrees and pour 1 cup of ice water over the roast. Roast for 30 minutes per pound. Approximately 30 minutes before the roast is scheduled to come out of the oven, pour the Cassis over the roast and baste often during this final cooking time. NOTE: Warn your guests about the peppercorns and bay leaves. SERVES 12.

Kentucky Bourbon Pork

2 1-pound pork tenderloins

MARINADE

¼ cup Kentucky Bourbon
¼ cup soy sauce
¼ cup brown sugar, packed
3 cloves garlic, minced
¼ cup Dijon mustard

1 teaspoon minced fresh ginger
   (or ¼ teaspoon ground)
1 teaspoon Worcestershire sauce
¼ cup vegetable oil

Combine marinade ingredients with a whisk or food processor. Place tenderloins and marinade in a sealed plastic bag in the refrigerator overnight. Grill 4 inches from a hot charcoal fire for 15-20 minutes. Baste often while cooking. Roasts may also be cooked under a broiler, approximately 6 inches from heat for 16-18 minutes. Slice in ½-inch thick slices to serve as a main course, or slice in ¼-inch slices to put on French bread for a picnic. NOTE: This traditional Kentucky Derby recipe is delicious when served with white zinfandel, Sauvignon Blanc or a light red wine. SERVES 6.

Maryland Rye-Whiskey Pork Chops

¼ cup vegetable oil
6 thick loin pork chops
Flour, seasoned with
   salt and black pepper
4 tart apples, pared, cored
   and sliced

¼ cup sugar
2 tablespoons freshly squeezed
   lemon juice
Nutmeg, freshly grated, to taste
¼ cup rye whiskey
Salt and black pepper to taste

Heat oil in heavy skillet. Dust pork chops lightly with seasoned flour and brown slowly on both sides (about 20-30 minutes). Remove chops from skillet onto heated dish. Pour off most of the fat from the skillet. Melt butter in skillet and add apples; sauté for a few minutes. Add sugar, lemon juice and a touch of nutmeg. Correct seasonings, if necessary. Sauté until apples are just tender, increase heat and add whiskey. Cook for 1-2 minutes. When ready to serve, spoon apples and sauce over pork chops. **SERVES 6.**

Bavarian Pork Chops

4 boneless loin pork chops,
   cut 1½-inches thick
Salt and pepper
2 tablespoons vegetable oil
1 oz. Kirsch, heated
¼ cup beef stock
1 17-oz. can pitted
   dark sweet cherries

½ teaspoon each of nutmeg,
   cloves, marjoram
½ teaspoon grated lemon rind
2 tablespoons freshly squeezed
   lemon juice
2 teaspoons cornstarch
1 teaspoon Bovril
½ cup chopped toasted walnuts

Season the chops with salt and pepper. Heat oil in skillet over medium heat. Add chops and cook until brown on both sides. Drain fat from pan and flambe chops with heated Kirsch. Pour in stock, cover, and simmer over low heat for 1 hour. While chops are cooking, drain syrup from cherries into a saucepan. Set cherries aside. Add nutmeg, cloves, marjoram and lemon rind to syrup. In separate small bowl, mix lemon juice and cornstarch together; slowly add to syrup mixture. Cook syrup over low heat until sauce is thick and glossy. Stir in Bovril. After chops have simmered for 45 minutes, pour syrup mixture into pan with chops. Just before serving, add reserved cherries and walnuts and cook over low heat until warmed through. **SERVES 4.**

Pork Tenderloin with Mustard Sauce

2 pork tenderloins (1½ to 2 pounds each)

MARINADE

½ cup soy sauce	1 tablespoon vinegar
1 tablespoon grated onion	¼ teaspoon cayenne pepper
2 cloves garlic, crushed	¼ cup water

MUSTARD SAUCE

⅓ cup mayonnaise	1 tablespoon grated onion
⅓ cup sour cream	Salt to taste
1 tablespoon dry mustard	

Blend marinade ingredients and pour over tenderloins placed in a shallow dish. Cover and refrigerate overnight or all day. Drain meat, reserving marinade. Bake uncovered, at 300 degrees for 1½ hours, basting frequently with reserved marinade. Also delicious grilled outdoors over medium heat for 45-60 minutes. While meat is cooking, prepare Mustard Sauce, blending ingredients in the order listed. To serve, slice thinly and top each serving with Mustard Sauce. SERVES 8-12.

Pork Normandy

1 5-pound boned loin of pork, rolled and tied	Garlic (optional)
	Madeira wine
Thyme	Normandy Sauce
Salt and pepper	Parsley or watercress, for garnish

Preheat oven to 325 degrees. Leave layer of fat on the loin. Rub loin with thyme, salt, pepper and a cut clove of garlic. Sear all sides in a hot skillet with small amount of cooking oil. Place loin on rack in roasting pan. Pour a cup of Madeira over loin. Cover and cook for 1½ hours or until meat thermometer registers 170 degrees. Do not overcook. Serve on a warmed platter decorated with parsley or watercress. Pass with Normandy Sauce. SERVES 10.

NORMANDY SAUCE

12 peppercorns, green or black	Degreased meat juices
½ cup vinegar	1 tablespoon butter
⅓ cup whipping cream	Salt
1 tablespoon flour or cornstarch	Chopped parsley
1 large tablespoon dry mustard	Thyme

Crush peppercorns, place in sauce pan with vinegar and bring to a boil. Reduce liquid by half. Add the flour or cornstarch, mustard and whipping cream to the vinegar. Heat, stirring constantly with wire whisk, until mixture thickens slightly. Add degreased pan juices from roast to the sauce. Add butter, a little salt and a bit of parsley and thyme for color and flavor. **MAKES 2 CUPS.**

Scottish Stuffed Pork Tenderloin

1 1-pound pork tenderloin

DRESSING

2 tablespoons butter	¼ teaspoon rosemary
1 cup fresh bread crumbs	Salt and pepper
½ cup chopped onion	1 egg, slightly beaten
¼ cup finely chopped parsley	1 bacon slice, cut in half
¼ teaspoon sage	String or skewers

Butterfly the tenderloin (cut partially in half horizontally, but do not cut completely through). Lay open the butterflied tenderloin and pound to flatten. In a small skillet, sauté onions in butter until tender. Add bread crumbs and cook until crisp. Add seasonings, remove from stove and cool slightly. Add egg to moisten. Spread stuffing on one half of the tenderloin and cover with the other half. Place bacon on top and tie with string or use skewers to secure. Bake at 350 degrees for 1 hour. **SERVES 4.**

Virginia Spareribs

4 pounds spareribs, cut into pieces
2 tablespoons butter
½ cup minced onions
3 cups apple juice
½ cup cider vinegar
3 teaspoons brown sugar

1½ teaspoons cinnamon
2 teaspoons cornstarch
4 apples, pared, cored and quartered
2 acorn squash, quartered
Salt and pepper to taste

Place ribs, meat-side up, in a large, shallow roasting pan. Bake for 1 hour in a 300 degree preheated oven. Drain fat. Meanwhile, combine butter, onions, apple juice, vinegar, brown sugar, cinnamon, and salt and pepper to taste. Bring mixture to a boil, simmer 15 minutes. Add cornstarch to thicken. Pour sauce over ribs and bake for an additional hour. Add quartered apples and squash; bake for 1 more hour. SERVES 6-8.

Alsace-Lorraine Spareribs

3 pounds spareribs
2-3 onions, sliced
3 tablespoons vinegar
3 tablespoons Worcestershire
  sauce
½ teaspoon salt
1½ teaspoons paprika

¾ teaspoon cayenne pepper
¾ teaspoon freshly ground
  black pepper
3 teaspoons chili powder
1 cup catsup
1 cup water

Place spareribs in roaster with sliced onions. Make a sauce of vinegar, Worcestershire sauce, salt, paprika, cayenne, black pepper, chili powder, catsup and water. Pour over spareribs. Cover and bake in 350 degree oven for 1½ hours. Baste and turn spareribs occasionally. During final 15 minutes of cooking time, remove the cover to brown the spareribs. NOTE: To deal with any accumulated fat, make this dish ahead of time and refrigerate for several hours. When completely cool, the fat will have risen to the surface and solidified. You can scoop it out easily with a slotted spoon and the spareribs can be reheated, gently, on the stove-top. SERVES 6.

Sausage Ratatouille

½ cup olive oil	2 teaspoons salt
2 large onions, sliced	1 teaspoon sugar
3 cloves garlic, minced	1 teaspoon dried oregano
1 medium unpeeled eggplant,	½ teaspoon dried thyme
cut into 1-inch cubes	24 sweet Italian sausages,
2 green peppers, chopped	cut into ½-inch slices
3 zucchini, cut into ½-inch pieces	Water
2 pounds fresh tomatoes, chopped	1 6-oz. can tomato paste

In a 5-6 quart saucepan, heat oil and brown onions and garlic for 5 minutes. Add eggplant and cook for 5 minutes. Add peppers and cook for 5 minutes. Add zucchini and cook for 5 minutes. Add tomatoes and seasonings and cook for 20 minutes, covered, at a simmer. (You can stop here and finish later if you wish.) Simmer sausages in enough boiling water to cover for 10 minutes. Drain well. Add to simmering vegetable mixture, along with the tomato paste. Continue cooking for 15 minutes, stirring occasionally. If done early in the day, cover and refrigerate. When ready to serve, bring to a simmer and cook for 15 minutes, uncovered. **SERVES 8.**

German Winter Stew

1 pound Italian sausages,	2 pounds potatoes, pared and cut
cut into pieces	in chunks
⅓ cup water	2 cloves or more of garlic, finely
1 pound knockwurst, cut into pieces	chopped
½ pound bratwurst, cut into pieces	Salt and pepper to taste
1 pound onions, peeled and chopped	

In a large pot, place Italian sausages in one layer and cover with the water. Cook over medium heat for 5 minutes. Add knockwurst and bratwurst to pot. Continue to cook for 10-12 minutes until sausages have browned. Remove from pot and set aside. Add onions and potatoes to drippings in pan and brown over medium heat for 20 minutes. Return sausages to pan, add garlic and salt and pepper to taste. Cover and simmer on low heat for 20 minutes. Serve with a slightly bitter, green salad. **SERVES 8.**

Lamb Ragoût

2 pounds boned lamb,
  cut into 1-inch cubes
Salt and freshly ground pepper
3 tablespoons vegetable oil
3 tablespoons olive oil
4 cups chopped onions

2 cloves garlic, minced
1 tablespoon flour
3 cups beef broth
1 cup Burgundy wine
⅛ cup tomato paste
2 bay leaves

Season lamb with salt and pepper in a bowl. Heat 1 tablespoon of each oil in a large, heavy skillet and add enough lamb to make one layer. Sear meat over a high heat to brown. Continue until all meat is seared. Drain in a colander, over a bowl, to retain all juices. Next, in a Dutch oven, sauté onions in 2 tablespoons of each oil for 10-15 minutes or until lightly browned. Add garlic and sauté for 2 minutes. Add flour and cook for 1 minute. Preheat oven to 350 degrees. Add broth and wine to onion/flour mixture. Add lamb, tomato paste and bay leaves. Add meat drippings and return to a simmer. Skim off any fat that rises to the surface. Cover pot and cook in the oven for 2-3 hours. You may need to skim fat occasionally while cooking. Remove bay leaves before serving. NOTE: Ragoût will keep for 4-5 days in the refrigerator and should be reheated thoroughly before serving. SERVES 8-10.

Carlyle Cassoulet

1½ pounds dried small
  white beans
Water
2 teaspoons dried thyme
2 bay leaves
2 cloves garlic, sieved
2 stalks celery, chopped
2 teaspoons salt
¼ teaspoon freshly ground pepper
1 pound lamb shoulder, cubed

1 pound pork shoulder, cubed
1 4-5 pound duck, cut into
  serving pieces
1 pound pork sausage, crumbled
2 tomatoes, cubed
1 onion, quartered
1 tablespoon butter, melted
1 cup dry bread crumbs
¼ cup chopped parsley

Soak beans, covered in water, overnight. Drain and cover with fresh water. Combine thyme, bay leaves, garlic and celery in a cheese cloth bag to make a bouquet garni. Add salt, pepper and bouquet garni to beans and cook for 45-60 minutes or until tender. Drain beans again and reserve the liquid. Set both aside. Discard bouquet garni. In a large, ovenproof Dutch oven, combine lamb, pork, duck, sausage, tomatoes and onion. Cook over high heat, stirring occasionally, until meats are lightly browned. Remove Dutch oven from heat. Mix beans with meats, stirring in cooking juices. Pour in enough of the reserved bean liquid to fill the Dutch oven only halfway up the sides of the dish. Cover, place in oven, and bake at 300 degrees for 3½ hours. Stir occasionally with a wooden spoon. Add more bean liquid if necessary. Mix melted butter with bread crumbs and parsley; spread over top of cassoulet. Bake, uncovered, at 400 degrees until crumbs are browned. SERVES **10-12.**

Lamb Navarin

2 tablespoons oil	2 13¾-oz. cans chicken broth
2 tablespoons butter or margarine	¼ cup chopped parsley, stems reserved
6-8 pounds shoulder of lamb, cut into 1½-inch pieces	1 bay leaf
2 cups chopped onions	½ teaspoon crumbled fresh thyme leaves
2 cloves garlic, minced	2 cups cooked peas, fresh or frozen
¼ cup all-purpose flour	2 1-lb cans small carrots, drained
1 teaspoon salt	
¼ teaspoon pepper	2 1-lb cans white onions, drained
2 cups dry white wine	
2 8-oz. cans tomato sauce	

Heat oil and butter in large skillet over medium heat. Brown meat in batches, adding more oil to pan if necessary. Transfer meat to large Dutch oven when browned. Add onion to fat left in skillet. Cook for 2-3 minutes, stirring occasionally. Add garlic; cook for 1 minute. Sprinkle with flour, salt and pepper. Mix well. Add wine. Bring to a boil and stir until all of flour mixture is dissolved. Add tomato sauce, chicken broth, parsley stems, bay leaf and thyme. Return to a boil. Pour sauce over meat. (If planning to freeze, stop cooking process at this point. Resume with instructions when mixture has been thawed.) Cover and simmer for 1 hour and 15 minutes or until meat is tender. Discard parsley stems and bay leaf. Add vegetables and simmer until vegetables are heated through. Sprinkle with parsley when ready to serve. SERVES **14-18.**

Grilled Lamb

1 boned leg of lamb (2½ to 3 lbs)
¼ cup Dijon mustard
1 teaspoon salt

4-6 cloves garlic, crushed
½ cup olive oil
2 tablespoons lemon juice

Combine mustard, salt, garlic, olive oil and lemon juice and use to coat lamb. Place in covered dish and chill overnight (or a minimum of 4 hours). Place lamb on grill about 4-6 inches above the coals. Grill approximately 20 minutes, turning frequently. Remove and slice. Serve rare or medium rare. SERVES **6.**

Lamb Korma

¼ cup cashews
2 small dried red chiles,
  seeded
1 1-inch piece of ginger root,
  peeled and chopped
1 cup cold water
1 stick cinnamon, crushed
¼ teaspoon cardamom seeds
¼ teaspoon ground cloves
3 cloves garlic, peeled
½ teaspoon turmeric
2 tablespoons poppy seeds

1 tablespoon coriander seeds
1 teaspoon cumin seeds
6 tablespoons butter or margarine
1 cup finely chopped onions
1 teaspoon salt
½ cup plain yogurt
1½ pounds lean boneless lamb,
  cut into 2-inch cubes
2 tablespoons minced fresh
  cilantro
1 tablespoon freshly squeezed
  lemon juice

Combine cashews, chiles, ginger and cold water in a food processor and purée. Add cinnamon, cardamom seeds, cloves, garlic, turmeric and poppy, coriander and cumin seeds. Blend into a thick, smooth sauce. Set aside. Heat butter in a heavy skillet and sauté onions until golden and tender. Stir in salt, cashew mixture and yogurt. Cook for 5 minutes, stirring occasionally. Add lamb cubes and reduce heat to low. Cook for 20 minutes more, covered. Add 1 tablespoon of the cilantro and stir. Cook for another 15 minutes or until lamb is tender. When ready to serve, sprinkle with lemon juice and remaining cilantro. SERVES **4.**

Lamb and Cucumber Stir-Fry

1 tablespoon corn starch
½ teaspoon salt
⅛ teaspoon pepper
½ cup chicken broth
2 tablespoons vegetable oil
1 cup sliced onions
1 clove garlic, minced

2 medium cucumbers, peeled,
   seeded and sliced
1 pound boneless lamb, trimmed
   and cut into thin strips
8 oz. plain yogurt
1 tablespoon finely chopped
   fresh mint

Combine corn starch, salt and pepper in a small bowl. Gradually add chicken broth and mix until smooth. Set aside. Heat oil in a large, heavy skillet and sauté onions and garlic for 2 minutes. Add cucumbers; stir-fry for 2 minutes. Remove vegetables from pan. Add lamb to pan and stir-fry for 1-2 minutes. (You may need to do this in two batches.) Return vegetables to pan. Reblend cornstarch mixture and add to skillet. Stir constantly over medium heat until mixture reaches a boil. Reduce heat to low and add yogurt and mint. Simmer, stirring constantly, until heated through. Serve over rice. **SERVES 4.**

Poultry

Menu

Twelfth Night On Captain's Row

This one short, cobblestoned stretch of Prince Street is famous as the street where many of Alexandria's seafaring captains chose to settle, close by the deepwater harbor on the Potomac just a block away. After two centuries, Captain's Row is still home to a lucky few who live in these 28 lovely, landmark houses.

Chicken Denise

4 chicken breast halves,
  skinned and boned
Flour
1 teaspoon butter
1 tablespoon vegetable or olive oil
½ cup orange juice

⅓ cup red wine vinegar
½ teaspoon allspice
2 bay leaves
Salt and pepper to taste
Orange slices and parsley
  for garnish

Dredge chicken breasts in flour. Set aside. Melt the butter and oil over medium to high heat in large, heavy-bottomed frying pan. Place chicken breasts in pan and sauté for 5 minutes on each side or until golden brown. Remove pan from heat and drain off excess fat. Add orange juice, vinegar, allspice, and bay leaves. Turn heat to low. Return pan to heat and cover. Simmer for 15-20 minutes, or until tender. Salt and pepper to taste. Garnish with orange slices and parsley. Serve with brown rice and vegetables. **SERVES 4.** *Denise Austin*

Baked Mustard Chicken

4 chicken breast halves,
  skinned and boned
¼ cup spicy brown mustard
  or Dijon mustard
½ cup bread crumbs

¼ cup butter, melted
2 tablespoons fresh lemon juice
2 tablespoons white wine
  (preferable) or water
Paprika

Brush chicken with mustard and dredge in bread crumbs. Place in 13x9x2-inch baking dish. Combine butter, lemon juice and wine; drizzle 1 tablespoon over each piece of chicken and pour remainder in dish. Cover and bake at 350 degrees for 45 minutes. Remove cover, sprinkle with paprika, and bake an additional 15 minutes. **SERVES 4.**

Elegant Chicken

4 chicken breast halves,
  skinned and boned

½ teaspoon salt
2 tablespoons vegetable oil

¾ cup butter or margarine
2 egg yolks
2 tablespoons dry white wine
1 tablespoon lemon juice
¼ teaspoon dried tarragon

10-12 oz. fresh spinach
2 tablespoons butter or margarine
¾ pound mushrooms, thinly sliced
1 carrot, pared and grated

Pound chicken breasts with mallet until ¼-inch thick. In a double boiler over hot (not boiling) water, beat ¾ cup butter, yolks, wine and lemon juice with a wire whisk until butter melts and mixture thickens. Stir in tarragon and salt. Cover and keep sauce warm. Be careful as sauce will separate if heat is too high. In a Dutch oven, heat oil until hot. Add spinach and cook until wilted, stirring constantly. Remove to a platter and keep warm. In a skillet, heat the 2 tablespoons of butter and add chicken breasts, cooking until tender and lightly browned on each side, about 5-7 minutes. Remove chicken and arrange over the spinach on the warmed platter. In pan drippings, cook mushrooms and grated carrot until tender. Ladle sauce over the chicken and top with mushroom and carrot mixture. SERVES 4.

Chicken Medallions

4 whole chicken breast halves,
  skinned, boned and halved
½ pound fresh spinach,
  finely chopped
¾ cup chopped fresh basil
5 oz. Mozzarella cheese, shredded

½ pound Ricotta cheese
Salt and pepper to taste
¼ teaspoon dried thyme
½ teaspoon dried tarragon

Place chicken breasts between two layers of waxed paper and flatten with mallet or rolling pin until ¼-inch thick. Combine spinach with basil, cheeses, salt, pepper, thyme and tarragon in a bowl. Spread mixture on each chicken breast, dividing mixture evenly. Roll up each breast, jelly-roll fashion, and secure with a toothpick. Place stuffed breasts, seam-side down, in a shallow baking pan and bake at 350 degrees for 1 hour. May be served hot or cold. Serve whole for a main course. To serve as a cold luncheon entrée, cut into ½-inch thick slices and serve on a platter lined with grape or lettuce leaves. NOTE: An unusual variation is to prepare breasts as directed and stuff with Diana's Sundried Tomato Spread. Bake as directed. These may be made a day ahead, but wrap well and refrigerate until ready to slice and serve. SERVES 6 AS A DINNER ENTRÉE, OR 12 WHEN CUT IN MEDALLIONS FOR A COLD LUNCHEON ENTRÉE.

Cold Marinated Chicken Breasts

2 cups water
½ teaspoon salt
6 whole chicken breasts
½ cup olive oil
½ cup vegetable oil
⅓ cup tarragon wine vinegar
1 teaspoon salt

½ teaspoon garlic powder
4 tablespoons sliced scallions
   (about 2 whole scallions)
¼ cup finely chopped parsley
Garnish:
   Olives, cherry tomatoes,
   green peppers, carrots, etc.

Heat water with salt to boiling in skillet. Put in chicken breasts and simmer just until all pink color disappears (about 12 minutes). Turn once during cooking. Drain and cool. When cool enough to handle, remove the bones and halve each whole breast to make 12 split breasts. Place in a bowl. Mix oils, vinegar, seasonings, scallions and 2 tablespoons of the parsley. Pour over chicken. Cover bowl and chill for at least 6 hours or overnight. Turn occasionally. To serve, arrange chicken on lettuce leaves, spoon some marinade over each piece and sprinkle with remaining parsley. Serve remaining marinade separately. Garnish with olives, cherry tomatoes, green pepper strips, carrot sticks, etc. Serve on a chilled platter with chilled plates on a hot summer day. SERVES 12.

Country Captain

4 chicken breast halves
Water
2 strips bacon
1 onion, chopped
1 green pepper, chopped
1 clove garlic, minced
3 tablespoons currants
½ teaspoon white pepper

2 teaspoons curry powder
2 cans tomatoes
1½ teaspoons chopped parsley
½ teaspoon thyme
2¾ oz. blanched,
   slivered almonds
6 cups cooked rice
Chutney

Remove skin and fat from chicken breasts. Place chicken in stockpot, cover with water and simmer for 45 minutes. Remove chicken from pot. When cool enough to handle, bone the chicken and cut into 1-inch chunks. Fry bacon in large skillet until crisp. Remove from pan; cool, crumble and set aside. Sauté onion, green pepper and garlic in bacon drippings until limp. Add remaining ingredients except rice and chutney and simmer for 30 minutes. Add chicken and crumbled bacon. Simmer just long enough to heat through. (May be refrigerated or frozen at this point.) Serve hot over rice with chutney. NOTE: This recipe was probably introduced to the English by a Sepoy ("Country Troops") Captain in India. It was known in America by 1854. SERVES **4-6.**

Indian Chicken

6 chicken breast halves,
  skinned and boned
½ cup dry white wine
1 teaspoon chicken bouillon granules

4 teaspoons chopped fresh
  parsley (or 2 teaspoons dried)
½ teaspoon curry powder

Place chicken in a lightly greased baking pan so all pieces fit snugly. In a small bowl, combine wine and dry ingredients with wire whisk until well mixed. Pour wine mixture over chicken. Cover pan tightly; bake at 350 degrees for 35 minutes or until chicken is done. SERVES **4-6.**

Chicken Tarragona

6 chicken breast halves,
  skinned and boned
Salt
Freshly ground pepper
¼ cup flour
4 tablespoons unsalted butter
1 tablespoon chopped shallots
  or onions

¼ cup dry white wine
¼ cup chicken broth
1 teaspoon chopped fresh tarragon,
  or ½ teaspoon dried
¼ cup heavy cream

Sprinkle chicken with salt and pepper and dredge with flour. Reserve remaining flour. In a large skillet, heat 3 tablespoons of the butter; add chicken and brown on both sides. Transfer to a heated platter. Sauté shallots in pan drippings. Add wine and cook over high heat until liquid is nearly evaporated, while scraping loose any particles in the pan. Whisk in the flour to make a thick mixture. Stir in chicken broth and tarragon. Add chicken to mixture; cover and simmer for 25 minutes or until chicken is tender. Remove chicken to platter and keep warm. Add remaining tablespoon of butter and the cream to skillet and heat. Pour the sauce over the chicken. SERVES **6.**

Lemon-Caper Chicken

¼ cup butter, unsalted
4-6 chicken legs or thighs
  (or combination)
½ pound fresh mushrooms,
  sliced
1 tablespoon capers, not drained

2 tablespoons freshly squeezed
  lemon juice
Salt and pepper to taste
Paprika
1 whole garlic clove, peeled

Melt butter in large, heavy skillet. Add chicken and brown on both sides. Remove from pan and keep warm. Add mushrooms, capers, lemon juice, salt, pepper, paprika and garlic to skillet. Bring to a boil and return chicken to pan. Cover and simmer for 30-40 minutes. Remove garlic clove. Serve with pan sauces spooned over chicken. **SERVES 2.**

Lemon Chicken

6 chicken breast halves,
  skinned and boned
Salt and pepper
Vegetable oil spray
1 tablespoon butter or margarine
¼ cup dry white wine or sherry
¼ cup chopped onion
2 tablespoons grated lemon rind
2 tablespoons fresh lemon juice

1 cup water
1 teaspoon chicken bouillon
  granules
¼ cup water
2 tablespoons flour
¼ cup freshly grated Parmesan
  cheese
¼ teaspoon paprika
2 tablespoons chopped fresh parsley

With mallet or rolling pin, flatten chicken breast halves until ¼-inch thick between two layers of waxed paper. Lightly sprinkle with salt and pepper and set aside. Spray a large skillet with vegetable spray and melt butter over medium heat. Quickly sauté the chicken, cooking for 3 minutes on each side. Remove chicken to a 13x9x2-inch baking dish which has been coated with vegetable oil spray. Do not remove juices from skillet. Add sherry, onions, lemon rind and lemon juice to skillet. Cook for 5 minutes over medium heat or until onions are tender. Add 1 cup of water and the chicken granules. Mix flour and ¼ cup water together until smooth. Add to mixture in skillet and cook for 5 minutes or until sauce thickens. Pour sauce over chicken in baking dish. Sprinkle with cheese, paprika and parsley, and bake at 350 degrees for 15 minutes. **SERVES 6.**

Chicken Fellini

1 medium green pepper
1 large or 2 small onions
6 medium zucchini
2 tablespoons olive oil
   or vegetable oil spray for pan
1 15-oz. can of tomato sauce

2 large whole chicken breasts,
   skinned, boned and halved
2 tablespoons flour
Salt and pepper
4 oz. Mozzarella, shredded

Cut pepper into bite-sized pieces and thinly slice the onions. Cut zucchini into quarters, then slice into ¾ inch-chunks. Flatten chicken breasts and coat in flour seasoned with salt and pepper. Heat oil in skillet or coat with vegetable oil spray. Sauté chicken on both sides over medium heat until almost done. Remove to plate. In pan drippings, cook vegetables until tender. Stir in tomato sauce. Pour into a baking dish, place chicken on top, and sprinkle Mozzarella over all. Bake at 350 degrees until bubbly. NOTE: This recipe can be made up to 2 days in advance and stored, covered, in the refrigerator. Proportions can be multiplied. It makes an economical buffet dish when served with rice, salad, and Italian bread. **SERVES 4.**

Chicken Queen Street

4 chicken breast halves,
   skinned and boned
1 pound feta cheese, crumbled
1 bunch fresh dill, chopped
1 teaspoon cracked black pepper

1 egg
½ cup milk
Bread crumbs
¼ pound butter

Slice open chicken breasts horizontally, making a pocket. Mix the cheese and dill together with the pepper to taste. Stuff chicken breasts with mixture. In a large bowl, beat together egg and milk. Dip stuffed chicken pieces into egg wash and then roll in bread crumbs. Melt butter slowly in a large oven-proof skillet. Add chicken breasts and bake at 400 degrees for 10-15 minutes or until golden brown. Turn chicken and bake for an additional 10-15 minutes. **SERVES 4.** *Bilbo Baggins Restaurant, 208 Queen Street*

Boursin Purses

4 chicken breast halves, skinned and boned	¼ cup pine nuts, toasted
1 package (4-oz.) garlic and herb spreadable cheese	3 tablespoons spicy-sweet mustard (or 2 tablespoons Dijon with 1 tablespoon honey)
2 scallions, chopped	

Preheat oven to 450 degrees. Blot chicken breasts dry with paper towels. Using a very sharp knife, butterfly the chicken breasts (make a horizontal slice, halving chicken breasts but leaving one side attached). Season with salt and pepper inside and out. Mix together cheese, scallions and pine nuts. Place a generous tablespoon in the pocket of each breast. Fold over one side of chicken breast to enclose filling, pressing gently around the edges. Spread the top of each stuffed breast with mustard. Place on lightly greased baking sheet and bake for 15-17 minutes. NOTE: Can be assembled earlier in day and refrigerated until baking time. SERVES 4.

Stuffed Chicken Breasts

2 large leeks	Salt
3 tablespoons butter	White and black pepper to taste
1 carrot, finely chopped	1 tablespoon chopped shallots
1 small onion, finely chopped	1 tablespoon finely chopped watercress
½ cup mushrooms, chopped	
1 egg, slightly beaten	1 clove garlic, finely chopped
2 tablespoons Port wine	4 chicken breast halves, skinned and boned
1 cup chicken stock	
1 cup crème fraîche or 1 cup heavy cream	2 egg yolks
	4 tablespoons water

From one leek, finely chop 1-inch of the light green portion plus all of the white portion. In a skillet, melt 1 tablespoon of the butter. Add the carrot, leek and onions. Sauté for 5 minutes. Add the mushrooms and cook until all liquid has evaporated (approximately 5 minutes). Add salt and black pepper to taste. Cool a bit, add egg and stir well. Set aside.

Thinly slice remaining leek. In another skillet, melt remaining 2 tablespoons of butter, add leek and cook for 10 minutes over low heat, covered. Stir occasionally. Add wine and stock; simmer for 10 minutes more, covered. Remove cover and continue to cook until liquid is reduced by half. Add cream, plus salt and white pepper. Bring just to a boiling point and remove from heat.

Mix shallots, watercress and garlic. Cut a pocket in each chicken breast by making a horizontal slice through the side. Stuff with 1 teaspoon of the shallot mixture. Add chicken breasts to the sauce and return to heat. Cover pan and simmer until chicken is done, about 6 minutes. Remove chicken from sauce and keep warm on a serving platter. In a small saucepan over low heat, beat egg yolks and water until yolks form a ribbon and triple in volume. Using a blender, on high speed, mix the sauce and egg yolk mixture together. Add more salt and white pepper if needed. Serve chicken breasts with a small amount of sauce spooned on top. Pass remaining sauce. SERVES 4.

Poulet Sauté au Basquaise

1 3-pound chicken	4 garlic cloves, minced
Chicken stock	10 tomatoes, peeled,
3 tablespoons vegetable	seeded and diced
or olive oil	2 tablespoons tomato paste
Salt and pepper	2 teaspoons sugar
Flour	Bouquet garni, with thyme
2 tablespoons vegetable	and bay leaf
or olive oil	7 oz. prosciutto ham
4 green onions, minced	Pinch of cayenne pepper
4 green peppers, minced	Fresh parsley, chopped

Cut the chicken into four serving pieces. Make chicken stock with remaining bony pieces (back, neck, wing tips). Season serving pieces with salt and pepper; coat lightly with flour. Heat 3 tablespoons of the oil in a large skillet and sauté the chicken over a quick flame. When chicken is evenly golden, cover the pan and simmer for 10 minutes over low heat. Remove the chicken. In the same skillet, pour 2 tablespoons of the oil and sauté the onions for 3 minutes. Add the green pepper, garlic, diced tomatoes, tomato paste, sugar, bouquet garni, ham, salt, pepper, and cayenne. Pour in 1 cup of chicken stock made from the bones, and cook this mixture to a sauce (about 15 minutes). Return chicken pieces to the skillet and simmer gently for 20 minutes. Place chicken on a warmed platter and sprinkle with chopped parsley. Serve with rice. SERVES 4. *La Bergerie Restaurant, 218 North Lee Street*

Baked Chicken in Wine

6-8 chicken breast halves	2 tablespoons tomato paste
½ cup butter or margarine	1 pint chicken stock
3 medium onions, sliced	1 beef bouillon cube
Mushrooms, sliced	½ cup dry red or white wine
2 tablespoons flour	

Preheat oven to 325 degrees. In skillet, sauté chicken breasts in butter or margarine until lightly brown. Place in a baking dish. Sauté sliced onions in skillet. Add mushrooms, flour, tomato paste and chicken stock. Stir in bouillon cube and simmer for 3-5 minutes. Add wine. Pour mixture over chicken breasts and cover. Bake in oven for 1½ to 2 hours. Uncover during final 20 minutes of baking time. NOTE: Can easily be prepared 1-2 days ahead and reheated before serving. SERVES 6-8.

Pollo Don Beverly

6 chicken breast halves, skinned and boned	¾ cup chopped mushrooms
Salt and pepper to taste	3 cups canned Italian plum tomatoes
¼ cup olive oil	½ cup chopped prosciutto ham
1 large onion, sliced	10 pitted black and green olives, halved
1 teaspoon chopped garlic	
2 green or red peppers, cut into strips	

Cut each chicken breast half into 2 or 3 pieces. Season with salt and pepper. Heat oil in skillet and quickly brown the chicken pieces. Transfer to a plate and keep warm. In the same skillet, sauté the onion, garlic and peppers over moderate heat for 8-10 minutes. Add mushrooms, tomatoes and ham. Simmer together for 2 minutes. Place chicken and vegetables in a casserole dish and bake at 350 degrees for 30 minutes (juices should have begun to reduce and sauce to thicken). Sprinkle olives over chicken and serve. SERVES 6.

Chicken Cacciatore

1 3-pound chicken, cut into
  small serving pieces
3 tablespoons olive oil
1¼ cups minced onions
1 handful or less finely chopped
  fresh parsley, or 1 teaspoon dried
1 handful or less finely chopped
  fresh basil, or 1 teaspoon dried

1 teaspoon salt
Freshly ground pepper to taste
3 fresh tomatoes, peeled and
  quartered, or 1 small can
  plum tomatoes
¼ cup dry white wine

Using a large, heavy skillet, brown chicken pieces on all sides in olive oil over medium heat. Chicken should become golden brown. Add onions, herbs, salt and pepper. Sauté, turning chicken and stirring to allow seasonings to blend. Add wine; cover and simmer for 2-3 minutes. Add tomatoes. Cover and simmer for 20-30 minutes or until tender. NOTE: This dish tastes best when made 24 hours in advance. Freezes well. **SERVES 4.**

Chicken Mexicana

1 whole chicken
1-2 onions, chopped
Water
1 cup rich chicken broth

1 stick margarine or
  3 tablespoons Molly McButter
10 flour tortillas
Salt and pepper to taste

In a large stockpot, boil chicken and onions in water until meat is falling off bones. To reduce fat, skim grease from top of broth. Remove chicken and bones from stock. Tear chicken into small pieces and return to broth. Add cup of rich chicken broth and margarine or substitute. Bring to a boil. Cut flour tortillas into 1-inch wide strips and slowly drop into boiling broth. Turn down heat and simmer, uncovered, for 15-20 minutes. Remove chicken and tortilla dumplings from broth with slotted spoon and serve. **SERVES 4.**

Mango Chicken

4 boneless chicken breast halves

MARINADE

1 tablespoon balsamic vinegar   ¼ cup olive oil
⅓ cup red or white wine   ⅓ cup red wine vinegar
½ cup mango chutney

Mix marinade ingredients. Remove skin from chicken if desired. Place chicken and marinade in sealed large plastic bag. Marinate overnight in refrigerator. Grill over hot coals, approximately 5 minutes per side, or until done. SERVES 4.

Chicken Sopa

4 chicken breast halves,   1 10-oz. package white corn
  skinned and boned   tortilla chips
5 cups water   1 pound grated Cheddar cheese
¼ cup butter or margarine   or slices of Monterey Jack
1 medium onion, chopped   Salt and pepper to taste
1 16-oz. can stewed tomatoes
1 10-oz. can diced tomatoes
  and green chilies

In large pot, simmer chicken in water for 20 minutes or until tender. Remove chicken, cool and shred; set aside pot with broth. While chicken is boiling, heat butter in large skillet and sauté onion until tender over medium heat. Add tomatoes and simmer for 10 minutes. Set aside. Preheat oven to 350 degrees. Spoon a small amount of tomato mixture into the bottom of a large shallow baking dish. Return reserved chicken broth to a rolling boil and * drop two large handfuls of tortilla chips into broth, stirring and cooking for 15 seconds. Work quickly, allowing broth to continue boiling, and remove barely softened chips with slotted spoon. Spread layer of chips over tomato mixture in dish. Layer one third of chicken over chips; top chicken with one third of the cheese. Spoon one third of tomato mixture over cheese. REPEAT FROM *, ending with tomato mixture. Cover and bake for 20 minutes. Uncover and continue baking for 15 minutes. NOTE: Can be prepared earlier in day and baked prior to serving time. SERVES 6.

Chicken Korma

MARINADE

1 8-oz. carton plain yogurt	1 teaspoon minced fresh ginger
2 teaspoons curry powder	4 cloves garlic, minced
1 teaspoon salt	½ teaspoon cayenne pepper
1 teaspoon ground coriander	½ teaspoon lemon juice
8 chicken thighs, skinned	Vegetable oil spray

Combine marinade ingredients in a deep bowl, add chicken and coat well. Cover and let stand at room temperature for 30 minutes, or refrigerate up to 24 hours. Drain chicken and grill over medium coals or broil in oven until golden brown. Spray grill or broiler pan with vegetable oil spray before cooking. **SERVES 4.**

Chicken and Peach Stir-Fry

1 pound chicken breasts, skinned and boned	2 tablespoons corn oil, divided
1 tablespoon corn starch	1 small sweet red pepper cut in strips
1 teaspoon sugar	⅓ cup sliced green onions
½ teaspoon salt	1 teaspoon minced fresh ginger
⅛ teaspoon pepper	2 cups peeled, sliced fresh peaches
¾ cup chicken broth, cooled	1 tablespoon lemon juice

Cut chicken breasts into strips and set aside. In a small bowl, combine corn starch, sugar, salt and pepper. Gradually stir in chicken broth until smooth; set aside. In a large skillet or wok, heat 1 tablespoon of the oil over medium-high heat. Add red pepper; stir-fry for 1 minute. Remove from pan and set aside. Heat remaining tablespoon of oil in same skillet. Add green onions and ginger; stir-fry for 1 minute. Add chicken strips; stir-fry for 2-3 minutes or until chicken turns white. Re-stir corn starch mixture and add to skillet. Stirring constantly, bring mixture to boil over medium heat and cook for 1 minute. Add red pepper strips, peaches and lemon juice. Cook for 1 minute or until heated through. **SERVES 4-6.**

Sampan Stir-Fry

1 pound chicken breasts, skinned and boned

MARINADE

¼ cup low-sodium teriyaki sauce
¼ cup low-sodium soy sauce
¼ cup Chablis or vermouth
2 cloves garlic, minced

½ teaspoon peeled, grated
  ginger root (or more to taste)
¼ teaspoon Chinese five-spice
  powder

1 4-oz. package uncooked wild
  rice or 1 cup uncooked white rice
1 teaspoon vegetable oil
1 cup sliced green peppers
⅔ cup sliced carrots

⅔ cup chopped onions
⅔ cup sliced mushrooms
1 cup frozen green peas, thawed
Vegetable oil spray
2 tablespoons slivered almonds, toasted

Cut chicken into 1-inch pieces and place in bowl. Whisk together marinade ingredients and pour over chicken. Cover and marinate in refrigerator for several hours. Cook rice according to package directions; keep warm. Heat oil in wok or skillet and stir-fry peppers and carrots for 2 minutes. Add mushrooms and peas; stir-fry for 2 minutes. Add vegetables to rice. Coat wok or skillet with vegetable oil spray. Add chicken with marinade liquid; stir-fry for 4 minutes or until done. Add rice and vegetables to chicken and cook for 1-2 minutes to heat. Sprinkle toasted almonds over all and serve. NOTE: Chicken, marinade and vegetables may be prepared early in the day of cooking. MAKES 4½ CUP SERVINGS.

Oriental Chicken

2 whole chicken breasts,
  skinned and boned
1 tablespoon corn starch
1 tablespoon sherry
1 tablespoon soy sauce
⅛ of whole jicama
  or 6 water chestnuts

1 green pepper
¼ pound fresh mushrooms
¼ pound snow peas
Salt to taste
3 tablespoons peanut oil
2 tablespoons Hoisin sauce
¼ cup chopped roasted peanuts

Cut chicken into cubes. In a large bowl, combine the corn starch and sherry. Stir in soy sauce. Add chicken to mixture and coat chicken evenly. Refrigerate until ready to use. Cut the jicama, or water chestnuts, and pepper into julienne strips. Slice mushrooms. Set aside. Remove tips and strings from snow peas and blanche in boiling water for 1 minute. Remove from boiling water, rinse in cold water, drain and set aside.

When ready to assemble, heat 2 tablespoons of the oil in a large wok or skillet until hot. Stir-fry vegetables for 2-3 minutes. Add a bit of salt and remove to warm plate. Add last tablespoon of oil to pan; heat and stir-fry chicken for 2-3 minutes. Add Hoisin sauce. Return vegetables to pan with chicken and continue to cook, stirring, for 1 minute more. Remove to warm serving dish and garnish with peanuts. **SERVES 4-6.**

Kung-Pao Chicken

MARINADE

1 pound chicken, skinned and boned
2 tablespoons soy sauce

1 tablespoon corn starch
2 tablespoons water

SAUCE

1 tablespoon white wine
2 teaspoons corn starch
1 teaspoon sugar
1 teaspoon vinegar
1 teaspoon sesame oil
2 teaspoons water

2 tablespoons vegetable oil
1 tablespoon sesame oil
12 dry hot red peppers
½ cup peanuts, unroasted and unsalted
12 scallions, cut ¼-inch thick
**   (including part of the green stalks)**

Cut chicken into small cubes and place in shallow dish. Blend soy sauce, corn starch and water and pour over chicken. Marinate for 1 hour. Make sauce by blending all ingredients until smooth. Set aside. Heat vegetable oil in wok or skillet. Add chicken when pan is very hot and fry until golden brown. Drain on paper towels. Add 1 tablespoon sesame oil to pan while still hot. Add hot peppers and cook 5-20 minutes until scorched. Remove peppers and discard. Add peanuts and scallions to peppered oil and cook for 30 seconds. Add chicken back to pan, pour sauce over. Cook and stir until chicken is tender, about 1 minute. NOTE: Serve with cooked white rice. Fewer peppers will decrease the "spicy" flavor; reducing the amount of time peppers are cooked in the oil also will decrease the "spiciness." Beef, shrimp or pork may be substituted for the chicken. **SERVES 2-4.**

Georgia Brunswick Stew

1 2-3 pound chicken
1 country ham bone, with
  some meat still on it
2 yellow onions, chopped
1 bay leaf
2 teaspoons salt
2 potatoes, peeled and chopped
1 16-oz. can peeled tomatoes,
  drained and chopped
1½ cups fresh lima beans,
  or 10-oz. package frozen
1½ cups fresh yellow corn,
  or 10-oz. package frozen

1½ cups sliced fresh okra,
  or 10-oz. package frozen
2 stalks celery, chopped
2 tablespoons fresh lemon juice
1½ teaspoons thyme
2 tablespoons Worcestershire
  sauce
2 tablespoons sugar
1 teaspoon pepper
1 tablespoon hot pepper sauce

In large stockpot, boil chicken until tender. Remove chicken and allow to cool. Remove bones and skin and cut meat into bite-sized pieces. Return chicken to liquid and add all remaining ingredients. Simmer for 2 hours or more. Stir occasionally to prevent sticking. Remove bay leaf and ham bone before serving. **SERVES 8-10.**

Southside Virginia Brunswick Stew

LAYER THE FOLLOWING IN A LARGE POT:

½ cup chopped onion
¼ pound salt pork
2 cups chopped, peeled potatoes
2 cups fresh corn kernels
2 cups lima beans

1 pound stew beef, cut into pieces
1 pound veal, cut into pieces
One whole chicken, cut into pieces
Salt and pepper to taste
1½ quarts boiling water

1 quart whole tomatoes, crushed
1 teaspoon salt
2 teaspoons pepper

¾ cup flour
1 stick butter, softened

Pour boiling water over layered ingredients in large pot. Simmer for 3 hours. Remove chicken from pot and allow to cool before removing bones and skin. Tear chicken into small pieces. Make sure stew beef and veal are in bite-sized pieces. Return chicken to pot and add tomatoes, salt and pepper. Cook for 1 hour longer, stirring occasionally. Mix together flour and butter. Pour into stew and stir well. Cook for 15 minutes or until thickened.

Roast Pheasant

BASTING SAUCE

1 tablespoon butter	3 whole cloves
4-5 oz. currant jelly	Dash cayenne pepper
Juice of ½ lemon	Salt to taste
½ cup water	½ cup Port wine

2 pheasants (approximately 2½ pounds each)	1 tablespoon butter, softened 6 slices bacon

Make sauce by combining butter, jelly, lemon juice, water, cloves, cayenne, and salt. Simmer for a few minutes and add wine. Brush pheasants with butter, place strips of bacon across breasts. Roast in a covered pan at 350 degrees for 2 hours or until tender, basting frequently with sauce. NOTE: Roast Pheasant is delicious prepared without stuffing; however, if Stuffed Roast Pheasant is preferred, use the recipe shown below. Stuff cavities and close with skewers before brushing pheasants with butter. Bake as directed, but lengthen baking time by 30 minutes. SERVES 2-4.

PHEASANT STUFFING

1 pound Italian sausages, casings removed	¼ cup chopped fresh parsley 1 tablespoon poultry seasoning
¼ cup unsalted butter	2 11-oz. packages chowder crackers,
2 large onions, chopped	lightly crushed
2 cups chopped celery	Chicken stock
8-oz. roasted chestnuts, chopped	

Cook sausages in a large, heavy skillet over medium-high heat until cooked through, crumbling with fork. Remove sausage to a large bowl. Add butter to skillet and melt over medium heat. Add onions and celery; sauté until tender. Mix in chestnuts, parsley and poultry seasoning. Add mixture to sausage. Stir in crackers and moisten with chicken stock. NOTE: This recipe is also excellent with turkey.

Roast Goose with Stuffing

STUFFING

1 cup dried apricots,
  coarsely chopped
½ cup golden raisins
2 cups Port wine
4 cups chicken broth
2 tablespoons butter
2 tablespoons olive oil
1 large onion, minced

3 celery stalks, chopped
2 cups long-grain white rice
½ cup chopped fresh parsley
3 tablespoons minced fresh
  thyme, or 3 teaspoons dried
1 teaspoon salt
½ teaspoon freshly ground pepper

Place apricots and raisins in separate bowls and pour 1 cup of Port over each. Let stand for at least 6 hours or overnight. In medium saucepan, bring chicken broth to a simmer. In large heavy skillet, melt butter over medium heat. Add onions and celery; sauté for 4-5 minutes. Add uncooked rice to skillet and stir for 3 minutes. Pour hot chicken broth over rice and vegetables and mix well. Reduce heat and cover. Cook for 20 minutes until rice is tender and liquid is absorbed. Drain Port from apricots and raisins; reserve 1 cup of Port. Stir raisins, apricots, parsley, thyme, salt and pepper into rice. Remove from heat and set aside. (May be prepared a day ahead, but bring to room temperature before stuffing goose.)

GOOSE STOCK

9 cups chicken broth
Neck, gizzard and heart from goose
2 celery stalks, chopped
1 carrot, peeled and chopped

1 bouquet garni (1 celery stalk,
  1 bay leaf, 2 sprigs thyme,
  6 peppercorns)

In a large, heavy pot, simmer all ingredients over medium heat until liquid is reduced to 6 cups. Skim surface occasionally. This should take at least 1-2 hours. Strain, cover and refrigerate. (May be prepared 2 days ahead.)

GOOSE

1 11-13 pound goose (neck, gizzard and heart reserved for Goose Stock)	1 tablespoon pepper
	Stuffing
1 lemon, halved	4 cups Goose Stock
1 tablespoon salt	

CIDER SAUCE

2 cups apple cider	1 cup reserved Port wine
2 cups Goose Stock	½ cup currant jelly

Boil in heavy sauce pan for 15 minutes or until reduced to 1 cup. Add 2 cups of the Goose Stock and 1 cup of the reserved Port. Reduce heat and simmer for 30 minutes, stirring occasionally. (May be prepared a day ahead.)

Preheat oven to 350 degrees. Cut off wing tips at joint. Squeeze lemon juice into main cavity and sprinkle inside lightly with salt and pepper. Prick goose skin (not meat) all over with fork. Rub outside of goose with salt and pepper. Fill main cavity and neck cavity loosely with rice stuffing. Skewer neck cavity closed. Tie legs together. Place any remaining stuffing in a small buttered baking dish (cover and refrigerate until later). Insert meat thermometer into thickest part of thigh. Place goose breast-side up on a rack set in large roasting pan. Use 3 cups of the Goose Stock for basting throughout baking period. Roast, uncovered, for 1¾ hours, basting every 30 minutes with Goose Stock and pan drippings. Pour off accumulated fat from pan.

Cover pan and roast for another 2½ hours, or until meat thermometer registers 180 degrees. Continue to baste goose during entire baking time. Place reserved stuffing in baking dish in oven during last hour of baking. Spoon 1 cup of the Goose Stock over stuffing after 30 minutes. (If Cider Sauce was not prepared a day ahead, it may be prepared at this point.)

When goose has finished baking, transfer to heated platter and keep warm. Strain roasting pan juices into bowl and degrease. Set roasting pan over medium heat. Return pan juices to roaster and bring to a boil, scraping up any browned bits. Transfer juices to heavy sauce pan. Add Cider Sauce and simmer for 10 minutes, or until reduced to 1½ cups. Add jelly and stir over medium heat until jelly melts. Serve goose with stuffing. Pass Cider Sauce separately. **SERVES 8-10.**

Roast Cornish Game Hens

2-4 Cornish game hens, thawed
  (approximately 1¼ pounds each)

10-oz. teriyaki sauce
10-oz. cooking sherry

Mix teriyaki and sherry; reserve ½ cup of mixture. Marinate hens in remaining liquid for at least 4 hours in refrigerator, turning often. Preheat oven to 350 degrees. Drain hens and place in roasting pan. Roast for approximately 1 hour, basting with reserved marinade throughout cooking period. Hens will be a beautiful, golden brown. SERVES 2-4.

Stuffed Cornish Game Hens

4 Cornish game hens, thawed
1 fifth Chablis (or other dry
  white wine)
4 cups cooked long grain rice
2 6-oz. jars marinated artichoke
  hearts, drained and chopped

1 2-oz. jar chopped pimentos
2 tablespoons chopped fresh parsley
Salt and pepper
Melted butter or margarine

Marinate hens in wine for 12 hours, turning once. Combine cooked rice with artichoke hearts, pimento, parsley, and salt and pepper to taste. Mix thoroughly. Stuff drained hens with rice mixture and close openings with skewers. Place hens in shallow baking pan and bake at 350 degrees for 1 hour, basting every 15 minutes with melted butter. NOTE: For stuffing variation, add slivered almonds, sliced water chestnuts or sautéed mushroom slices. SERVES 4.

Duck Francais

2 5-pound ducks
3 tablespoons olive oil
Salt and pepper to taste
2 cups orange juice
2¼ cups Burgundy wine
2 tablespoons fresh lemon juice

2 yellow onions, sliced
2 tablespoons grated orange or lemon rind
1 teaspoon dried rosemary
1 teaspoon dried oregano
4 tablespoons corn starch
¼ cup Cointreau liqueur

Cut each duck in quarters and remove as much fat as possible. Add olive oil to heavy, oven-proof pot and heat. Brown duck pieces well. Add salt and pepper, orange juice, 2 cups of the Burgundy wine, lemon juice, onions, orange or lemon rind, and herbs. Bring pot to a simmer. Remove from heat, cover and bake in oven at 275 degrees for 3 hours. Remove duck from sauce and skim fat. Place pot on top of stove over medium heat. Add corn starch and remaining ¼ cup of the Burgundy wine to sauce, stirring constantly until thickened. Add liqueur and correct seasonings. Serve immediately, or cool and reheat later in a 375 degree oven for 30 minutes or bring to simmer on stove top. SERVES 6-8.

Roast Duck

1 5-pound duck	1 onion, peeled and chopped
1 tablespoon pepper	1 tablespoon vegetable oil
1 tablespoon salt	Currant Sauce
5 sprigs parsley	

Clean duck by running under cold water and removing excess skin from neck, tail and inside cavity. Preheat oven to 450 degrees. Prick skin 10-12 times to release fat during cooking. Sprinkle cavity with pepper and half of the salt. Add whole parsley sprigs and chopped onion to cavity. Rub skin with remaining salt. Grease bottom of duck with oil and place on rack in roasting pan. Roast at 450 degrees for 20 minutes. Reduce heat to 325 degrees and roast for 2¼ hours more, or until leg moves freely. Remove from oven and let stand for 15 minutes. Carve and serve with Currant Sauce. SERVES 4.

NOTE: For cocktail buffets, thinly slice small slivers of duck and serve cold on toast points drizzled with Raspberry Sauce for Duck.

CURRANT SAUCE

3 shallots, finely chopped	½ cup red currant jelly
1½ cups Burgundy wine	Tabasco sauce
1 tablespoon balsamic vinegar	¼ cup Port wine
2 cups Chasseur Sauce	Salt and pepper to taste

Combine shallots, Burgundy wine and vinegar in a saucepan. Reduce to about 2 tablespoons. Add Chasseur Sauce and bring to a boil. Lower heat and simmer for 5 minutes. Add jelly and stir until melted. Add a few drops of Tabasco sauce and Port wine. Return sauce back to a simmer. Add salt and pepper, stir and remove from heat.

Seafood

Menu

Picnic At Jones Point Lighthouse

Crab Gazpacho   PAGE 55

Grilled Salmon Steaks with Cucumber and Mint
PAGE 178

Indian Cabbage Salad   PAGE 35

Linguine Genovese   PAGE 67

Lemon Cookies   PAGE 225

Chocolate Toffee Bars   PAGE 224

Beer and White Wine

Jones Point was named by the enterprising English surveyor and mapmaker (and later Governor of the Bahamas) Cadwalader Jones who began trading with the Indians on this spot in 1682. The Lighthouse was erected in 1855 near the District of Columbia's southern boundary marker, to guide ships to Alexandria's busy seaport for the next 70 years. It is the oldest inland waterway lighthouse in America.

Grilled Swordfish Steak

4 swordfish steaks, about 1-inch thick	Salt and white pepper
	Papaya Salsa
¼ cup olive oil	Ginger Bean Sauce

Salt and pepper steaks. Brush with oil and grill about 5-6 minutes. Prepare Papaya Salsa by combining all salsa ingredients. Add steaks to salsa and marinate over night. Prepare Ginger Black Sauce. When ready to serve, put salsa on top of swordfish and place in a buttered baking pan. Bake in a 375 degree oven for about 5-8 minutes. Garnish plate with 3 cilantro leaves and 3 slices starfruit. Heat this plate in oven with garnish on it. Put a pool of Ginger Black Bean sauce onto the hot plate and place the swordfish on top of sauce to serve. SERVES 4.

PAPAYA SALSA

1 papaya, peeled, cored and diced into ½-inch pieces	2 cloves garlic, diced fine
	¼ cup lime juice
½ red onion, diced fine	2 tablespoons cilantro, chopped
¼ green pepper, diced fine	¼ teaspoon cayenne pepper

GINGER BLACK BEAN SAUCE

½ can cooked black beans, drained	1½ tablespoons sherry wine vinegar
1 tablespoon minced garlic	⅓ bunch scallions, diced
1 tablespoon minced ginger or 1 teaspoon ground ginger	1¼ cup chicken stock
1½ tablespoons soy sauce	3 tablespoons sugar or 2 packets Equal

Combine ingredients in a saucepan and simmer until tender. Transfer to blender or food processor and blend well. *The Bleu Rock Inn, a beautiful country inn owned by Jean and Bernard Campagne of La Bergerie — the perfect getaway just a short drive from Alexandria. The Bleu Rock Inn, Route 1, Box 555, Washington, Virginia 22747.*

Turkish Skewered Swordfish

2 pounds swordfish steaks cut into 1-inch cubes Juice of 1 lemon	½ cup olive oil 2 tablespoons grated onion Salt and freshly ground pepper
4 ripe tomatoes, cut into chunks 3 Spanish onions, cut in wedges	18-20 bay leaves, cut in half Lemon wedges

Combine oil, lemon juice, grated onion and salt and pepper. Cut swordfish steaks into 1-inch cubes and place in a large bowl. Pour over cubes for at least 2 hours. Drain, reserving marinade. Thread cubes onto skewers alternating with tomato and onion chunks and bay leaf. Use about 10 bay leaf pieces per skewer and make sure there is a bay leaf between each two pieces of fish. Grill or broil, turning frequently and basting with marinade. Cook for about 15 minutes or until fish is golden brown on all sides. **SERVES 4-6.**

Gingered Bluefish

4, 6 to 8-oz. bluefish filets, with skin, marinated

MARINADE

½ cup lemon juice
2 cloves garlic, minced finely
  or pressed
1 tablespoon fresh ginger root,
  peeled and grated
1 teaspoon finely chopped
  lemon peel
	3 tablespoons vegetable oil
	3 tablespoons olive oil
	¼ teaspoon salt
	¼ teaspoon white pepper

Mix all marinade ingredients in a bowl. Place bluefish in glass pan, cover with marinade and refrigerate, covered, 2-4 hours, turning occasionally. When ready to grill, remove fish from marinade. Place fish on grill close to flame. Grill skin side down for 3 minutes. Turn carefully and grill 3 more minutes. Transfer to heated serving platter. Remove skin. Heat marinade in non-aluminum pan and pour over fish to serve. **SERVES 4.**

Stir-Fried Snapper

½ pound snow peas,
  cleaned and strings removed
⅓ cup peanut oil
4 spring onions, sliced diagonally,
  with 3-inches of green
1 tablespoon fresh ginger,
  peeled and minced
2 medium tomatoes, peeled,
  seeded and chopped

1½-pounds red snapper filets,
  sliced in 3-inch strips
Salt and pepper to taste
½ cup finely chopped fresh
  cilantro leaves
2½ teaspoons red wine vinegar

Blanch snow peas for 1 minute in boiling water. Rinse in cold water and drain. Heat oil in skillet or wok until hot. Add onions and ginger and stir-fry for 2 minutes. Add tomatoes and cook for 1 minute. Turn heat down to medium-high and add fish. Cover and cook about 3-4 minutes or until fish flakes. Add salt, pepper, cilantro, peas and vinegar. Cook until heated, stirring constantly. **SERVES 4-6.**

Red Snapper al Pesto

4 red snapper filets
Salt and pepper
2 ripe tomatoes, peeled,
  seeded and chopped

4 anchovy filets, chopped
2 tablespoons olive oil
1 cup Pesto Sauce

Rinse, pat dry and place filets in baking dish. Sprinkle with salt and pepper. Combine tomatoes, anchovies and 2 tablespoons olive oil in a saucepan. Cook gently over medium heat for about 5 minutes. Add salt and pepper to taste. Broil steaks for 5 minutes on each side. While steaks are cooking, heat tomato sauce if making ahead and just before serving add 1 cup Pesto Sauce. Heat through and pour over fish. Serve immediately. **SERVES 4**

Sweet and Sour Rockfish

¼ cup pine nuts, toasted
2¾ cups Sweet and Sour Sauce
1 whole rockfish (about 4 pounds),
    fileted and cut in two pieces
2 tablespoons dry sherry

White pepper to taste
½ cup corn starch
Vegetable oil
1 cup chopped cilantro leaves
1 recipe Sweet and Sour Sauce

Prepare Sweet and Sour Sauce and set aside. Score flesh of fish in a diamond pattern. Sprinkle with sherry and rub into crevices. Sprinkle with corn starch and pepper and rub into crevices. Heat enough oil to cover fish, in large skillet or wok to 375 degrees. Add fish and cook until browned, about 5 minutes. Using 2 slotted spatulas, carefully remove fish from pan and place on warmed serving platter. Keep warm up to 15 minutes in a 150 degree oven. Heat sauce to boiling and spoon over fish and sprinkle with cilantro to serve. **SERVES 4.**

SWEET AND SOUR SAUCE

¼ cup vegetable oil
⅓ cup carrots diced
⅓ cup thinly sliced green onion,
    including tops
3 cloves garlic, minced
1¼ cups chicken broth

6 tablespoons soy sauce
6 tablespoons sugar
6 tablespoons red wine vinegar
2½ tablespoons corn starch
2½ tablespoons water

Heat oil and add carrots, onions and garlic and cook, stirring, for about 1 minute. Add broth, soy sauce, vinegar and sugar and mix well. Combine corn starch and water. Add to broth mixture and cook until sauce boils and thickens. This can be made ahead, up to four hours, and returned to boil to serve over fish. **MAKES 2¾ CUPS.**

Dilled Orange Roughy

1 pound orange roughy filets	2 tablespoons chopped fresh parsley
¼ cup butter	1 teaspoon dried dill weed
2 tablespoons fresh lemon juice	2 pinches cayenne pepper
2 tablespoons chopped chives	Salt to taste

Wash and dry fish. Place in single layer in square baking dish. Combine all other ingredients, except salt, in a small pan and heat until well mixed. Pour mixture over fish and bake at 400 degrees about 8 to 10 minutes or until fish is cooked but not dry. Remove fish to a heated platter. Drain all juices into saucepan. Heat to boiling and cook until reduced to about ⅓ cup. Pour over fish to serve. Season to taste with salt if desired.

Melbourne Roughy

⅓ cup olive oil	2 tablespoons balsamic vinegar
⅓ cup capers, drained	Flour
8 tablespoons unsalted butter	1½ pounds orange roughy filets
4 tablespoons vegetable oil	

SAUCE: In a saucepan, heat olive oil until very hot. Add capers and cook until they pop open. Drain oil from capers. Set aside capers. In same saucepan, melt 6 tablespoons of butter until starts to brown. Add vinegar and capers and mix well. Keep warm but do not allow to boil.

Flour fish. Heat vegetable oil and remaining 2 tablespoons butter. Cook fish about 2-3 minutes per side or until golden. Place on a heated platter and cover with sauce. SERVES 4.

Bombay Fish

3 pounds halibut or haddock	½ - 1 pound shrimp
1 cup peanut oil	1 cucumber, thickly sliced
Juice of 2 fresh limes	2 bunches scallions, cut in pieces
3 tablespoons soy sauce	Curry Sauce

Cut filets into 1-inch cubes. Combine rest of ingredients, except shrimp, in a small bowl. Mix well and pour over halibut. Marinate in refrigerator about 1 hour. Remove fish from marinade and reserve sauce for basting. Skewer fish cubes with cucumber, scallion and shrimp. Grill for about 10 minutes or until fish is opaque and flakes easily. Serve with rice and your favorite condiments for curry, such as peanuts, chutney, toasted slivered almonds, raisins, toasted coconut and curry sauce. SERVES **6-8.**

CURRY SAUCE

5 tablespoons butter	**3 cups chicken stock**
1 onion, minced	**¼ to ½ cup cream**
1 apple, peeled, cored and minced	**Salt and freshly ground pepper**
1 stalk celery, minced	**to taste**
4 tablespoons flour	**Fresh lemon juice to taste**
1-3 tablespoons curry powder	**2 tablespoons mango chutney**

In a saucepan, heat butter and sauté onion, apple and celery until slightly brown. Sprinkle with flour and curry powder and cook about 2 minutes more or until flour is cooked thoroughly as for a roux. Add stock a little at a time, stirring constantly. Simmer 45 minutes. Add cream, seasoning and lemon juice. Add chutney just before serving. MAKES 3 CUPS.

Trout and Almonds

4 pan-dressed trout, about 5-oz. each	**¼ cup slivered almonds**
¼ cup butter	**2 teaspoons almond liqueur**

Place butter in small bowl. Microwave on high until melted. Stir in almonds and liqueur. Microwave on high until almonds are light brown, about 3-3½ minutes, stirring after every minute. Remove almonds from butter with a slotted spoon and set aside. Place trout in a rectangular baking dish. Pour almond butter over top. Cover with waxed paper. Microwave on high until fish flakes in center with fork, about 5-9 minutes. Turn fish over once during cooking time and rotate dish halfway through cooking time. To serve, sprinkle with almonds and sauce. Fish can also be grilled. SERVES **4.**

Crab and Sole Ricky

1-1½ pounds filet of sole
4 tablespoons flour
6 tablespoons butter
Salt and pepper
⅔ cup chicken broth
⅓ cup milk
⅓ cup sherry

½ pound mushrooms, chopped
1 green pepper, chopped fine
¼ Bermuda onion, chopped fine
1 small jar pimentos,
   drained and chopped
1 pound backfin crabmeat

Combine 2 tablespoons flour with salt and pepper in a small plastic or paper bag. Add sole and shake to coat evenly. In a skillet, melt 2 tablespoons butter, add sole, and sauté until lightly browned. Line a low casserole dish with sole. In a double boiler, combine butter and flour to make a roux. Add chicken broth, milk and sherry. While sauce is thickening, sauté together mushrooms, pepper and onion in remaining 2 tablespoons butter, until tender. Add to sauce along with crab and pimentos. Pour crab sauce over filets. Can be made ahead and refrigerated to this point. When ready to serve, heat at 350 degrees for 20 to 30 minutes. **SERVES 4.**

Stuffed Filet of Sole

3 good-sized filets of sole
3 tablespoons flour
5 tablespoons butter
3-oz. can sliced mushrooms
About ¾ cup milk
   or light cream
3 tablespoons cream sherry
Salt and white pepper to taste
6 oz. crab, tiny shrimp
   or lobster

1 tablespoon chopped parsley
Pinch of thyme
Pinch of tarragon
Parmesan cheese, freshly grated
Fine white bread crumbs
Parsley sprigs for garnish
Lemon wedges

With 3 tablespoons of flour and 3 tablespoons of butter, make a roux in a saucepan. Drain mushrooms and add liquid to a measuring cup. Add light cream to measure ¾ cup. Add to roux and cook and stir until thickened. Add 2 tablespoons sherry and salt and white pepper to taste. Set aside. In a skillet, sauté crab, shrimp or lobster in 2 tablespoons butter. When warmed through, add mushrooms, 1 tablespoon or more of sherry, chopped parsley, thyme, tarragon and salt and white pepper to taste. Butter 6 scallop shells and place on cookie sheet. Spoon 1 tablespoon of sauce in each shell. Divide filets in half. Top each shell with ½ filet. Top with remaining sauce. Top with Parmesan cheese and fine white bread crumbs. May be prepared ahead to this point, covered and refrigerated. When ready to serve, bake 15-20 minutes at 400 degrees or until lightly browned and bubbly. Garnish with parsley sprigs and lemon wedges. **Serves 6.**

Sizzling Monkfish

3 pounds monkfish
½ cup + 1 tablespoon peanut oil

3 tablespoons soy sauce
3 bunches green onions, sliced

Preheat oven to 450 degrees. Line pan with foil. Brush foil and monkfish with 1 tablespoon oil. Sprinkle soy sauce and rub on all sides. Bake 7 minutes for each ½-inch thickness. Cut monkfish into cubes. Arrange on warm platter. Heat remaining ½ cup oil and add onions to sauté. Sprinkle with onions and oil over fish. **Serves 6.**

Fiorino's Smoked Salmon

1 8-14 pound salmon, split open
  as if to filet
¼ cup wine vinegar
1 cup fresh lemon juice
1 whole lemon, chopped in chunks
1½ cups salad oil
2 cloves garlic

⅓ medium onion, chopped
1 cup white wine
2 teaspoons chopped parsley
Salt and pepper to taste
1 tablespoon soy sauce
Few drops of Worcestershire sauce

Mix all ingredients above, except salmon, in blender or processor until well blended. Place the two sides of fish in roasting pan skin-side down. Pour marinade over both halves to cover. Refrigerate at least overnight. Make a tray of heavy-duty aluminum foil to fit grill. Place salmon skin-side down on the tray. Continue to baste fish using the marinade. Cook, covered, until the fish flakes easily with a fork. On a kettle grill, cooking takes about 25 minutes. **Serves 10-12.**

Grilled or Broiled Salmon

8 fresh salmon steaks
  or one very large boned filet
½ cup salad oil
⅔ cup soy sauce

⅔ cup bourbon
1 stick butter, melted
Juice of one lemon
1 lemon, sliced

Rinse fish and dry with paper towel. Mix oil, soy sauce, bourbon and pour into shallow pan. Place fish in mixture, refrigerate 2 hours, turning once. Remove fish from marinade and grill or broil 5-10 minutes. Fish should just barely flake and be lightly pink. Do not overcook. Remove to platter and top with some of the melted butter and lemon juice. Garnish with lemon slices. **SERVES 8.**

Grilled Salmon Steaks with Cucumber and Mint

8 salmon steaks, about ½-inch thick

MARINADE

3 tablespoons olive oil
2 cloves garlic, crushed

2 tablespoons finely chopped fresh mint

CUCUMBER GARNISH

2 small cucumbers, pared,
  halved lengthwise, seeded,
  cut in thin crosswise slices
½ cup plain low or nonfat yogurt
1 scallion, trimmed and
  thinly sliced
1 tablespoon finely chopped
  fresh dill

1 tablespoon finely chopped
  fresh parsley
1 teaspoon finely chopped
  fresh mint
Salt and freshly ground pepper
Whole sprigs of mint, dill
  and/or parsley for garnish
Lime wedges

Prepare marinade by combining oil, garlic and mint on a large platter. Add salmon steaks and turn to coat evenly with the marinade. Cover and refrigerate for 2 or more hours. To prepare garnish, combine cucumber, yogurt, scallion, dill, parsley, chopped mint, salt and pepper to taste; stir to blend. Cover and refrigerate at least 2 hours. On a hot grill, cook salmon steaks, turning once, until flesh is opaque throughout except for a thin, translucent line in the center, about 6 to 10 minutes per side. Place salmon steaks on a serving platter. Spoon cucumber garnish on top of each steak. Top with sprigs of mint, parsley or dill and lime wedges. NOTE: To keep fish from sticking to a grill, use a non-stick grill liner, brush the grill rack lightly with oil, or use a grilling basket lightly brushed with oil. **SERVES 8.**

Baked Salmon in Parchment (Papillote)

4 7-oz. salmon filets
1 carrot, julienned
1 celery, julienned
1 leek, white only, julienned
1 oz. Spice Mixture

1 oz. vermouth
1 oz. clam juice or fish stock
4 sheets parchment paper
  or aluminum foil

Fold foil in half, reopen, place salmon next to fold. Top salmon with spice mixture, vegetables then liquids. Refold foil and crimp edges together to seal. Place in 450 degree oven for 8-10 minutes. **SERVES 4.**

SPICE MIXTURE

4 parts or less salt
  (Salt can be reduced
  if desired)
3 parts paprika
2 parts black pepper

1 part each white pepper,
  onion powder, garlic powder,
  dry mustard, cayenne pepper,
  filé powder, dried basil
  and dried thyme

NOTE: This is a good entrée to serve at a dinner party for it can be made 4-5 hours before cooking. To keep it health-oriented, serve with boiled new potatoes and steamed vegetables. To serve, cut foil pouch on one side carefully, remove salmon to plate, pour liquid over and serve. For a variety try baking with orange or grapefruit slices. *The Dining Room at Morrison House, 116 South Alfred Street*

Japanese Salmon

Salmon steaks, one for each guest
Thick slices of lemon

White wine
Foil

Place each steak in a square of foil large enough to wrap steak. Place one slice of lemon on top. Bring edges of foil up to form a boat. Add ¼ cup white wine to each steak. Continue wrapping to seal. Bake at 400 degrees for 10-15 minutes or barbecue about 20 minutes until tender. Unwrap carefully to reserve liquid. Place on plate and cover with reserved sauce.

Tracy Austin's Fresh Scallops Sauté

15 sea scallops
2 sprays of non-fat,
** non-stick cooking spray**
½ teaspoon minced garlic

½ cup white wine
¼ cup water
Juice of ½ lemon
1½ teaspoons dill

Wash and pat dry scallops. Spray skillet with cooking spray. Sauté garlic for two minutes in pan. Add scallops. Stir in pan to coat garlic. Cook for five minutes; add wine and water. Sprinkle with lemon juice and dill. Stir to combine. Cook until done. NOTE: This recipe has only 2.9 grams of fat per serving. **SERVES 4.**

Montrachet Shrimp

⅓ cup olive oil
¾ cup finely chopped onions,
1 28-oz. can whole tomatoes,
** undrained**
3 small garlic cloves, pressed
¼ teaspoon salt
2½ teaspoons fresh oregano, finely
** chopped, or ¾ teaspoon dried**

⅛ teaspoon dried
** red pepper flakes**
2 pounds large raw shrimp,
** peeled and deveined**
¾ cup fresh parsley
8 oz. Montrachet cheese,
** crumbled**

Sauté onions in oil about 5 minutes until clear and tender. Add tomatoes and seasonings, except parsley. Simmer 15-20 minutes, stirring to break up tomatoes. Add shrimp and parsley and cook 2 minutes or until shrimp is just pink. Place shrimp mixture in a shallow baking pan, top with cheese and bake at 325 degrees for 15-20 minutes. **SERVES 6.**

Shrimp in Parmesan Butter

36 large raw shrimp, peeled,
  deveined and butterflied
1 cup butter
3 tablespoons capers,
  including liquid

1½ tablespoons fresh
  lemon juice
2 large cloves garlic, minced
1 cup freshly grated
  Parmesan cheese

Microwave butter on high 1¼ minutes until melted. Add capers, lemon juice and garlic and stir well. Pour ⅔ of mixture into an 8 x 8-inch shallow glass baking dish. Arrange shrimp in sauce. Top with cheese and remaining butter. Cover with waxed paper and microwave on high 6-7 minutes until shrimp is opaque and firm. Turn ½ turn after 3 minutes. **SERVES 3-4.**

Barbecued Shrimp

2-3 pounds fresh large raw shrimp,
  unpeeled
¼ pound butter or margarine
¾ cup olive oil
8 oz. chili sauce
3 tablespoons Worcestershire sauce
2 lemons, sliced
3 cloves garlic, minced
2 teaspoons dry mustard

3 tablespoons lemon juice
1 tablespoon parsley, chopped
2 teaspoons paprika
2 teaspoons oregano
½ teaspoon cayenne pepper
1 teaspoon Tabasco
3 tablespoons liquid smoke
1 teaspoon salt

Rinse shrimp in cold water. Spread out in several shallow glass pans, approximately 8 x 11-inches. Combine all ingredients, except shrimp, in medium sauce pan over low heat. Pour over shrimp in pans. Make sure sauce is on all shrimp. Refrigerate. Baste and turn every 30 minutes while marinating several hours. Preheat oven to 300 degrees. Bake for 30 minutes, turning shrimp at 10-minute intervals. Serve in soup bowl with French bread for dipping in sauce and plenty of napkins! NOTE: This recipe works easily as well on the grill. **SERVES 6-8.**

Szechuan Shrimp

2 tablespoons vegetable oil
½ pound medium to large raw
  shrimp, shelled and deveined
½ cup celery, diced
1 green pepper, diced
½ teaspoon ground ginger
¼ cup minced green onions
2 cloves garlic, pressed
3 tablespoons dry sherry

3 tablespoons soy sauce
2 teaspoons sugar
½ teaspoon salt
6 tablespoons ketchup
½ cup water
2 tablespoons chili sauce
¼ teaspoon red pepper flakes
  or a few dashes hot sauce

Heat oil in wok or large heavy skillet. Sauté shrimp, celery, green pepper, ginger, onion and garlic. Stir-fry over medium to high heat until shrimp are pink. Add sherry, soy sauce, sugar and salt. Stir well. Blend in ketchup, chili sauce and red pepper flakes or hot sauce. Serve over rice. SERVES 2.

Texas Cloaked Shrimp

16 large shrimp,
  peeled and deveined
8 slices hickory smoked bacon
2 jalapeño peppers,
  julienned into 16 pieces
1 oz. sweet butter
1 large onion, chopped fine
14 oz. ketchup

3 oz. Worcestershire sauce
1 oz. cider vinegar
½ bottle steak sauce,
  such as A-1
3 oz. brown sugar
½ cup water
½ oz. Tabasco

Melt the butter in a large, heavy sauce pan. Add the onions and cook over low heat until translucent. Add everything but the shrimp, bacon and peppers and mix thoroughly, making sure the sugar dissolves. Simmer uncovered for about 30 minutes until the sauce thickens slightly. Put the julienned peppers on the back of each shrimp and wrap around with half piece of bacon. Thread the shrimp onto metal or wooden skewers and grill or broil for 2-3 minutes per side, basting with the sauce. Remove the shrimp from skewers and top with more sauce. Garnish with a sprig of parsley and a lemon quarter. NOTE: Texas Cloaked Shrimp makes an excellent entrée when served over rice or can be served as an appetizer. *The Warehouse Bar and Grill, 214 King Street*

Mardi Gras Shrimp

½ cup olive oil
1 tablespoon soy sauce
1 tablespoon honey
2 tablespoons lemon juice
2 tablespoons chopped
  fresh parsley

2 tablespoons Creole
  or Cajun seasoning
Dash of cayenne pepper
  to taste
1 pound large shrimp,
  peeled and deveined

Mix all ingredients, except shrimp, in a 9x13 inch baking dish. Add shrimp and coat it with some sauce. Let it marinate for 1 hour. Preheat oven to 450 degrees. Bake until shrimp are cooked, stirring a few times, about 10 minutes. Garnish with lemon slices. Serve with crusty bread and a green salad. SERVES 4.

Potomac Crab Cakes

⅓ cup unseasoned bread crumbs
2 tablespoons mayonnaise
2 teaspoons minced parsley
1 teaspoon minced celery leaves
  (optional)
1 teaspoon Worcestershire sauce
1 teaspoon dry mustard

½ teaspoon salt
½ teaspoon pepper
1 medium egg, slightly beaten
1 teaspoon lemon juice
1 pound cooked crabmeat
3 tablespoons butter or margarine
1 lemon, cut in wedges

Mix egg, bread crumbs, mayonnaise and seasonings in large bowl. Sprinkle lemon juice over crab meat and add to mixture in bowl. Stir with fork until blended. Divide into 6-8 portions. Melt butter in 10-inch skillet over medium heat. Spoon 4 portions into skillet; lightly flatten tops to form patties. Fry until golden on one side; turn and brown remaining side. Remove to platter and keep warm. Repeat with remaining portions. Serve with lemon wedges and tartar sauce. SERVES 4.

Crabmeat Croquettes with Parsley Sauce

1 cup dry bread crumbs
6 oz. crabmeat, well-drained
1 cup grated carrots
½ cup milk
½ cup celery, diced

1 egg, beaten
1 tablespoon minced onion
¼ teaspoon salt
⅛ teaspoon pepper
1 recipe Parsley Sauce

Combine all ingredients except Parsley Sauce; mix well. Divide mixture into equal portions for appetizers or entrées, shaping into a mound or cone shape. Place on a baking sheet that has been coated with cooking spray. Bake at 400 degrees for 20 minutes. Serve with Parsley Sauce on the side. SERVES **3-4** AS AN ENTRÉE, MORE IF AN APPETIZER.

Dijon Crab

1 tablespoon butter
1 pound backfin crabmeat,
  well-picked
2 tablespoons or more mayonnaise,
  as needed
Salt, white pepper and cayenne
  to taste
2 tablespoons capers, drained

1 pound sharp Cheddar cheese,
  grated
¾ cup flat beer
1 teaspoon Dijon mustard
1 teaspoon Worcestershire sauce
1 egg yolk, beaten
6 English muffins, toasted
  and buttered

In a bowl, gently combine crab and just enough mayonnaise to bind it together and not break up crab. Season lightly with salt and peppers and add capers. Melt 1 tablespoon butter in small saucepan. Add cheese, beer, mustard and Worcestershire sauce. Season with salt and peppers. Stir until cheese is blended and melted. Stir in egg yolk. Heat thoroughly, stirring constantly. Toast and butter muffins. Place on cookie sheet and cover with a mound of crab mixture. Spoon sauce over crab just to cover. Bake at 400 degrees for 10 minutes and then place under broiler until cheese is browned. SERVES **3-6.**

Maryland Crab Imperial

2 pounds crabmeat,
  backfin or lump
1 stick butter
4 tablespoons flour
1 cup half and half
1 teaspoon pepper
1 teaspoon dry mustard
1 teaspoon salt or salt substitute

4 tablespoons sherry
4 tablespoons bourbon
Dash of Tabasco, Worcestershire
  sauce or hot pepper sauce
Croutons or cracker crumbs,
  basted lightly with butter
  as garnish
Grated Cheddar cheese for garnish

Make a roux of flour and butter in a medium sauce pan. Gradually add half and half
and cook until sauce begins to thicken. Add rest of ingredients except garnishes. Pour
into a buttered casserole or buttered individual shells. Add croutons and cheese to top.
Bake at 350 degrees for 30 minutes. **SERVES 4**

Melt-In-Your-Mouth Crab

1 pound lump crab meat
¼ cup onion, minced
¼ - ½ cup green bell pepper,
  minced

¾ cup low-fat mayonnaise
3 tablespoons margarine or butter,
  melted
½ cup fresh bread crumbs

Sauté onion and green pepper in margarine until limp. This can be done in the
microwave as well as on the stove top. In a, oven-proof serving dish, combine crab,
onions and peppers which have been drained of butter. Reserve butter. Gently fold in
mayonnaise. Combine melted margarine and bread crumbs and put on top of crab
mixture. Bake for 12 minutes in a 350 degree preheated oven until the crumbs are
golden brown and casserole is heated through. Serve immediately. **SERVES 4.**

Cozze al Vino Bianco (Mussels in White Wine)

10 dozen mussels
2 cloves garlic, minced
2 small shallots, minced
4 teaspoons chopped fresh parsley

½ wine glass of olive oil
1 wine glass very dry white wine
1 wine glass clam juice
Black pepper to taste

Heat olive oil in heavy kettle that can hold all of the mussels and sauté garlic and shallots until golden over medium heat. Raise heat to high and add mussels, clam juice and white wine. When mussels open, add pepper and serve with a sprinkling of fresh parsley. **SERVES 8.** *Geranio Restaurant, 722 King Street*

Old Port Mussels

3 dozen mussels, well-scrubbed,
  beards removed
2 tablespoons flour
4 tablespoons water
6 shallots, minced
1 large garlic clove, minced
2 tablespoons olive oil

1 16-oz. can tomatoes, well-drained
  or 2 chopped fresh tomatoes
4-6 tablespoons chopped fresh basil
  or 1½ teaspoons dried
2 tablespoons vermouth
¼ cup fresh parsley

Mix flour and water. Fill a large bowl with cold water and add flour mixture and mussels. Soak for 30 minutes and drain well. In a heavy pan, sauté shallots and garlic in oil until soft. Add tomatoes and basil and simmer for 2-3 minutes more. Add mussels and cover pan. Steam mussels for 4 minutes, shaking pan occasionally. Remove mussels with slotted spoon to bowls and keep warm. Throw away any mussels that did not open. Add vermouth to pan and bring to boil. Pour over mussels and sprinkle with parsley. **SERVES 4-6.**

Sicilian Mussels

1½ pounds mussels
1 cup dry vermouth
1 cup olive oil

1 cup freshly grated Parmesan cheese
3 large cloves garlic, pressed
1 tablespoon finely chopped parsley

Clean mussels and remove beards. Add to a large pot with vermouth. Cover and simmer over medium-high heat just until shells open, about 5 minutes. Remove from heat. While cooking, mix oil, 3 tablespoons of cheese and garlic. When shells open and are cool enough to handle, remove one half of shell. Arrange remaining half with mussel in a single layer in a baking dish. Drizzle with oil mixture. Broil 4-inches from heat until cheese begins to melt, about 5 minutes Sprinkle with parsley and remaining cheese. **MAKES ABOUT 3 DOZEN.**

Spicy Mussels

¼ cup olive oil
¾ cup onion, chopped
4 anchovy filets, chopped
3 large garlic cloves, chopped

¼ teaspoon crushed red pepper
1 mashed anchovy filet
3 pounds fresh mussels
1 cup white wine

Thoroughly clean mussels, removing all grit. Soak 4 hours in salt water, keeping cold; change water twice. Heat oil in heavy skillet. Sauté onion until tender. Add chopped anchovies, garlic and crushed pepper. Sauté 5 minutes. Add anchovy which has been mashed to a paste. Combine mussels and wine in sauce pan. Cook approximately 7 minutes until mussels open. Transfer to 2 large bowls. Pour juice from the mussels into onion mixture and heat 2 minutes. Pour over mussels. Serve with French bread or fettucini. NOTE: The most important step in cooking fresh clams or mussels is to select ones that are tightly closed and have no broken shells. Be sure to soak them thoroughly. When cooked, discard any which have not opened. **SERVES 4-6.**

Washboiler Clambake

Seaweed, well washed
1 quart water
4 Idaho potatoes, wrapped in foil
2 chickens, cut up and parts
  wrapped in cheesecloth

2½ pound lobsters
4 ears of corn, husked and
  wrapped in foil
24 steamer clams

Fill the bottom of a washboiler or large enamel pot with seaweed, add water, and place over high heat. When water boils, add more seaweed and the potatoes. Cover and cook for 15 minutes. Add another layer of seaweed and the chicken, cover and cook 15 minutes. Add seaweed layer, lobsters, then more seaweed. Cover and cook 8 minutes. Add corn and cook 10 minutes. Add clams and cook, steaming, until clams open up. Serve with butter and kettle liquid. NOTE: Great when served with cold beer or white wine. SERVES 8.

Potomac Seafood Stew

6 tablespoons butter
¾ cup diced onions
2 leeks, quartered and chopped
2 small cloves garlic, chopped
4 tablespoons flour
⅔ cup diced Smithfield ham
4 cups clam juice
1 cup dry white wine
2 cups peeled, quartered tomatoes
1 cup peeled, diced potatoes

1 teaspoon salt
4 threads saffron, ground
  or finely minced
½ pound bass or cod filets,
  cut in chunks
1 pound soft-shelled clams,
  well-washed
½ pound backfin crabmeat,
  picked over for shells
1 bay leaf

In a heavy-bottomed soup pot, melt the butter and sauté the onions, leek, and garlic until soft. Stir in the flour and cook, stirring constantly, 3 minutes. Add ham, stock, wine, tomatoes, potatoes, salt, saffron and bay leaf. Bring to a boil, reduce the heat and simmer for 40 minutes. Stir in the fish, clams and crabmeat. Cover and cook until the clams open. Serve in bowls with Tabasco on the side and lots of crusty bread. SERVES 6.

Oysters Rockefeller en Casserole

3 packages frozen chopped spinach
8 tablespoons melted butter
1 cup fine bread crumbs
1 tablespoon Anisette
½ onion, grated
1 clove garlic, crushed

1 teaspoon anchovy paste
Salt, pepper and Tabasco to taste
1 quart oysters, drained
½ cup grated Parmesan cheese,
   or more to taste

Cook spinach slightly. Drain well. Add melted butter, bread crumbs, Anisette, onion, garlic, anchovy paste, salt, pepper and Tabasco. Cut up oysters into quarters and combine with spinach mixture. Mix well. Put into greased casserole. Sprinkle with Parmesan cheese. Bake, covered, 20 minutes at 350 degrees. Remove cover and bake 10 minutes more. **SERVES 10.**

Cioppino

1 large green pepper, chopped
1 large onion, chopped
2 cloves garlic, minced
2 16-oz. cans Italian tomatoes
½ cup minced parsley
1½ cups dry red wine
1 can chicken broth
½ teaspoon basil,
   or more if desired

½ teaspoon ground pepper
½ pound medium shrimp
½ pound scallops or lobster
½ pound firm fish,
   such as grouper
1 dozen clams, washed
¼ cup olive oil

Sauté onion, pepper and garlic in olive oil. Add tomatoes, parsley, wine, broth, basil and ground pepper. Simmer 25 minutes. Add clams and simmer until clams open. Discard any unopened clams. Add fish. Cook 5 minutes. Add scallops and shrimp and cook a few minutes until done. Serve with fresh bread. **SERVES 6-8.**

Seaport Seafood Delight

1 medium onion, chopped	¾ pound Cheddar cheese,
1 small green pepper, chopped	grated
1 cup of green onion tops,	1 small can evaporated milk
chopped	2 tablespoons corn starch
1 stalk of celery, chopped fine	1 pound lump crabmeat
1 stick butter	Salt, cayenne pepper
1 cup oysters	and black pepper to taste
1 pound shrimp, peeled	1 cup bread crumbs
and deveined	

Preheat over to 350 degrees. In a medium sauté pan, sauté onions, pepper, onion tops and celery in butter. When the onions are clear and limp, add the oysters and shrimp and simmer the water out of them, about 5 minutes. Remove from heat. In a small pot, add milk and corn starch. Stir until the corn starch is dissolved. Place the pot on medium heat, add the cheese and heat until the cheese is melted and the sauce is smooth. Remove from heat and add cheese sauce to shrimp and oyster mixture. Mix thoroughly. Fold in the crabmeat and season to taste. Pour the mixture into a 2-quart casserole and top with bread crumbs. Bake for 20 minutes at 350 degrees. Serve hot. **SERVES 8.**

Seafood Risotto

2 tablespoons olive oil	Pinch of marjoram
2 tablespoons butter	1 cup cooked shrimp
1 clove garlic, peeled and pierced	Butter
with a fork several times	¼ cup freshly grated
2 whole fresh sage leaves	Parmesan cheese
1 cup uncooked risotto	Garnish: more shrimp and/or
½ cup white wine	canned whole baby clams
2 cups chicken stock, heated	or mussels

In a large skillet, heat oil and butter. Sauté the garlic and sage, add risotto and cook, stirring until golden brown. Add white wine and cook over low heat until absorbed by risotto. Add 1 cup chicken stock, cover and cook for 20 minutes. Remove garlic and sage. Add marjoram, shrimp and 1 more cup stock. Stir once with fork, cover and cook slowly until risotto is tender, approximately 20 minutes. At 15 minutes, check to make sure there is enough liquid. May be made ahead to this point. Just before serving, add a few bits of butter and Parmesan cheese. Garnish with seafood. **SERVES 4-6.**

Les Spaghettis de Courgettes des Pêcheurs (Zucchini with Seafood in Cream)

**1 zucchini, 5-oz., cut into
 lengthwise strips,
 ¼-inch in diameter
1 teaspoon minced shallot
1 tablespoon clarified butter
8 bay scallops
8 frozen baby shrimp, thawed,
 peeled and deveined
1 tablespoon dry vermouth
⅓ cup fresh tomato, peeled,
 seeded and diced in
 ⅓-inch pieces**

**¾ cup heavy cream
3 tablespoons lump crabmeat
6 mussels, steamed to open
1 teaspoon buerre manie
1 tablespoon fresh lemon juice
Salt and fresh ground pepper
 to taste**

In sauté pan, sauté zucchini and shallot for 30 seconds over high heat. Push to one side; add scallops and shrimp; cook 1 minute, turning seafood occasionally. Add vermouth, tomato and heavy cream. Bring to full boil, reduce heat to medium, and cook 30 seconds. With skimmer, remove zucchini, seafood and tomato to heated serving plate and top with crabmeat and mussels. Return cream to heat and boil rapidly 1 minute. Then whisk in buerre manie to thicken. Add lemon juice, salt and pepper. Pour over zucchini and seafood. Serve immediately with buttered rice. **SERVES 1.** *Le Gaulois, 1106 King Street*

Confections

uchello

Menu

Washington's Birthday Celebration At Gadsby's Tavern

Gadsby's Tavern Fudge Pye   PAGE 204

Katie Couric's Lemon Loves   PAGE 221

Tipper Gore's Tennessee Treats   PAGE 224

Willard Scott's Red Velvet Cake   PAGE 194

Patsy Ticer's Pecan Pie   PAGE 194

Champagne

In the 18th century Gadsby's Tavern was considered by its many guests, including the Marquis de Lafayette and Thomas Jefferson, to be the finest 'Public House' in America. It was here in 1787 that George and Martha Washington attended the first Birthday Ball in his honor — still an Alexandria tradition after more than two hundred years.

Patsy's Pecan Pie

3 eggs	½ cup brown sugar
1 cup dark corn syrup	⅛ teaspoon salt
1 teaspoon vanilla	1 cup pecans, chopped
¼ cup melted butter	1 9-inch pie shell, pre-baked

Mix all ingredients together except pecans. Put pecans into pie shell and pour mixture over them. Bake in a hot, 450 degree, oven for about 25 minutes. **SERVES 8.** *The Honorable Patricia S. Ticer, Mayor of Alexandria, Virginia, and Past President of The Twig*

Willard's Red Velvet Cake

1½ cups sugar	1 teaspoon baking soda
2 oz. red food coloring	2 eggs
2 tablespoons cocoa	1 tablespoon vinegar
1 cup buttermilk	½ cup shortening
2¼ cups flour	1 teaspoon vanilla
1 teaspoon salt	

Cream shortening with sugar, add eggs and beat well. Make a paste of cocoa and food coloring, add to creamed mixture. Sift flour and salt twice. Add buttermilk alternately with flour to creamed mixture. Add vanilla. Put vinegar in deep bowl, add soda (it will foam). When blended, add to creamed cake batter. Do not beat; just blend well. Grease and flour two 9-inch cake pans; pour batter into pans and bake at 350 degrees 25-30 minutes.

CREAM CHEESE ICING

3 oz. cream cheese	1 teaspoon vanilla
1½ cups confectioners sugar	

Cream all ingredients together until fluffy and smooth. Will frost 1 cake. *Willard Scott*

Chocoholic Cake

1 cup butter, softened
1½ cups sugar
4 eggs
6 1.55-oz. milk chocolate
    candy bars, melted
2 ½ cups flour
¼ teaspoon baking soda

Pinch of salt
1 cup buttermilk
1 cup chopped pecans
1 5½-oz. can chocolate syrup
2 teaspoons vanilla extract
Powdered sugar

Cream butter and sugar. Add eggs one at a time. Add melted candy bars. Add flour, soda and salt to chocolate mixture alternately with buttermilk. Add pecans, chocolate syrup and vanilla, blending well. Pour batter into greased and floured 10-inch bundt pan. Bake at 325 degrees for 1 hour and 15 minutes. Use toothpick to test for doneness. Cool in pan 10 minutes before removing. Sift powdered sugar over cake, if desired.

Cocoa Crème Cake

1 teaspoon cinnamon
¼ cup sugar
2 tablespoons unsweetened
    cocoa
¼ cup walnuts or pecans,
    chopped
1 stick of butter (4 oz.)
1 cup sugar

2 eggs
2 cups flour
¼ teaspoon salt
1 teaspoon baking soda
1 teaspoon baking powder
1 cup sour cream
1 teaspoon vanilla

Mix cinnamon, sugar, cocoa and pecans well and set aside. In a bowl, beat butter, sugar and eggs until creamy. In a separate bowl, combine flour, salt, baking soda and baking powder. Add flour mixture to dry ingredients and cut in. Add sour cream and vanilla extract and mix until well blended. Spray or grease a tube or 9x9 inch pan. Spoon in half of the batter. Add half of the sugar mixture and evenly spoon in rest of batter. Top with remaining sugar mixture. Bake in a 375 degree preheated oven for 40 minutes or until toothpick comes out clean. Serve with a dollop of whipped cream. **SERVES 8-10** and can be made ahead and frozen.

Christmas Hermit Cake

1 pound brown sugar
1 pound butter or margarine
4 cups sifted flour
6 eggs
2 cups shelled walnuts or pecans

2 pounds dates
Juice of 1 lemon
1 teaspoon vanilla
1 teaspoon cinnamon

Cream butter and sugar. Add 1 egg at a time and cream until smooth. Cut up dates and nuts and mix with flour which has been sifted with cinnamon. Combine with eggs and sugar. Add lemon juice and vanilla. Bake in floured and greased tube pan at 275 degrees for 2¼ hours. Store like a fruit cake.

Prunella Cake

2 cups flour
½ teaspoon salt
1 teaspoon baking soda
1 teaspoon cinnamon
1 teaspoon nutmeg
1½ cups sugar

1 cup vegetable oil
3 eggs
1 cup buttermilk
1 cup cut-up cooked prunes
1 cup chopped pecans
1 recipe Topping

Mix dry ingredients and add oil, eggs and buttermilk. Once batter is well mixed, add prunes and pecans. Bake in 10x14 inch greased and floured pan for 40 minutes at 325 degrees. Remove from oven and pour on topping while hot.

TOPPING

½ cup buttermilk
½ teaspoon baking soda
1 cup sugar

1 tablespoon light corn syrup
⅓ stick butter
½ teaspoon vanilla

Put all ingredients, except vanilla, in sauce pan over medium heat. Cook until just before soft ball stage, about 15-20 minutes. Mixture will turn light brown. Remove from heat and add vanilla. Pour over hot cake. Cake can be pierced with fork so that icing can penetrate cake. NOTE: If you do not have buttermilk, you can create your own by adding 1 teaspoon of lemon juice to sweet milk.

Yankee Bog Cake

1 cup sugar
4 tablespoons margarine
2 cups flour
1 teaspoon salt
1 tablespoon baking powder
2 cups fresh cranberries

1 cup milk
1 cup brown sugar
½ cup margarine
4 tablespoons heavy cream
½ teaspoon vanilla

Mix flour, salt, baking powder, cranberries and milk together. Pour batter into greased 9-inch cake pan. Bake in a preheated 350 degree oven for 30 minutes. Cake can be made ahead or served warm. Heat remaining ingredients for sauce in a double boiler until warm. Spoon sauce over cake. **SERVES 8.** NOTE: This very rich cake is excellent for the holidays.

Zuppa Inglese (Italian Rum Cake)

8 egg yolks
8 half egg shells full of
   Marsala sherry
8 level teaspoons sugar
1 sponge cake,
   10-12 inches in diameter

1 cup sweet rum
2 tablespoons sugar
½ pint whipping cream
½ cup chopped glazed fruit
   (optional)
Sliced almonds

Make the zabaglione, or Marsala custard, by breaking egg yolks into top of a double boiler. Add sugar. Beat with an egg beater until light lemon-colored and thoroughly blended. Add Marsala. Beat thoroughly. Boil water in lower part of double boiler. Cook egg yolk mixture over water about 5 minutes or until it begins to thicken. While cooking be sure to beat constantly. Do not allow to boil. Remove from fire immediately on first sign of bubble. Set aside to cool. Slice sponge cake into 3 layers.

    Place one layer on cake platter, sprinkle with ½ almonds and pour ⅓ cup of rum over it. Cover with ½ of the zabaglione custard. Place second layer over this. Alternate with almonds, rum and zabaglione. Top with last layer and cover with remaining rum. Place in refrigerator. When ready to serve, pour cream in mixing bowl, add 2 tablespoons sugar and beat until stiff. Spread over top and sides of cake. Just before serving, sprinkle with glazed fruit, if desired.

Cherry-Coconut Cake

1½ cups self-rising flour
½ cup margarine
2 beaten eggs
½ cup sugar

⅓ cup unsweetened coconut
¼ cup chopped cherries
   (glace type and rolled in flour)
2 tablespoons milk

Cream sugar and margarine together. Beat in eggs, then add flour and coconut to mixture. Add milk, then cherries last. Rolling the cherries in flour will prevent them from sinking to the bottom of the cake. Bake for approximately 1¼ hours in a loaf tin in a 300 degree preheated oven. Test cake with toothpick to make sure cake is cooked all the way through. *The Tea Cozy, 119 South Royal Street*

Buttermilk Apple Cake

3 cups flour
1 cup sugar
1½ teaspoons baking soda
½ teaspoon salt
1 teaspoon cinnamon
¼ teaspoon allspice

¼ teaspoon nutmeg
1 cup buttermilk
½ cup butter, melted
1 large egg
2 cups chopped, unpeeled apples
½ cup chopped almonds

Preheat oven to 325 degrees. Grease a 10-inch tube pan. In a large bowl, combine flour, sugar, soda, salt, cinnamon, allspice and nutmeg. Stir in buttermilk, butter and egg until just combined. Fold in apples and almonds. Spoon into pan. Bake 50-60 minutes or until center springs back when lightly pressed. Cool in pan 10 minutes. Turn out onto a serving plate and cool completely.

Marlene's Meringue Cake

8 egg whites
1 cup sugar
1 teaspoon vinegar

2 cups whipping cream
2 teaspoons confectioners
   sugar

1 teaspoon vanilla extract   Hazel nuts, chopped and without skins

Beat the 8 egg whites until stiff and slowly add the 1 cup sugar. Keep beating after sugar has been added. Add 1 teaspoon vinegar and 1 teaspoon vanilla. Continue beating. Butter 2 round springform pans and place waxed paper cut to the size of the bottom of the pan in the pans. Divide the batter evenly and put it into the pans, pushing the batter down a bit. Bake for 1 hour in a very moderate oven, 250 degrees. Turn oven off, leaving the pans in the oven for 15 minutes to dry. Turn the cakes onto 2 separate plates and peel off the waxed paper. When cakes have cooled, whip the cream and add powdered sugar. Spread it between the layers and on top. Sprinkle with hazel nuts. Place in refrigerator. Let stand two hours before serving. NOTE: Serve this cake with Raspberry Sauce for a truly scrumptious dessert. SERVES 8.

Bittersweet Chocolate Torte with Raspberries

10 oz. semisweet chocolate
4 oz. bittersweet chocolate
½ cup margarine or butter
¼ cup milk
5 eggs
1 teaspoon vanilla
½ cup sugar

¼ cup all-purpose flour
¼ cup seedless red raspberry
   jam
1½ to 2 cups fresh
   red raspberries
Powdered sugar, sifted

Grease the bottom of a 10-inch springform pan. In a heavy medium saucepan, combine both chocolates, margarine and milk. Cook and stir over low heat until chocolate melts. Cool 20 minutes. In a mixing bowl, beat eggs and vanilla on low speed until well combined. Add sugar and flour and beat on high speed for 10 minutes. Stir chocolate mixture into egg mixture. Transfer to the prepared pan. Bake in a 325 degree oven for 30 minutes. Cool on a wire rack for 20 minutes. Cool completely. In a small saucepan, melt raspberry jam and cool. Spread jam on top of torte, cover jam layer with raspberries, stem-side down. Dust with sifted powdered sugar just before serving. Cut with a knife that has been dipped in hot water. SERVES 16.

New England Pumpkin Roll

1 cup all-purpose flour
1¼ teaspoons double acting
  baking powder
1 teaspoon ground cinnamon
¾ teaspoon ground ginger
½ teaspoon salt
⅛ teaspoon ground nutmeg
4 large eggs at room temperature

1 cup granulated sugar
1½ teaspoons vanilla extract
1 teaspoon lemon juice
⅔ cup solid pack canned pumpkin
¾ cup finely chopped walnut
  halves
Confectioners sugar

CREAM CHEESE FILLING

10 oz. cream cheese
4 tablespoons (½ stick)
  unsalted butter, softened

1¼ cups sifted confectioners
  sugar
1 teaspoon vanilla extract

Whipped cream for garnish,
  optional

Raspberry Sauce for garnish,
  optional

To make the pumpkin sponge cake, position rack in center of the oven and preheat to 350 degrees. Line the bottom of a 17½-inch x11½-inch jelly roll pan with aluminum foil, leaving a 2-inch overhang on each short end. Fold the overhang underneath the pan. Butter the aluminum foil and the sides of the pan. Lightly dust the bottom and sides of the pan with sifted cake flour and tap out the excess. In a small bowl, stir together the flour, baking powder, cinnamon, ginger, salt and nutmeg. Sift the flour mixture onto a piece of waxed paper.

In a large bowl, using a hand-held mixer set at medium-high speed, beat the eggs until frothy. While continuing to beat, add the sugar in a slow, steady stream. Continue beating the egg mixture for 10-12 minutes or until it has tripled in volume and the batter is pale yellow and forms a thick ribbon when beaters are lifted. Beat in the vanilla and lemon juice. Fold in the pumpkin. Resift one-half of the flour mixture over the batter.

Using a large rubber spatula, fold the resifted flour mixture into the batter, making sure to bring the spatula to the bottom of the bowl to free any flour that may be clinging to the bottom and side of the bowl. Resift the remaining flour mixture over the batter and fold in. Scrape the batter into the prepared pan and spread it evenly with a spatula. Sprinkle the walnuts evenly over the batter.

Bake the sponge cake for 15 to 18 minutes, or until the center of the cake springs back when gently pressed. Do not overbake or it will crack when rolled. Run the tip of a knife around the edges of the pan. Lightly dust a clean kitchen towel with sifted confectioners sugar. Invert the cake onto the towel and remove the pan. Carefully peel off the aluminum foil. Starting at a long side, roll the cake and towel together into a tight cylinder. Cool the rolled cake completely on a large wire rack.

While cooling, prepare the cream cheese filling. In a large bowl, using a hand-held mixer set at medium-high speed, beat the cream cheese, butter and confectioners sugar for 8 to 10 minutes, or until very light and almost white in color. Beat in the vanilla. When cake is completely cool, assemble the roll. Carefully unroll the cooled cake so as not to crack it. Using an offset metal cake spatula, spread the filling over the cake in an even layer. Using the towel as a guide, reroll the cake into a tight cylinder. Wrap the roll in a piece of aluminum foil. Twist the ends of the foil to secure the round shape of the roll. Refrigerate the roll for 1 to 2 hours or until it is firm enough to slice. Cut the roll into ½-inch slices. Slightly overlap two slices on each serving plate. If desired, coat plate with dessert Raspberry Sauce, and then pieces of pumpkin roll. Top with a dollop of whipped cream. NOTE: Although this recipe seems quite complicated, it is really very simple. The roll can be made the day before serving and makes an elegant fall or winter dessert. **SERVES 8-10.**

Virginia Pound Cake

3 cups sifted flour	⅓ cup solid shortening,
3 cups sugar	such as Crisco
5 eggs	3 tablespoons vanilla extract
1 cup milk	1½ tablespoons lemon extract
1 cup margarine or butter	

Cream butter and shortening. Add sugar and beat thoroughly. Add eggs one at a time and beat thoroughly after each addition. Add flour and milk alternating one with the other. Be sure to begin with milk so that you end with flour. Add extracts and blend. Pour into a greased and floured bundt pan or 2 jelly roll pans. Bake at 300 degrees for 1 hour and 15 minutes. Cake will be done when it begins to pull away from the sides of the pan. Turn off oven and leave pans in oven for 20 minutes. Remove from oven. Turn out to cool. Wrap tightly in foil to keep for later use. NOTE: Pound cake is excellent served with seasonal fruits or can be the base for another dessert.

Chocolate Torte

6 oz. semisweet chocolate chips   1 small pound cake
  (or any flavored chip), melted   Raspberry Sauce
8 oz. sour cream

Slice pound cake horizontally into five layers. Mix melted chocolate chips and sour cream together. Spread mixture between layers and on top and sides. Refrigerate or freeze until ready to serve. Slice thinly and garnish with dessert Raspberry Sauce. It is very rich! SERVES 12.

Brazilia Torta

CAKE

½ cup unsalted butter, cut in 8 pieces   2 large eggs, at room temperature
2 tablespoons espresso   ¾ cup sugar
  or very strong coffee   1 teaspoon vanilla
8 oz. semisweet chocolate bits   ¼ cup flour

PIE CRUST

9-oz. package crushed chocolate wafers 6 tablespoons unsalted butter

PIE FILLING

1 quart raspberry sherbert   1 recipe Amaretto Chocolate Sauce
1 quart vanilla ice cream

To prepare cake mixture, preheat oven to 375 degrees. Line a 9 x 9 inch pan with foil. Butter and flour the pan. In a small saucepan, melt the butter in the coffee, add chocolate and stir until chocolate is melted and smooth over a low heat. Cool about 5 minutes. In a large bowl, beat eggs, sugar and vanilla until eggs are pale yellow. Add cooled chocolate mixture. By hand, stir in flour. Pour into prepared pan and bake at 375 degrees for about 25 minutes or until cake cracks around edges.

    In a 9-inch springform pan, melt butter and add crushed cookies. Mix. To form crust, pat mixture onto bottom and sides of pan. Bake for 10 minutes at 375 degrees. Cool completely.

Spread raspberry sherbert on crust. Break up cake into small pieces and sprinkle one half on sherbert. Drizzle one cup of Amaretto Chocolate Sauce on top. Top with vanilla ice cream. Add rest of cake on top and freeze until firm. Just before serving, take from refrigerator and let stand a few minutes before cutting. Pass remaining sauce.

Rebecca's Chocolate Pound Cake

1½ cups butter, softened
3 cups sugar
5 eggs
3 cups all-purpose flour
½ cup cocoa
1 teaspoon baking soda

¼ teaspoon salt
2 teaspoons vanilla
8 oz. sour cream
1 cup boiling water
Powdered sugar, sifted, if desired

Cream butter, gradually adding sugar and beat well. Add eggs, one at a time, beating after each addition. Combine flour, cocoa, soda and salt. Add to creamed mixture alternating with sour cream, beginning and ending with flour mixture. Mix well after each addition. Add boiling water and vanilla and mix well. Pour batter into a greased and floured 10-inch tube pan. Bake at 325 degrees for one hour or until toothpick comes out clean. Cool cake in pan 10-15 minutes. Remove and cool completely. If bundt pan is used, you may have extra batter (use to make cupcakes). Dust with powdered sugar when cooled and serve with dessert Raspberry Sauce.

Lemon Torte

½ bag lemon crunch cookies,
  crushed
3 tablespoons butter, melted
4 eggs, separated
1 cup sugar

1½ cups whipping cream
½ cup lemon juice
1½ teaspoons grated lemon rind
1 10-oz. carton frozen raspberries,
  thawed

Combine crushed cookies and butter in small bowl. Press into bottom of a 9-inch springform pan. Beat egg whites and add sugar gradually. In a separate bowl, beat egg yolks and add lemon juice and rind. Set aside. Beat cream. Fold all mixtures together. Pour into crust and freeze. Let thaw 10 minutes before serving. Place raspberries in blender until liquefied. Pass as sauce.

Perfect Pie Pastry

1⅓ cups unbleached
  all-purpose flour
1 tablespoon sugar
½ teaspoon salt

1 stick unsalted butter (4-oz.),
  cut into 8 parts
½ teaspoon fresh lemon juice
3½ teaspoons ice water

Using a food processor with metal blade, combine flour, sugar, salt and butter for about 10 seconds until mixture looks like coarse meal. Mix lemon and juice and ice water and, while processor is running, pour in liquid in a steady stream. When dough begins to form a ball, stop processing. You may stop at this point, wrap ball tightly, and store in the refrigerator until ready to use. To continue, roll dough on a lightly floured board into a 14-inch circle, ⅛-inch thick. Move dough to a 10-inch pie plate and trim to ½-inch along edge. Turn the ½-inch to inside and press to seal. Crimp dough with your finger to make a pretty edge. Refrigerate the shell for 20 minutes. Preheat oven to 425 degrees. For a partially baked shell, line shell with aluminum foil and fill with uncooked beans or pie weights. Bake 10-12 minutes, or until set but not brown. For a fully baked shell, bake 20-25 minutes until lightly browned. **Makes one 10-inch pie crust.**

Gadsby's Tavern Fudge Pye

1 10-inch fresh or frozen
  pie crust, unbaked
2½ oz. flour
4 oz. cocoa mix

Dash of cinnamon
¼ cup chopped walnuts
4 eggs
¾ pound butter

Mix flour, cocoa and cinnamon. Cream margarine and eggs. Add the flour mixture to the margarine and eggs. Mix in the walnuts. Pour into crust. Bake at 350 degrees until the top breaks, about 25 minutes. **Makes one 10-inch pie.** *Gadsby's Tavern, 134 North Royal Street*

Black-Bottom Cherry Pie

2 cups walnuts, finely chopped
3 tablespoons butter or margarine,
 softened
2 tablespoons brown sugar
1 16½-oz. to 17-oz. jar or can
 of pitted dark sweet cherries
1½ cups heavy or whipping cream

1 3½ to 3¾ oz. instant vanilla
 pudding package
1 cup milk
¼ teaspoon vanilla extract
2 squares semisweet chocolate,
 melted

Preheat oven to 400 degrees. In a 9-inch pie plate, mix the walnuts, brown sugar and butter. Press mixture onto the bottom and side of plate forming a thin crust. Bake 7-8 minutes or until golden. Cool on a wire rack. Drain cherries and pat dry with paper towels. Save 10 cherries for garnish. Cut each of the remaining cherries in half and set aside. In a bowl, beat 1 cup heavy or whipping cream until stiff peaks form. In another bowl, prepare instant pudding according to package directions, but use only 1 cup of milk. Cool. With wire whisk or spatula, gently fold whipped cream and vanilla into pudding mixture. Reserve 1½ cups of pudding mixture. With a wire whisk, fold melted chocolate into remaining vanilla pudding. Spoon chocolate mixture into crust. Top with cherry halves. Evenly spread reserved vanilla pudding over cherries. Refrigerate pie at least one hour. When ready to serve, beat remaining ½ cup cream and spoon dollops on top of pie. Add whole cherries on top as garnish.

Carlyle Oatmeal Pie

2 eggs, beaten
⅔ cup melted butter
⅔ cup sugar
⅔ cup white corn syrup

⅔ cup uncooked regular oatmeal
½ teaspoon vanilla extract
¼ teaspoon salt
1 unbaked deep-dish pie shell

Beat eggs and then blend in all other ingredients. Pour mixture into pie shell. Bake at 350 degrees for 45 minutes to 1 hour. Serve warm with a scoop of vanilla ice cream on top.

Southern Pecan Pie

½ cup brown sugar
3 tablespoons butter, softened
4 eggs
2 tablespoons flour
1 teaspoon vanilla

1 teaspoon vinegar
⅛ teaspoon salt
1½ cups light corn syrup
1½ cups pecans
1 8-inch unbaked pie shell

Cream butter with sugar and then add eggs, one at a time. Blend in remaining ingredients. Pour mixture into an 8-inch unbaked pastry shell. Bake in a hot 425 degree oven for 10 minutes. Reduce temperature to 325 degrees and bake for 30-40 minutes more. Dark corn syrup may be used in place of light syrup for a slightly more robust taste. Whipped cream may be used as a topping.

Pecan Chocolate Pie

1 partially baked pie shell
5 oz. bittersweet chocolate,
   finely chopped
1 cup + 2 tablespoons sugar
4 oz. unsalted butter (1 stick)

1 cup light corn syrup
2 cups pecan halves, chopped
¼ cup dark Crème de Cacao
½ cup heavy cream, whipped

Preheat oven to 350 degrees. Combine chocolate and sugar. Melt butter in corn syrup over a moderate heat. Add chocolate mixture and stir continually until the chocolate is smooth and melted. Add eggs, pecans and creme de Cacao and mix until eggs are incorporated. Pour mixture into warm, prebaked pie shell. Place shell on baking sheet and bake for 1 hour on center rack of the 350 degree oven. If crust begins to brown too early, cover crust edges with foil. Cool to room temperature and serve with whipped cream. SERVES 10-12.

Mapheson Pumpkin Pie

3 egg yolks, beaten
¾ cup brown sugar
1½ cups cooked pumpkin
½ cup milk

½ teaspoon nutmeg
1 envelope unflavored gelatin
¼ cup cold water
2 egg whites, stiffly beaten

½ teaspoon salt

1 teaspoon cinnamon

¼ cup granulated sugar

Combine beaten egg yolks, brown sugar, pumpkin, milk, salt and spices. Cook in double boiler until thick, stirring constantly. Soak gelatin in cold water and stir into hot mixture. Chill until partially set. Beat egg whites, add granulated sugar and beat again until stiff. Fold into gelatin mixture. Pour into baked pie shell and chill until set. Garnish with whipped cream. Makes one large pie or 8 individual tarts. NOTE: For a nice alternative to pie, spoon pumpkin mixture alternating with whipped cream into parfait glasses.

Pumpkin-Pecan Pie

6 oz. apricot preserves

1 tablespoon brandy

3 cups canned pumpkin

1¼ cups sugar

¾ teaspoon ground cloves

½ teaspoon ginger

¾ teaspoon nutmeg

¾ teaspoon salt

4 eggs

¾ cup milk

⅓ cup bourbon

1 unbaked deep-dish pie shell

PECAN TOPPING

⅔ cup firmly packed brown sugar

¼ cup melted butter

1 tablespoon heavy cream

⅛ teaspoon salt

¾ cup chopped pecans

½ cup pecan halves

¾ cup heavy cream

2 tablespoons bourbon

Preheat oven to 425 degrees. Liquefy preserves in a double boiler over hot water. Combine preserves and ⅓ cup bourbon. Set aside. Combine pumpkin, sugar, cloves, ginger, nutmeg, salt, eggs, and ¾ cup milk in a large bowl and mix thoroughly. Paint pie shell with 2 teaspoons or more of preserve mixture. Pour in pumpkin mixture and bake for 15 minutes. Reduce heat to 350 degrees and bake 40-50 minutes more or until filling has set. Cool pie to lukewarm. Meanwhile combine brown sugar, butter, 1 tablespoon of cream, salt and chopped pecans. Reserve pecan halves. Spread mixture over pie and arrange pecan halves on top. Broil 3-4 inches from heat until surface begins to bubble. Do not burn. Whip remaining ¾ cup of cream, fold in remaining 2 tablespoons bourbon and serve as garnish on wedges of warm pie.

Northeaster Crisp

1 quart fresh blueberries
1 tablespoon lemon juice
1 cup flour
¼ teaspoon cinnamon

1 cup brown sugar
½ cup butter
Vanilla ice cream (optional)

Place washed berries in 1½-quart casserole dish. Add lemon juice. Sprinkle with cinnamon. Mix sugar and flour together. Cut in butter until mixture is crumbly. Spread over berries. Bake at 375 degrees for 45 minutes. Serve with ice cream if desired.

Fruit Tart

TART SHELL

1¼ cups unbleached,
    all-purpose flour
½ cup cold unsalted butter,
    cut up

2 tablespoons grated lemon peel
2 tablespoons sugar
1 large egg yolk
2 tablespoons ice water

CREAM FILLING

½ cup sugar
1 tablespoon fresh lemon juice
2 cups raspberries

5 large egg yolks
6 tablespoons unsalted butter

TOPPING

2 kiwi fruit, peeled and sliced thinly
1½ cups fresh, washed raspberries

½ cup apricot jam
¼ cup Cointreau liqueur

To prepare shell, process sugar, butter, lemon peel and flour with a steel blade until it looks like coarse meal. Add yolk and process a few seconds to combine. With processor running, add enough ice water, a drop at a time, to allow dough to just hold together. You may not use all the water. Wrap dough tightly in a ball and refrigerate a minimum of 2 hours.

Next purée lemon juice, sugar and raspberries in a blender. Strain purée to remove seeds. Mix purée and butter in a double boiler and stir until butter is completely melted. Using a whisk, add yolks and continue to stir and cook over a low heat until it thickens to a custard. Remove and chill a minimum of 2 hours in the refrigerator.

When ready to assemble, preheat oven to 375 degrees. Roll dough into a 12-inch circle. Using a tart pan with removable bottom, line pan with dough and turn and crimp edges. Freeze shell for 30 minutes. Bake, weighted, for 20-25 minutes or until golden brown. Cool shell. Fill shell with cream filling and arrange fresh fruit on top. Melt jam with liqueur in a small saucepan. Cool slightly and cover tart with jam glaze. SERVES 8.

Cranberry Chess

1 cup sugar	1 teaspoon almond extract
1 cup flour	1 bag cranberries
2 eggs	1 cup walnuts, chopped
¾ cup butter	

Toss cranberries, walnuts and ½ cup sugar together. Mix all other ingredients and pour over cranberries. Bake at 350 degrees for ½ hour.

Cranberry Pie

¾ cup raisins	¼ cup brandy
3 cups cranberries	1½ teaspoons vanilla
2 tablespoons corn starch	Dash salt
1¾ cups sugar	2 recipes Perfect Pie Pastry
¼ cup orange juice	

Combine raisins and cranberries. Mix in corn starch and sugar. Add orange juice, brandy, vanilla and salt. Pour over cranberry and raisin mixture and blend well. Roll out half the pastry and fit into a 9-inch pie plate. Fill pastry with fruit mixture. Roll remaining pastry dough and cut into 1-inch strips. Arrange strips on top of fruit in a lattice pattern. Trim and flute the edges of the pie. Bake at 425 degrees about 15 minutes. Reduce heat to 350 degrees and bake another 30 minutes.

Chocolate Kahlúa Cheesecake

1¼ cups chocolate wafers,
  finely crumbled
5 tablespoons butter, melted
3 8-oz. packages cream cheese,
  softened
1 cup sugar
3 eggs

8 oz. semisweet chocolate, melted
2 tablespoons Kahlúa
1 teaspoon vanilla extract
1½ cups sour cream
Sweetened whipped cream
  for garnish

In a bowl, stir to combine wafer crumbs and butter. Press into a 9-inch springform pan to make a crust. Chill crust. In a bowl, beat cream cheese until light and fluffy. Gradually add sugar while continuing to beat. Add the eggs, one at a time, beating after each addition. Add melted chocolate and beat mixture until smooth. Add Kahlúa and vanilla and beat well. Fold in sour cream. Preheat oven to 350 degrees. Pour mixture into the chilled crumb shell. Bake at 350 degrees for 1 hour. Turn off oven and let pie stand for 30 minutes more with the door of the oven partially open. Remove from oven, cool, and refrigerate, covered, for at least 8 hours. Garnish top with sweetened whipped cream, if desired.

Cookie Cheesecake

CRUST

1¼ cups crushed chocolate-vanilla
  sandwich cookies
⅓ cup melted unsalted butter

1 teaspoon cinnamon
¼ cup firmly packed
  light brown sugar

FILLING

2 pounds cream cheese
1¼ cups sugar
2 tablespoons all-purpose flour
4 large eggs
2 egg yolks

⅓ cup heavy cream
1½ teaspoons vanilla
1½ cups chopped chocolate-vanilla
  sandwich cookies

TOPPING

2 cups sour cream   ¼ cup sugar
1 teaspoon vanilla

To prepare crust, blend cookies, butter, brown sugar and cinnamon in a 9 to 10-inch springform pan and press to bottom and sides. Refrigerate for 10 minutes.

While crust is chilling, prepare filling. Beat cream cheese until smooth. Add sugar and flour and beat until blended. Beat in eggs and yolks until all the mixture is smooth. Fold in cream and 1 teaspoon vanilla by hand. Pour half of the mixture into the crumb crust. Sprinkle with the coarsely chopped chocolate crumbs. Pour over remaining batter, smoothing surface. Bake for 15 minutes in a preheated 425 degree oven. Reduce oven temperature to 225 degrees. Bake 50 minutes more. If pie is browning too quickly, cover loosely with foil. Remove from oven and increase temperature to 350 degrees.

For topping, blend sour cream, sugar and vanilla in a bowl. Spread over pie. Bake for 7 more minutes. Refrigerate immediately, covered with plastic wrap, and chill overnight.

Pumpkin Cheesecake

6-8 oz. cream cheese   2 cups canned pumpkin
1½ cups sugar   1½ teaspoons cinnamon
2 teaspoons vanilla   ½ teaspoon ground nutmeg
6 eggs   2 9-inch graham cracker pie crusts

Combine all ingredients in a large bowl, mixing well. Pour into graham cracker crusts. Bake in a 350 degree preheated oven for 55 minutes. Serves 16. *Bilbo Baggins Restaurant, 208 Queen Street*

Seasonal Pizza

1 roll sugar cookie dough	½ cup apricot preserves
8 oz. cream cheese	1 tablespoon hot water
½ cup sugar	
1 teaspoon vanilla	
3 or 4 varieties of seasonal fruits, such as bananas, grapes, strawberries, blueberries, washed and sliced	

Slice cookie dough into ⅛-inch thick slices. Overlap the slices on a cookie sheet or pizza pan and press into a 10-inch circle. Bake in a preheated 375 degree oven for 12 minutes. Cool completely. Mix cream cheese, sugar and vanilla together to blend well. Spread over cooled crust. Decorate with fruits. Melt preserves and water in a small saucepan. When preserves are melted, brush or pour over fruit and place in refrigerator until well chilled. SERVES 12.

Winter Solstice Pudding

1 cup flour	1 cup grated potato
1 teaspoon each nutmeg, cinnamon, salt, baking soda and ground cloves	1 cup raisins
	½ cup butter
1 cup sugar	1 recipe Hard Sauce
1 cup grated carrot	

Butter a 1-pound coffee can or 8 individual desert cups. Combine flour, spices and sugar together in a large bowl. Add carrot, potato, raisins and butter and combine thoroughly. Using your hands may work best. Spoon into desired baking tin, leaving room at the top of can or cups for expansion. Place can or cups into a large, covered kettle which has a small amount of water in the bottom and steam for 1 to 1½ hours. Serve warm with Hard Sauce. If using a coffee can, slice in ½-inch slices. NOTE: This is a dessert traditionally served on Christmas Eve in England. SERVES 8.

Scotch Pudding

1 cup dark brown sugar	1 teaspoon vanilla
¾ cup light corn syrup	½ teaspoon salt
4 eggs	1 cup toasted walnuts
¼ cup whiskey	1 cup raisins
¼ cup melted butter	½ cup toasted walnut halves

Preheat oven to 400 degrees. Butter a 9-inch square or round baking dish. Combine brown sugar, corn syrup, eggs, whiskey, butter, vanilla and salt with an electric mixer until well blended. Sprinkle raisins and chopped nuts over bottom of prepared baking pan. Cover with egg mixture. Place nut halves in a decorative pattern over the top. Bake for 10 minutes at 400 degrees in middle of oven. Reduce oven to 325 degrees and bake about 20-25 minutes more or until firm. Serve with Scotch Cream or vanilla ice cream.

Crème Brûlée

1 pint whipping cream	Pinch of salt
6 egg yolks	2 teaspoons vanilla
½ cup sugar	Brown sugar

Heat cream to just below boiling. While heating, beat sugar, yolks and salt until yolks are thick. Stir in hot cream and add vanilla. Pour into a soufflé dish. Place in a pan of hot water and bake for 25 to 30 minutes at 350 degrees. Cool and chill.

When ready to serve, sprinkle top with brown sugar about ¼-inch deep. Place dish in ice water and broil until brown sugar has melted and is bubbly. Do not let the sugar burn! Chill again. The topping will stay crunchy for 3-4 hours. **SERVES 6.**

Grand Marnier Crème

5 egg yolks
2 tablespoons sugar

⅓ cup Grand Marnier liqueur
1 cup heavy cream

In a double boiler, mix egg yolks and sugar. Cook mixture until it thickens, stirring constantly. Mixture will coat a wooden spoon when ready. Do not let mixture curdle. Add Grand Marnier and cool to room temperature. Beat heavy cream. Add, by folding, the cooled mixture into the beaten cream. Pour into a serving bowl and chill at least 4 hours. SERVES 4-6.

Old Fashioned Cranberry Dessert

1½ cups washed, unblemished
   fresh cranberries
⅓ cup + ½ cup sugar
⅓ cup walnut pieces

8 tablespoons butter
1 egg
½ cup flour
Fresh whipped cream

In an 8-inch pie tin, spread 2 tablespoons butter on the bottom and sides. Cover with 1½ cups cranberries mixed with walnut pieces. Sprinkle ⅓ cup sugar on top. In a bowl, beat the egg. Add ½ cup sugar and the ½ cup flour, by tablespoons, beating as each tablespoon is added to the egg. Melt the remaining 6 tablespoons of butter and add to flour mixture. Mix well. Pour batter over cranberries and nuts. Place in a preheated 350 degree oven for 45 minutes or until top is golden brown. Remove from oven and cool slightly. Invert on a serving platter. Serve at room temperature with whipped cream on top or on the side. NOTE: You can divide this mixture into two or three pie tins, bake and place in a glass bowl with the whipped cream between the layers. An elegant dessert for a winter menu!

Almond-Baked Apples

¼ cup brown sugar,
   firmly packed

¼ teaspoon salt
6 large Pippin apples

3 tablespoons butter or margarine, softened

2 tablespoons apricot preserves

3 tablespoons toasted slivered almonds

¾ cup orange juice

½ cup sugar

2 teaspoons quick-cooking tapioca

1 large size cooking bag

Place bag in a baking dish large enough to hold the six apples. Combine brown sugar, apricot preserves, almonds and salt in a bowl. Hollow apples, leaving small end intact. Pare some skin from upper half of apples. Fill apple holes with brown sugar mixture and place apples in bag. In another bowl, combine orange juice, white sugar and tapioca and stir until sugar is dissolved. Pour over apples. Close bag and secure. Make at least 6 fork punctures in top of bag. Bake in microwave on high for 8-10 minutes, turning dish once halfway through cooking. Spoon sauce in bag over top of apples to serve. SERVES 6.

Apricot Mousse

8 oz. dried apricots

3 cups water

1 cup sugar

Zest of 1 orange, no white, grated

Zest of 1 lemon, no white, grated

⅛ cup vanilla

⅛ cup Cointreau or brandy

1 pint whipped cottage cheese

1½ pints whipping cream

Orange juice, French vanilla ice cream and fresh whipped cream for garnish

Cover apricots with 3 cups water and let soak for 2-3 hours. Add one cup sugar. Cook on low heat, simmering until apricots are mushy, fall apart and become syrupy. Purée in a processor. Place apricots in bowl and add zests, vanilla, liqueur and stir. Allow to chill in refrigerator. When chilled, whip with mixer until the consistency of cream. Add whipped cottage cheese and whip again until well blended. In a separate bowl, whip cream and add to apricot mixture by folding in. Set in refrigerator for 6-8 hours before serving. To serve, top each serving with 1 teaspoon orange juice, 1 teaspoon French vanilla ice cream and one teaspoon whipped cream.

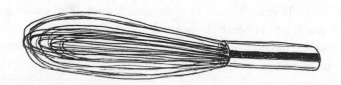

Mousse au Citron Vert

¾ tablespoon unflavored gelatin

¼ cup cold water

4 eggs, separated
1½ cups sugar
1 teaspoon corn starch
½ cup fresh lime juice
2 tablespoons lime peel,
   no white, grated

4 tablespoons rum
1½ cups whipping cream
3 tablespoons powdered sugar
Raspberry Sauce

Soften gelatin in cold water. Put in top of double boiler and heat until dissolved. Meanwhile beat egg yolks with an electric mixer with sugar until pale yellow. Combine corn starch with 3 tablespoons lime juice and stir until smooth. Add to corn starch mixture rest of lime juice, peel and dissolved gelatin. Stir until well blended. Add corn starch mixture to egg yolk and whisk into a custard. Put entire mixture back into double boiler and cook over hot water until custard thickens, about 20 minutes, stirring. Add 2 tablespoons rum and stir and cook for 1 minute more. Do not allow to boil. Chill mixture, covered, until it begins to set. Whip cream and slowly add remaining rum and powdered sugar. Whip until stiff. Whip egg whites until stiff. Fold whipped cream and egg whites into lime custard with a wooden spoon. Chill mixture until ready to serve. When ready to serve, spoon into large bowl or individual dessert dishes. Serve with dessert Raspberry Sauce. **SERVES 6-8.**

Soufflé au Citron

1⅔ cups unbleached flour
¼ teaspoon salt
1 tablespoon sugar
¾ cup unsalted butter,
   cut into pieces

¼ cup cold water
1 recipe lemon soufflé filling
Powdered sugar
Fresh Raspberry Sauce
10-12 fresh whole raspberries

In a mixing bowl, combine flour, salt and sugar. Cut in butter until mixture resembles coarse meal. Add cold water and mix until dough is formed. Roll out dough into a 12-inch circle and fit into a 10-inch tart pan with removable bottom. Trim and crimp edges. Pierce bottom with fork. Line pie shell with foil and weigh down bottom as with any pastry crust. Bake in a 425 degree preheated oven for 15-20 minutes. Remove foil and weights and bake another 5 minutes until crust is golden. Cool on a wire rack. Fill shell with lemon soufflé filling and bake at 375 degrees for 15 minutes or until soufflé is puffed and lightly browned. Remove from oven and cool on a wire rack. When ready to serve, dust with powdered sugar and serve garnished with fresh raspberries on top and Fresh Raspberry Sauce on the side.

FILLING

4 eggs, separated	¼ cup unsalted butter, melted
½ cup plus 3 tablespoons sugar	Dash salt
⅔ cup fresh lemon juice	

Beat egg yolks with ½ cup sugar until pale. Add in lemon juice. Put melted butter in a saucepan and add yolk mixture. Heat over low heat until thickened to custard, about 6 minutes. Stir continually while cooking. Pour mixture into a bowl and cool about 3 hours. Beat egg whites with salt until soft peaks form. Add remaining sugar, 1 tablespoon at a time, beating constantly. Whites should be stiff and glossy. Add ⅓ whites to custard and fold in. Return custard to rest of egg whites and fold in. Mix gently but thoroughly.

Raspberry-Chartreuse Bombé

1 pint raspberry sherbert	½ cup crushed almonds
½ gallon French vanilla ice cream	¾ cup crushed macaroons
½ cup bittersweet chocolate, grated	½ cup green Chartreuse liqueur
	1½ cups whipping cream

Slightly unthaw sherbert until malleable but not liquid. While unthawing, place a charlotte mold or large mixing bowl in the freezer. Remove from freezer and coat the walls with sherbert. Refreeze. Remove vanilla ice cream and allow to soften slightly as you whip the cream. Fold whipped cream, chocolate, almonds, macaroons and liqueur into the ice cream. You must work fast so that the ice cream does not become too soft. Remove sherbert mold from freezer and fill with ice cream mixture. Cover tightly with plastic wrap and return to freezer. Allow to set in freezer for several days to flavor. To unmold, place bombé in hot water for ½ minute to release. Invert onto serving platter. Bombé should not be too hard when served. At Christmas, garnish top of bombé with holly. On Valentine's Day, garnish with shaved chocolate and cinnamon hearts.

Mardi Gras Pralines

4 cups sugar
½ teaspoon salt
1 cup water
2½ cups evaporated milk

4 cups pecans
1 stick butter
1 teaspoon vanilla

Cook sugar, salt, water and milk over low heat in a large heavy pot until soft ball is formed when dropped in cold water. For best results, test with a candy thermometer. Take off heat and add pecans. Then add butter and vanilla. Stir vigorously until butter is melted. Drop onto waxed paper. Two sheets of waxed paper will help prevent breakage of pralines when lifted. **Makes about 45 pralines.**

Meringue Rings

4 egg whites
Pinch of salt
4 drops vanilla or almond extract

¼ teaspoon cream of tartar
1 cup fine sugar

Beat egg whites until stiff but not dry with salt and vanilla. Beat in cream of tartar and sugar, a tablespoon at a time. Put into a pastry bag or spoon in circles about the size of an egg onto a buttered cookie sheet using the back of a spoon to form a well. Bake for 10 minutes in a 300 degree preheated oven. Reduce heat to 275 degrees and continue to bake for 20-25 minutes or longer but do not allow to brown. Remove from oven and cool completely before filling. These can be made early in the day and, when cool, wrapped airtight until ready to use. Note: When an elegant but simple dessert is in order, consider meringue rings filled with fresh fruit and topped with Amaretto Chocolate Sauce.

Gourmet Chocolate Brownies

½ pound unsalted butter
¼-lb unsweetened chocolate, chopped
3.1 oz. dark Mexican chocolate,
   such as Ibarra, chopped (one disk)

1½ cups sifted flour
2 tablespoons ground cinnamon
1 teaspoon baking powder
¼ teaspoon salt

4 large eggs, room temperature   ¾ teaspoon vanilla extract

TOPPING

½ cup sliced almonds   2 teaspoons sugar
1 tablespoon unsalted butter,   Large pinch of cinnamon
  melted and cooled

Butter the inside of a 10-inch square pan. Line the bottom of the pan with a square of parchment, cut to size, and dust sides with flour. Set aside. Melt ½-pound butter and chocolate in a saucepan over low heat; stir well, then cool completely. Beat 2 cups sugar and eggs in a large bowl with electric mixer on moderate speed 5-6 minutes or until mixture is light and lemon colored. Resift flour with 2 tablespoons cinnamon, baking powder and salt onto a large sheet of waxed paper. Blend melted chocolate-butter mixture into egg mixture on low speed. Blend in vanilla. By hand, stir in the sifted flour. Pour and scrape the batter into the prepared pan. Combine almonds, 1 tablespoon melted butter, 2 teaspoons sugar and pinch of cinnamon in a small bowl. Sprinkle over top. Bake at 350 degrees 30-35 minutes. Do not overbake. Cool on rack 3-4 minutes before cutting into squares.

Maple Brownies

8 tablespoons melted butter   2 teaspoons baking powder
2 cups brown sugar   1 teaspoon vanilla
2 eggs   ½ cup coconut
1 teaspoon salt   1 cup chopped nuts
1½ cups flour

FROSTING

½ cup butter   1¾-2 cups powdered sugar
½ cup brown sugar   1 teaspoon maple extract
¼ cup half & half, at room temperature

Mix all cake ingredients together. Put into a greased 9x13 pan. Bake for 25 minutes at 350 degrees. Cool. For the frosting, melt the butter until brown but do not burn. Add brown sugar and cook over low heat until melted. Pour in half and half, stir and let cool. Beat in powdered sugar until smooth. Brownies can be frozen and are also excellent unfrosted. **MAKES 2 DOZEN.**

Almond Crunch Cookies

1 cup sugar
1 cup sifted powdered sugar
1 cup margarine, softened
1 cup vegetable oil
2 eggs
2 teaspoons almond extract
3½ cups all-purpose flour
1 cup whole wheat flour

1 teaspoon baking soda
1 teaspoon salt
1 teaspoon cream of tartar
2 cups chopped almonds
1 6-oz. package almond brickle
   chips, such as Heath Bits
Sugar

Combine sugar, powdered sugar, margarine and vegetable oil. Beat at medium speed with electric mixer until blended. Add eggs and almond extract, beating well. Combine flours, soda, salt, cream of tartar and gradually add to creamed mixture, beating after each addition. Stir in almonds and brickle chips. Chill dough 3-4 hours before shaping into small balls. Flatten cookies with fork dipped in sugar making crisscross pattern. Bake at 350 degrees 14-15 minutes or until lightly browned. Cool on racks and store in airtight container. **MAKES 5-6 DOZEN AND FREEZES WELL.**

Fresh Lemon Fingers

1½ cups self-rising flour
2 cups sugar
¾ cup margarine or butter

2 eggs
Rind of one lemon, grated
Juice of one lemon

Line a 8x12-inch baking tin with foil and butter. Preheat oven to 350 degrees. Beat 1½ cups sugar and butter together until pale in color. Add eggs, one at a time, with a spoonful of flour and beat together. Gently fold in flour with a metal spoon until well blended. Mix in lemon rind. Put mixture into tin and bake for 15-20 minutes. Take out of oven. Make a paste with lemon juice and remaining ½ cup sugar. Pour over sponge mixture while still hot. Leave to cool and crisp and then cut into fingers. Excellent for afternoon tea! **MAKES APPROXIMATELY 16 FINGERS.** *The Tea Cozy, 119 South Royal Street*

Katie Couric's Lemon Loves

CRUST

1 cup butter
½ cup confectioners sugar

2 cups flour
Pinch of salt

FILLING

4 eggs
2 cups sugar
6 tablespoons flour

6 tablespoons lemon juice
Grated rind of one lemon

Blend dry ingredients, cut in butter until mixture is crumbly. Press into an oblong 9x12 lightly greased pan. Bake 20 minutes at 350 degrees. To mix filling, beat with mixer eggs, sugar, flour and lemon juice. Add grated rind. Spread on top of baked crust and bake 25 minutes at 350 degrees. When cool, sprinkle with confectioners sugar. Cut into bite size squares. *Katie Couric*

Mrs. Randolph's Mince Meat Cookies

3 cups sifted flour
½ teaspoon salt
1 teaspoon baking soda
½ cup sugar

3 eggs, well beaten
1 small package mince meat
Brandy or bourbon

Soak mince meat in small amount of brandy or bourbon to moisten. Sift together flour, salt and soda. Cream shortening; add sugar gradually to shortening and beat until fluffy. Add eggs, beat. Add mince meat broken into small pieces. Add flour, mix. Drop by teaspoon on greased cookie sheet. Bake at 375 degrees for 12-15 minutes. **MAKES ABOUT 5 DOZEN.**

Macadamia Nut Cookies

½ cup butter (1 stick)
1 cup sugar
1 egg
1 teaspoon vanilla

1½ cups flour
½ teaspoon each salt, soda
   and cream of tartar
1 cup chopped macadamia nuts

Heat butter until it foams and is richly browned. Pour over sugar in a mixing bowl and mix well. Stir in egg and vanilla. Sift together flour, salt, soda and cream of tartar. Stir into mixture. Stir in nuts. Drop by teaspoons onto a baking sheet. Bake at 375 degrees for 10 minutes or until golden brown. Cool. MAKES 5 DOZEN.

Scottish Shortbread

2 cups butter, softened
1 cup sugar

5 cups flour

Preheat oven to 300 degrees. Cream butter and sugar until light and fluffy. Beat in flour, 1 cup at a time, until well mixed. Divide dough into 4 equal pieces. Pat each piece evenly into the bottom of an 8-inch pie plate. With the tines of a fork, prick the dough either randomly all over or in a pattern to prevent bubbles from forming during baking. The dough can also be put into molds or rolled and cut into cookie shapes. Bake 30 minutes or until pale and golden. Do not allow to brown. Cool in pans 10 minutes and then cut into wedges. MAKES 32 WEDGES.

Almond Shortbread

1 cup margarine
½ cup sugar
2½ cups sifted flour

1 teaspoon vanilla
½ teaspoon almond extract
2 oz. almond paste for decoration

Preheat oven to 300 degrees. Combine all ingredients except almond paste in a large bowl. Turn dough onto a board and roll thinly. Cut in strips, squares, or shapes. Bake for 10-15 minutes or until a pale golden brown. Cool on wire rack. Shape thin slices

from almond paste and use to decorate cookies. Dust with additional sugar if desired.
MAKES ABOUT 3 DOZEN COOKIES

Maple Oatmeal Cookies

1½ cups flour
½ teaspoon baking soda
1 teaspoon cinnamon
½ teaspoon salt
½ cup granulated white sugar
½ cup firmly packed brown sugar
1 egg, beaten
½ cup vegetable shortening,
    melted and cooled

1 stick butter, melted and cooled
    (4 oz.)
1½ tablespoons maple syrup
¼ cup milk
1¾ cups rolled oats
1 cup raisins

In a large bowl combine flour, baking soda, cinnamon, salt and both sugars. Mix well.
Add egg, shortening, butter, maple syrup, milk, oats and raisins. Stir batter until well
combined. Drop by heaping teaspoons onto ungreased baking sheets. Bake in 350
degree oven for 10-12 minutes or until edges are golden. **MAKES ABOUT 45 COOKIES.**

Williamsburg Pecan Cookies

1 cup white sugar
1 cup brown sugar
3 eggs
1¼ cups shortening
4½ cups flour
2 teaspoons soda

1 teaspoon cinnamon
1 teaspoon salt
½ teaspoon cloves
½ teaspoon nutmeg
1 cup finely chopped pecans

Preheat oven to 375 degrees. Cream sugar and shortening; add eggs. Mix together flour
plus all spices. Mix well together. Add pecans last. Form in 3 rolls, wrap in plastic wrap
and refrigerate up to 3-4 days. When ready to bake, slice in ⅓-inch slices and bake at
375 degrees for 8-10 minutes.

Tipper's Tennessee Treats

2 cups dark brown sugar,
  firmly packed
2 whole eggs and 2 egg whites
2 tablespoons honey
1 teaspoon baking powder,
  dissolved in ¼ cup boiling water
2 cups flour

½ teaspoon cinnamon
⅛ teaspoon allspice
⅛ teaspoon ground cloves
½ teaspoon salt
½ cup raisins
½ cup chopped dates
½ cup walnut pieces

Preheat oven to 350 degrees. In a large mixing bowl, mix brown sugar and eggs. Add honey and stir. Add baking powder to water and mix. Add water to mixing bowl. Combine flour and spices and stir into mixture. Add remaining ingredients and stir. Pour into a greased 8x12 inch baking pan. Bake 350 degrees for 30-40 minutes. To determine when treats are ready, insert toothpick. A nearly dry toothpick indicates they are done. Cut into squares while warm. *Tipper Gore*

Chocolate Toffee Bars

2 sticks of margarine (8-oz.)
1 cup firmly packed brown sugar
1 large egg yolk
1½ teaspoons vanilla
3 tablespoons instant cappuccino
  or espresso coffee dissolved
  in 2 tablespoons boiling water

½ teaspoon salt
8 oz. semisweet chocolate
¾ cup salted cashews, chopped

Cream butter and brown sugar with an electric mixer until light and fluffy. Beat in egg yolk, vanilla and coffee mixture until well combined. Add salt and flour, beating until well mixed. Spread the batter evenly in a jelly roll pan, 15 ½ x 10 ½ x 1-inch, and bake in preheated 350 degree oven for 15-20 minutes or until it pulls away from the edge of the pan. Melt chocolate and spread over baked layer and sprinkle cashews on top. Cool and cut into bars. Chill until chocolate is firm. Freezes well and can make **48 BARS.**

Lemon Cookies

1 medium lemon
1 cup sugar
4 oz. unsalted butter, cut into
   8 pats, at room temperature

1 large egg
1½ cups all-purpose flour
¼ teaspoon salt

Remove zest from lemon, mix sugar and finely chop in a food processor. Add butter and continue to blend until creamy. Add juice of lemon and egg and blend well. Add flour and salt and blend until flour is well mixed. If dough is very soft, refrigerate up to 1½ hours. Form dough into an 8x2-inch roll. Wrap in plastic wrap and refrigerate overnight. Dough can be stored up to 10 days in refrigerator or 6 months in freezer. If dough is frozen, defrost in refrigerator overnight. When ready to use, preheat oven to 350 degrees. Cut dough with serrated knife into ¼ inch slices. Place on a greased baking sheet and bake for 8-10 minutes or until cookies are firm. Cool on wire racks.

Great Pumpkin Cookies

2 cups flour
1 cup oats
1 teaspoon baking soda
1 teaspoon ground cinnamon
½ teaspoon salt
1 cup butter or margarine
1 cup brown sugar, firmly packed
1 cup granulated sugar

1 egg
1 teaspoon vanilla
1 cup mashed canned
   or freshly cooked pumpkin
1 cup semisweet chocolate pieces
Icing of choice (even peanut butter!)
   to affix assorted candies, raisins or nuts

Combine flour, oats, baking soda, cinnamon and salt. Set aside. Cream butter. Gradually add sugars, beating until light and fluffy. Add egg and vanilla, mixing well. Alternately add dry ingredients and pumpkin, mixing well after each addition. Stir in chocolate pieces. For each cookie, drop ¼ cup dough onto lightly greased baking sheet. Spread into pumpkin shape using a thin metal spatula. Add a bit more dough to form stems. Bake at 350 degrees for 20-25 minutes until cookies are firm and lightly browned. Remove from baking sheets and cool on wire racks. Decorate using icing of choice and assorted candies, raisins, or nuts for mouth, eyes, etc. **MAKES ABOUT 20 COOKIES.**

Chocolate Chip Crispies

1 cup solid shortening
1 cup brown sugar
1 cup granulated sugar
2 eggs, well beaten
1 teaspoon vanilla
1½ cups sifted enriched flour

1 teaspoon salt
1 teaspoon soda
3 cups quick-cooking oats
½ cup chopped walnuts
6 oz. chocolate chips

Thoroughly cream shortening and sugars. Add eggs and vanilla. Beat well. Sift together dry ingredients. Add to creamed mixture. Add oats, nuts and chocolate chips. Mix well. Shape into rolls and wrap in plastic wrap or waxed paper and chill thoroughly, preferably overnight, in the refrigerator. Slice ¼-inch thick. Bake on an ungreased cookie sheet in a 350 degree oven for 10 minutes. **MAKES 5 DOZEN.**

Hard Sauce

½ cup unsalted butter
1½ cups powdered sugar

2 tablespoons or more brandy,
   rum or any liqueur

Cream butter well and gradually beat in powdered sugar and liqueur. Serve at room temperature and refrigerate any leftovers for later use.

Amaretto Chocolate Sauce

1½ cups sugar
3 tablespoons butter
4 oz. unsweetened chocolate
1 cup cream

1 teaspoon vanilla
¼ cup Amaretto (rum, sherry
   or Cointreau can be substituted)

Place the first 4 ingredients into a heavy bottomed saucepan. Place over medium heat and stir until sugar is dissolved. When mixture comes to a boil, lower the heat and boil for 7 minutes without stirring. After 7 minutes remove from heat and add vanilla and Amaretto. Stir. NOTE: This sauce can be kept indefinitely if frozen. Thaw and reheat slowly when needed. Vary the flavor with the liqueur.

Fresh Raspberry Sauce

1 pint raspberries	⅓ cup water
1 cup sugar	Pinch of cream of tartar

Press raspberries through a sieve to remove all seeds. In a small saucepan combine sugar, water and cream of tartar. Bring to boil, covered. Remove cover and boil syrup rapidly until spoon forms a thin ribbon when lifted. Add boiled mixture to raspberry purée. Stir well and cool.

VARIATION: FROZEN RASPBERRY SAUCE

2 10-oz. boxes frozen raspberries	Sugar to taste
2 tablespoons Cointreau	

Purée raspberries in a processor and strain seed through a fine sieve. Add Cointreau and sugar to taste if desired.

Banana Dessert Sauce

2 tablespoons butter	1 oz. banana liqueur
4 tablespoons brown sugar	2 oz. white rum
Dash cinnamon	

Heat ingredients together in saucepan. Cool and refrigerate until ready to use. Reheat slowly. Sauce can be served over vanilla ice cream or over bananas sliced and heated through in a chafing dish.

Scotch Cream

1 cup whipping cream	2 tablespoons Scotch whiskey,
1 tablespoon powdered sugar	rum or brandy

Combine all ingredients in a cold bowl and whip until it forms soft peaks. Makes about 2 cups. SERVES **2.**

A Walking Tour

A WALK THROUGH Alexandria is a walk through history. A few short blocks can take you from the Revolutionary War to the Civil War and back again. Turning a corner, you can stand at attention where Washington mustered his troops, find the spot where Lee answered his country's call, climb the steps where the Marquis de Lafayette received a hero's welcome, or slip into the quiet church where Roosevelt and Churchill prayed for peace in Washington's family pew.

As you walk, you will be following the footsteps of a 17-year-old George Washington who tradition says staked out the city's first streets as a surveyor's apprentice. Passing by landmarks that sprang from lots laid down in his youth, you can retrace not only the course of his daily life in his hometown but the unfolding history of a young nation.

You can step from the tavern where Washington dined with his family and friends and cross the square where he drilled as a young militia officer — in front of the Town Hall where he conducted his business as a gentleman planter and next to the Courthouse where he voted for resolutions against British tyranny. From there you can walk past the little townhouse where he often stayed when pressing business kept him in town, to the church where he worshipped as the Commander of the Continental Army, turn back down the street to the inn where he celebrated his birthday as the nation's first President — and finally stand in silence for a moment in the Meeting House where the citizens of Alexandria mourned the man from Mount Vernon at his memorial service.

Today, you can still walk those same streets, and see what Washington saw — not some charming contrivance created for the tourist trade, but a living, breathing city where the business of daily life is still being conducted against a background of 250 years of unbroken history.

Of course, Alexandria does have more than its share of the picturesque: wooden gates and brick archways, walled gardens of fragrant boxwood and blooming azaleas, improbable flounder houses, tortuous cobblestones, converted tobacco warehouses, obsolete horsewalks and the hidden grave of the Unknown Revolutionary Soldier.

But quaint architecture is not what makes Alexandria such a remarkable place to live. The fine Federal, Georgian and Greek Revival homes that grace its streets are indeed historic — not just because *someone famous once lived there* — but because more than a few of them have been occupied by the same family for generations, while descendants of Alexandria's less well-known founders may live next door or across the street. Together with more recent arrivals, they are living in a town that Washington would still recognize — and living a life he would find more than a little familiar.

Not only can you step into the shop where legend says the first President picked up his mail, or dine in an inn where a helpful young naval officer named John Paul Jones is remembered for arranging accommodations for a newly-arrived French nobleman named Lafayette — you can sit in the square and read a newspaper that's been published for more than 200 years (half of that time by one family) and cross the street to deposit your valuables with a family that's been banking in Alexandria for two centuries.

Just as you could in Washington's time, you can rise early in the morning and find Market Square filled with stalls of fruit, flowers and fresh vegetables. You can watch as shopkeepers arrive to open their stores, artisans walk to their studios, tradesman tote their tools, merchants line up at the bank, lawyers gather at the courthouse, citizens enter town hall and all manner of ladies and gentlemen, in town to conduct business of one kind or another, exchange greetings and pass on news as they meet one another.

At midday you can retire, as Washington did, to any one of a dozen inns, taverns and coffeehouses, where you will rub elbows with travelers from New York and Boston, Charleston and New Orleans, and over the sea from England, Spain, France, Holland, Germany or Russia. In the evening, you will see the local gentry passing by — just as Washington did in his day — dressed in their finest and on their way to the theatre, a concert or a party, a ball or a banquet, a meeting of this Society or that Club.

T HAT ALEXANDRIA'S HERITAGE has survived — let alone become the fabric of a living city — is due both to the forces of history and the determination of its citizens to preserve it. To see how history has shaped the city's fate, you only have to follow where Alexandria's streets lead you — down to the river.

It was on the banks of this river that Native Americans planted, fished and traded for 10,000 years. It was up this river that Captain John Smith — the first recorded European to see it — sailed in 1608, reporting back that its name, Potomac, meant "trading river." It was down this river that Indians from this area came in 1619, seeking trade with the new English settlement at Jamestown. It was across the river to this spot that Margaret Brent, the first woman lawyer in America, came from Maryland to take possession of 700 acres granted to her in 1654. It was on the riverbank just above her land, at the foot of the ancient Oronoco Trail, where Scottish traders built the first sheds for storing tobacco on its way to England. It was that riverbank, together with Margaret Brent's land, which the Scotsman John Alexander purchased for 10,500 pounds of tobacco in 1699. And it was there in 1748 — on a part of "Alexander's Land" deemed to be the the best harbor on the river — that the General Assembly in Williamsburg directed 60 acres to be set aside for the purposes of building a port, appointing trustees to survey and subdivide the land and supervise the construction of a new city.

The seaport they built grew with the trade brought by ships up the river from across the Atlantic. By the beginning of the Revolution, Alexandria was the third busiest port in the colonies — important enough to be considered as a site for the new nation's capital. But it was passed over in favor of the final choice a few miles upriver, which in time took on the name of its most famous native son — Washington. What might have been a fatal blow was instead a saving grace.

Coming down the river five days after they burned the Capitol, the White House and the Navy Yard in August of 1814, British frigates sailed into the harbor at the foot of King Street. Commandeering food and munitions from Alexandria's warehouses, as well as ships from the harbor, they retreated downstream after putting the port's remaining vessels to the torch — but not the city, which escaped the fate of the capital.

Thirty-five years later, on the very day Virginia seceded from the Union, federal troops streamed across the Potomac under orders from Abraham Lincoln. A contingent of New York Zouaves arrived by boat in Alexandria's harbor under the command of one Colonel Ellsworth — who is said to have marched up King Street alone, ripped down a Confederate flag flying in front of a tavern, and been shot dead on the spot by the innkeeper — becoming the first casualty of the War.

From that day the presence of the Federal troops sorely tried the Southern sympathies of its citizens, who saw its economy devastated and its finest homes, churches and schools taken over as hospitals for wounded Union soldiers. But Robert E. Lee's hometown, by remaining an occupied city from the first day of the war, was never threatened with combat — and Alexandria was spared the bloody conflict that ravaged so much of the country.

Thus preserved, first by fate and later through perserverance, Alexandria is a living legacy of two and a half centuries of history. Those who call it home today walk her streets with a deep pride in that history — and they welcome you to share it with them.

We suggest that you begin a walking tour from King and Union Street.

The Torpedo Factory

105 North Union Street Originally built for the manufacture of munitions during World War I, the restored Torpedo Factory Art Center is now home to more than 150 craftsmen and artists. One of the first city-funded centers for the visual arts in the country, it provides studio space and showrooms to working artists — and a chance for the public to watch them at work.

Upstairs is a museum exhibiting artifacts from 5,000 years of Alexandria's history. Alexandria Archaeology also offers tours, seminars and publications about the fascinating achaeological research still being conducted in Alexandria. Established in 1973, it is one of the first city-sponsored programs dedicated to conservation of sites in an urban environment.

Walking south on Union Street and turning right at Prince Street, you will arrive at Captains Row.

Captains Row

Just as early Virginians considered Alexandria to be the most favorable location on the Potomac for a seaport, many of Alexandria's sea captains chose this stretch of Prince Street, just steps from the river, to build their homes in the new city. The 28 fine houses in this short block were more than just residences when they were first built: shipping offices often occupied the main level, with family quarters on the second. The seaport brought more than prosperity to Prince Street — its original cobblestone paving is believed to have first arrived in Alexandria as ballast in ships, and later laid by Hessians during the Revolutionary War.

Continuing up Prince Street one block, you will arrive at the corner of Lee Street, and the Athenaeum.

The Athenaeum

Ten years after opening its doors as the Bank of the Old Dominion, this beautiful Greek Revival building was the scene of great drama the day Union troops invaded Alexandria at the outset of the Civil War, when Old Dominion's cashier is said to have daringly removed the bank's deposits during the night to a secret location. After the War they were safely retrieved, and Old Dominion became the only bank in Virginia to redeem all of its outstanding currency. Rescued from neglect one hundred years later, the Athenaeum is today home to the Northern Virginia Fine Art Association's art exhibits.

Walk one block further on Prince Street, turn right on South Fairfax Street, and walk one block north where you will discover the Old Apothecary Shop at 105-107 South Fairfax.

Old Apothecary Shop

The Stabler-Leadbeater Apothecary Shop, known in Alexandria as the Old Apothecary Shop, first opened in 1792 and remained in the Stabler family until it closed in 1933, making it the second oldest shop in continuous operation in America. This is where Martha Washington bought castor oil and where George is said to have picked up his mail. A plaque inside marks the spot where Robert E. Lee was standing when he received orders to put down John Brown's insurrection at Harper's Ferry. Saved by a local civic society, this perfectly preserved shop today houses the largest medicinal glass collection in the country, with hundreds of valuable hand-blown bottles, as well as the store's original wooden clock, an antique cast iron sewing machine and many other items.

Turning back towards Prince Street, walk down South Fairfax Street one and one-half blocks to the Old Presbyterian Meeting House.

The Old Presbyterian Meeting House

The Scottish merchants of early Alexandria engaged John Carlyle, who had just completed construction of Christ Episcopal Church, to build the first Presbyterian Meeting House in 1774. Popularly referred to as the Dissenting Church, it was also used by other unofficially recognized groups, such as the Methodists, who had no churches of their own. On a cold December day in 1799, George Washington's funeral service was held here — the snow being so deep that the road to Christ Church (the "Church in the Woods") was said to be impassable. When the Meeting House was stuck by lightening in 1834, it was badly damaged by fire. Rebuilt within two years, a bell tower was added in 1843 and the church was enlarged in 1855. Unchanged since then, it is an outstanding example of Georgian architecture. During the Battle of Bull Run, it was used as a hospital. In its graveyard are buried John Carlyle, Dr. James Craik, Washington's friend and doctor, as well as the Unknown Soldier of the American Revolution.

Leaving the Meeting House garden on Royal Street, walk north to Duke Street, turn left on Duke and walk three blocks west to Washington Street. Cross Washington, turn right and walk one block north toward Prince Street and the Lyceum.

The Lyceum

201 South Washington Street In 1834, a group of civic-minded citizens, led by Benjamin Hallowell, a Quaker schoolmaster, organized the Alexandria Lyceum Company. By 1838, its membership had grown considerably, while the Alexandria Library Company led by Dr. James Muir, the Presbyterian pastor, had also outgrown its quarters at the Meeting House. The two organizations agreed to share a new building, which was constructed in 1839 and quickly became Alexandria's first cultural center. The first floor of the Lyceum housed the library, a large reading room and historical exhibits, while the second floor was used for lectures and concerts. During the Civil War, the Lyceum was requisitioned as a hospital and then sold in 1868 to John B. Daingerfield to use as a residence. One of the few Greek Revival buildings in Alexandria — in fact, one of a very few in Virginia — the Lyceum was rescued from demolition in 1969 when Alexandria was the first city in the state to exercise the right of eminent domain for the purposes of preservation. Restored by the City with the help of a modern group of civic-minded citizens, the Lyceum opened its doors to the public once again, this time as Alexandria's history museum.

Walking west on Prince Street, turn right on South Alfred Street, where you will find the Friendship Firehouse.

Friendship Firehouse

107 South Alfred Street The Friendship Fire Engine Company was organized in 1774 as one of Alexandria's first volunteer fire companies. History says that George Washington, one of the original members, purchased the city's first fire engine (now on display here), sending it as a gift to Alexandria from Philadelphia where he had gone to take command of the Continental Army in 1775. By 1855, the Company had acquired the present building, which was later dedicated as a National Shrine in honor of George Washington. The members of the Friendship Veterans Fire Engine Company organized the first parades to honor Washington, and the honor roll of this historic association has included presidents, congressmen, governors and many other distinguished Americans. Restored in 1993, the firehouse is open to the public.

From the Firehouse, continue on South Alfred one block to King Street. Turn right and proceed one block east to Columbus Street. Turn left and walk one block north to Christ Church.

Christ Church

Christ Church has been in continuous use longer than any other church in Alexandria. Completed in 1773, its design is credited to James Wren, a descendant of the great English architect Sir Christopher Wren. Constructed well beyond where the young town of Alexandria had yet grown, it was often called the "Church in the Woods." Already a vestryman of the unfinished church, George Washington is on record as being the first to buy a pew for his family, purchasing number 15 for £36. It has become traditional for the President of the United States and his family to worship in Christ Church on the Sunday nearest to Washington's birthday and sit in his pew. Nearby is the pew that belonged to Robert E. Lee. Outside, the beautiful brick tower and steeple were added in 1818. Inside, the sanctuary is noted for its six-sided pulpit covered by a canopy and centered under a Palladian window, flanked by two tablets inscribed by James Wren with the Lord's Prayer and the Apostle's Creed.

Walk one block north of Christ Church on Washington Street to Lloyd House.

Lloyd House

220 North Washington Street One of Alexandria's finest examples of late Georgian architecture, Lloyd House was built in 1797 as a private residence. It was used by the Quaker Benjamin Hallowell for his school, before being purchased in 1832 by John Lloyd, whose wife Anne was a cousin of Robert E. Lee. Restored in 1976 by the Alexandria Historical Restoration and Preservation Commission under the supervision of the White House's restoration architect, Lloyd House is now part of the Alexandria Public Library and houses a large collection of family papers, rare books and historical documents.

Continuing North on Washington Street two blocks to Oronoco Street will bring you to two historic sites: the Lee-Fendall House and Lee's Boyhood Home.

The Lee-Fendall House

614 Oronoco Street The first of the three Lee family homes to rise on Oronoco Street was built in 1785 by Phillip Richard Fendall, a founder of the Bank of Virginia, on a lot he purchased the previous year from his relative "Lighthorse Harry" Lee. Known today as the Lee-Fendall House, it was home to 21 members of the Lee family for the next 118 years. This historic home is graced with a growing collection of the furniture and personal belongings of members of this distinguished family who lived here. More recently, Lee-Fendall House was the home of labor leader John L. Lewis and his family.

Across Oronoco Street you will find Lee's Boyhood Home.

Lee's Boyhood Home

607 Oronoco Street One of a pair of fine homes constructed in 1795, this house was purchased by Colonel William Fitzhugh, who fifty years earlier had become one of Alexandria's first landowners. A former member of the Virginia House of Burgesses, the Revolutionary Conventions of 1776 and 1776, and later the Continental Congress, Colonel Fitzhugh moved his family here in 1799 from Chatham, his elegant home on the Rappahannock. Long a friend of fellow patriot George Washington, his youngest daughter, Mary Fitzhugh, was married in this house to George Washington Parke Custis — Martha Washington's grandson — in 1804.

Seven years later, in 1811, the house was purchased by the famous Revolutionary War General "Lighthorse Harry" Lee, who, after serving as governor of Virginia, left Stratford, his magnificent estate in the country, to bring *his* growing children — including a four-year-old son named Robert Edward — to attend school here. Growing up in this house, Robert E. Lee attended the Alexandria Academy, leaving after his appointment to West Point. Later, as a young officer, he married Mary Custis — the only daughter of Mary Fitzhugh and George Custis who had been married in the same house years earlier.

Continuing east on Oronoco Street, turn right on St. Asaph Street and proceed south three blocks. Turn left on Cameron Street, and walk two blocks east to Royal Street, where you will find Gadsby's Tavern on your right.

Gadsby's Tavern

134 North Royal Street Opening its doors not long after Alexandria was founded in 1749, this building has been a tavern or inn for over 250 years, known variously as Mason's Ordinary, Fountain Tavern, the Bunch of Grapes, the City Tavern (and the City Hotel, when a new addition opened in 1793), and finally as Gadsby's — after the man who leased it in 1795. During its heyday, Gadsby's was described as the finest public house in America by its many famous guests, from George Washington and the Marquis de Lafayette, to Thomas Jefferson, James Madison, and John Adams. The scene of frequent dancing parties and celebrations throughout the 18th century, Gadsby's ballroom welcomed George and Martha to the first Birthday Ball in his honor, which continues to be held in this same ballroom today. On November 5, 1798, on his way home from Philadelphia, the nation's first President was escorted to Gadsby's, where he dined and then stood in review on the tavern's steps as Alexandria's Independent Infantry Blues passed by, honoring him with a sixteen-round salute. Restored in 1976 to celebrate America's Bicentennial, food, drink and entertainment are still available in the tavern.

Continue south down Royal Street toward King Street, and you will find Market Square on your left.

Market Square and City Hall

Surrounding Alexandria's City Hall is Market Square. Before the first lots in Alexandria were auctioned on July 13, 1749, two half-acre lots had already been set aside for the Town Hall and the Market Place. Within three years, the new town's trustees had authorized semi-annual fairs in the Market Place, and construction (financed by a lottery) had begun on the first Court House, which was the county seat of Fairfax until 1800. Market Square is where a young Major George Washington drilled his troops from the Virginia Militia in 1755, preparing to march with Braddock's British troops against the French and Indians. The Courthouse is where, little more than fifteen years later, Washington presided over a meeting of Fairfax's freeholders where George Mason drew up the Fairfax Resolutions protesting British tyranny on July 18, 1771. And the Courthouse is where, as the nation's first President, Washington went to cast his final vote in 1799. The first Town Hall, which had grown with the city, was destroyed by fire in 1871. The new, Victorian-style City Hall was constructed two years later in a U-shape, which was enclosed in 1962 by a modern addition in colonial style. Today, Market Square hosts the oldest, continuously operating market in the country. On Saturday mornings, Alexandrians still congregate here to meet friends, buy fresh produce and select bouquets of flowers and herbs.

Leaving Market Square and heading east (toward the river) on King Street, just past Fairfax Street, brings you to Ramsay House.

Ramsay House

The oldest house in Alexandria was in fact the very first house in the new town, built on land purchased by William Ramsey when the first lots were auctioned by the town's trustees on July 13, 1749. An enterprising Scot, Ramsey is reported to have towed the original portion of his clapboard cottage up the Potomac on a barge to the spot where it rests today, three blocks from the Potomac River in the heart of Old Town. Hardworking and resourceful like so many of Alexandria's founders, Ramsay was more than a successul businessman — at one time or another he served as the town overseer, census taker, and postmaster — even being honored in 1761 as the founder and "Lord Mayor of Alexandria" by members of the St. Andrew's Society. Leaving for Philadelphia to assume command of the Continental Army, George Washington had breakfast here on May 5, 1775 with William and his wife Anne — who once served as the treasurer of Fairfax County, and was busy raising large sums of money for the Revolutionary cause. One of their eight children was elected Mayor of Alexandria, in which capacity he became the first official to address George Washington as "Mr. President," as Washington was leaving Alexandria — this time for his first inauguration in New York in 1789. Despite major alterations in the late 18th century and a fire in 1942, the city's oldest house survived until the City of Alexandria was able to purchase the house and restore it. Dedicated in 1956 as an historic site, Ramsay House is today Alexandria's official Visitors Center. They will gladly assist you with any further information that you made need regarding Alexandria.

Returning to the corner of King Street, turn right on South Fairfax Street and walk one-half block to Carlyle House.

Carlyle House

Modeled after an imposing manor in West Lothian, Scotland named Craighall, the Carlyle House was built in 1752 by the Scottish merchant John Carlyle for his bride, Sara Fairfax, on a lot he purchased at the original auction on July 13, 1749, and an adjacent lot purchased from his neighbor William Ramsey. One of the first trustees of Alexandria, John Carlyle was a merchant and shipowner appointed in 1758 as Collector of His Majesty's Customs for the Port of Alexandria. Together with his business partner John Dalton, he also owned Mason's Ordinary, the forerunner of Gadsby's Tavern.

His stately home was certainly the frequent scene of social activity in the early days of Alexandria, but Carlyle House became the center stage of American history on April 14, 1755. It was on this day that the British General Edward Braddock, who had made his headquarters at Carlyle House, met with the colonial Governors of Virginia, Maryland, Pennsylvania, New York and Massachusetts to discuss the growing threat posed by the French and Indian encroachment upon the British colonies. The most important recommendation of the Carlyle House Conference: "laying a tax" upon the colonists in order to finance the British military campaign. This led directly to the Stamp Act, the beginning of "taxation without representation," and, consequently, the American Revolution.

It was also from this house that Braddock departed, with the young George Washington as an aide-de-camp, to march against the French at Fort Duquesne, only to be ambushed and slain in the wilderness. Washington not only survived, he learned from this defeat the effectiveness of "guerilla" tactics against regular troops — knowledge which served him well during the Revolution. Now the property of the Northern Virginia Regional Park Authority, Carlyle House has been restored to its 18th Century elegance, when it was host to history itself.

BEYOND OLD TOWN

To the west of Old Town, away from the river and straight up King Street, you will see the spire of the Masonic Memorial.

George Washington National Masonic Memorial

This towering monument was erected by the Masonic Fraternity of the United States as a memorial in honor of the nation's first president, who was also the first Worshipful Master of the Alexandria Lodge, organized here in 1783. It was in both those capacities that George Washington laid the cornerstone of the United States Capitol in a Masonic ceremony on September 18, 1793. 130 years later, the cornerstone of the Memorial was laid with the same trowel that Washington had used in the Capitol ceremony. Dedicated in 1932, the monument rises 333 feet above the top of Shuter's Hill, one of the highest points in Alexandria—a location once heartily recommended by both James Madison and Thomas Jefferson as the site for the nation's new capitol, but rejected by George Washington because his family happened to own property nearby. Today, this shrine and its museum houses an important collection, long safeguarded by Washington's Lodge, of historic items and family relics associated with Washington's family, friends and fellow Masons.

Two and one-half miles to the west, on Braddock Road, is Fort Ward Park, a must for Civil War enthusiasts!

Fort Ward

When the Civil War began in 1861, the capital city of Washington was practically on the front lines, vulnerable to attack. On the very day of Virginia's secession from the Union, Lincoln ordered Federal troops across the Potomac River, quickly seizing Alexandria and Arlington Heights — even as the Sixth Alexandria Battalion, answering the call to join the Confederate forces, hastily assembled and marched to the train depot. As part of a defense network that would eventually include 68 forts and batteries surrounding the capital, Lincoln's troops marched up Braddock Road and immediately began construction on Fort Ward, the fifth largest fort in the chain, with 36 guns and 5 bastions. Named for Commander James Harmon Ward, the first Union naval officer killed in the Civil War, this historic landmark is today a 40-acre park, purchased by the City of Alexandria in 1964. The Northwest Bastion has been carefully restored to look as it did over 100 years ago, while a headquarters building and officers' hut have been reconstructed according to Matthew Brady photographs. The museum located in the headquarters building features changing exhibits of one of the country's largest and finest collections of Civil War items. Fort Ward is also the site of several Civil War and Revolutionary War reenactments and encampments throughout the year, as well as symphony concerts in the summer.

Last, but not least, down the George Washington Memorial Parkway, lies:

Mount Vernon

First patented in 1669, this 5,000-acre site on the Potomac was named by Lawrence Washington — George's elder half-brother — for Admiral Vernon, the British naval officer under whom he had served. George Washington acquired Mount Vernon in 1754, enlarged the main house while incorporating the latest architectural styles and conveniences, built several outbuildings, and landscaped the grounds, making it one of the finest estates of his era. It was here that he and Martha entertained friends, family and an unending stream of visitors. The rescue, painstaking restoration and continuing maintenance of this national treasure are all due to the efforts of the Mount Vernon Ladies' Association, which purchased the historic estate in 1858. It is a grateful visitor today who steps onto the wide veranda that overlooks exactly what the father of our nation saw two centuries ago — a sweeping view of broad lawns descending to the river below and the Virginia and Maryland countryside beyond.

Index

Contributors

The Twig, Junior Auxiliary of Alexandria Hospital, would like to thank our members and friends who contributed with their recipes and talents for *Seaport Savories...*

CHERRY ABBOT
LYNN ABRAMSON
CARDIOVASCULAR SERVICE
  PROGRAM AT ALEXANDRIA
  HOSPITAL
MRS. JOHN B. ALLEN
CINDY ANDERSON
MRS. ROBERT H. ANDERSON
SHELLEY M. ANNAND
DENISE AUSTIN
TRACY AUSTIN
MRS. GLENN BACKUS
VIVIEN BACON
JANET BAKER
ANNE BALDWIN
MRS. E. DARRYL BARNES
MRS. RENNY H. BARNES
KRISTINE BARR
CINDI BARTOL
BERNARD BAUDRAND
BONNIE BAXLEY
MARY BEATLEY
CHRISTINE BELLINO
LUCIO BERGAMIN
ANN BERMINGHAM
TOM BESHORNER
WALTER E. BEVERLY, JR.
NANCY BIEGING
BILBO BAGGINS
GAIL BLACHLY
MARY PAT BLANTON
BLEU ROCK INN
CONNIE BLOOD
BETTY H. BLOUNT
BLUE POINT GRILL
REBECCA BOSTICK
CAROL BOYD

GINNY BRADLEY
MRS. JAMES S. BRADY
DEBBIE BRAY-LESSANS
SALLY GUY BROWN
MICHAEL G. BRUNER
JOAN BURCHELL
JANE BURNS
REBA BURNS
TRISH CALLOWAY
BERNARD CAMPAGNE
JEAN CAMPAGNE
CAROL CARBAUGH
CATHERINE A. CARTER
KATHLEEN CHARLES
MARY CLARK
MRS. FRANK W. CLARKE
HARLENE CLAYTON
JAN S. COLLINS
CINDY COOLBAUGH
COLLEEN CORBETT
KATIE COURIC
MRS. PETER J. COVER
FARRIS CRAIG
MONTA LEE DAKIN
DIANA M. DAMEWOOD
PATRICIA DAY
PAT DE PUY
VIRGINIA TURNER DEDI
MRS. DAVID W. DELLEFIELD
MRS. CAROL P. DEMERY
SHERRYL DODD
MARY DOYLE
MRS. THOMAS R. DYSON, JR.
ECCO CAFE
EMILY ERICKSON
BONNIE FAIRBANK
JEAN TAYLOR FEDERICO

PATRICIA M. FISKE
ROBIN FITCH
JOAN S. FLETCHER
CATHERINE HARE FOLTZ
BONNIE FOWLER
MAUREEN M. FRANKS
GADSBY'S TAVERN
MRS. KEVIN GALLEN
GINA GALLOWAY
ROSANNE GARBER
MRS. ROBERT E. GASSER
GERANIO RISTORANTE
GLADYS GILES
PATRICIA S. GILL
STEVIE GILLESPIE
CYNTHIA GOLUBIN
NANCY L. GRAY
ANNE GROSS
LAVONA HAAS
MARGITTA HANFF
LINDA HARDING
ROBIN E. HARRELL
MARCY HARRIS
LOUISE E. HART
BRENDA HATTON
DEIRDRE HEARN
MRS. WILLIAM HERSEY
S. M. HILLEARY
DAVID M. HIRSCH
BETTY HOLLIS
MRS. HERBERT A. HOLT III
CAROLE SCHNEIDER HOUK
SUSANNE HOWARD
MRS. JAMES L. HOWE III
TOD R. HULLIN
BARABARA HULTMAN
SUNNY HUNNICUTT
SUSANNE HYMAN
CAROL JOHNSON
MRS. BRUCE KARRH
MARY KASIK
KAREN KAUFMAN
JOCIE KAZANJIAN
DEBBIE KELLER

MARY KELLEY
MRS. JOHN H. KELSO
MARY BETH KETCHUM
ELIZABETH KIDNEY
MRS. BRIAN D. KIDNEY
KAREN KILDAY
VIVIAN KILEY
PAULA KLEIN
JEAN KLINGE
LEE KLOUSIA
LA BERGERIE
LYNN LADY
LANDINI BROTHERS RESTAURANT
JEANIE LANGE
KATHY LARKIN
KATHY LAZARUS
LE GAULOIS
MARIANNE LEARD
ELEANOR LINDEMAN
JULIE ROBBEN LINEBERRY
ANN LOGSDON
CAROL LOWE
KATHRYNE HOLLIS LYONS
KATHIE MADDEN
MRS. WILLIAM T. MAHOOD
GAIL MALMGREN
KATHLEEN MANAFORT
DR. GEORGE W. MAPHESON
JACKIE MASON
JOUMANA MASTERSON
SARA MASTERSON
MRS. FRANK McCABE
BARBARA McCAFFREY
MAUREEN BRESNAHAN McCARTY
JOANNE McCASKILL
CARY D. McDANIEL
CONNIE McELHINNEY
KRISTI McELROY
LEE McGETTIGAN
JEAN McGUINNESS
SUSAN McLEOD
JUDY McMILLIN
DIANE MERIWETHER
AMANDA MERTINS

CAROLYN MEYER
STEVE MEYERSON
CHRISTINE CHAPIN MONCURE
CATHERINE MONZEL
SUZANNE MORRISON
MORRISON HOUSE
MRS. EDWARD M. MOSES
MRS. BRIAN MURPHY
SEEMA NAWAZ
GEORGEEN NEWLAND
THOMAS O'BRIEN
SHEILA O'SHAUGHNESSY
JOAN O'TOOLE
MARY LOU PALMER
AMY FORTNEY PARKS
ALISON PAYNE
ALEXANDRA PEKATOS
SHARON A. PENNY
BARBIE POOLE
MRS. LEWIS B. PULLER, JR.
EMMA PURSE
RADIO FREE ITALY
WANDA RAGLAND
LUCY RHAME
HOPE RHOADS
JANE RING
CLAUDIA RITT
KAREN ROBERTS
CAROLYNE ROEHRENBECK
ED ROLLINS
SHERRIE ROLLINS
BROOKE ROSS
MARIE B. ROSS
EM RUSCH
PAT SCHELHORN
J. SCOTT
MARJORIE SCOTT
WILLARD SCOTT
GERALD SEAGER
MRS. THOMAS F. SHEA
HELENMARIE SHIPP
W. LEWIS SHIPP
ANNE MARIE SHUYLER

TINA SIMS
BARBARA FOLEY SMITH
WENDY SMITH
ANN SPARKS
ASHLEY SPENCER
JACKIE SPIGAR
MERYL STAFMAN
MRS. HERBERT P. STEWART
ANNA STOCKER
MARSHA R. SULLIVAN
REBECCA M. SULLIVAN
MARCIA TALMADGE
NANCY OLSON TAMEZ
VALERIE TARVER
THE TEA COZY
CATHERINE THOMPSON
MAURINE V. THURMAN
MAYOR PATRICIA TICER
NANCY TOMION
JO TORPY
BETTY TOWERS
RICKY TROWBRIDGE
TWO-NINETEEN RESTAURANT
CARLO UCHELLO
PATSIE UCHELLO
ANITA VERGNE
JOYCE VONDERAHE
BETTYE WALKER
JEFF WALLINGFORD
CHARTLEY WARD
MRS. NATHANIEL P. WARD, III
WAREHOUSE BAR AND GRILL
JANE HORINE WARFIELD
JUDY WILLIAMS
STUART WINELAND
SUSAN WINN
ANNE WITHERS
JANICE WOLK-GRENADIER
MRS. WALTER N. WOODSON
STARLET G. ZAREK
MRS. RONALD ZIEGLER
MRS. JOSEPH ZIEMBA

SEAPORT SAVORIES

SEAPORT SAVORIES, P.O. BOX 3614, ALEXANDRIA, VA 22302   (703) 504-3364   FAX: (703) 504-3378

Please send me _____ copies of *Seaport Savories* at $14.95 per copy plus $1.75 for postage and handling. (Virginia residents please add 4.5% sales tax.)

☐ Enclosed is my check or money order for $ _____

Please charge my ☐ VISA ☐ MasterCard ☐ Amex Expiration Date ___/___/___

Account# _____ Signature _____

Name _____

Address _____

City _____ State _____ Zip _____

Please make your check payable to: Seaport Savories

SEAPORT SAVORIES

SEAPORT SAVORIES, P.O. BOX 3614, ALEXANDRIA, VA 22302   (703) 504-3364   FAX: (703) 504-3378

Please send me _____ copies of *Seaport Savories* at $14.95 per copy plus $1.75 for postage and handling. (Virginia residents please add 4.5% sales tax.)

☐ Enclosed is my check or money order for $ _____

Please charge my ☐ VISA ☐ MasterCard ☐ Amex Expiration Date ___/___/___

Account# _____ Signature _____

Name _____

Address _____

City _____ State _____ Zip _____

Please make your check payable to: Seaport Savories

SEAPORT SAVORIES

SEAPORT SAVORIES, P.O. BOX 3614, ALEXANDRIA, VA 22302   (703) 504-3364   FAX: (703) 504-3378

Please send me _____ copies of *Seaport Savories* at $14.95 per copy plus $1.75 for postage and handling. (Virginia residents please add 4.5% sales tax.)

☐ Enclosed is my check or money order for $ _____

Please charge my ☐ VISA ☐ MasterCard ☐ Amex Expiration Date ___/___/___

Account# _____ Signature _____

Name _____

Address _____

City _____ State _____ Zip _____

Please make your check payable to: Seaport Savories